Play It Again

Play It Again

Baseball Experts on What Might Have Been

Edited by JIM BRESNAHAN

Foreword by Pete Palmer

McFarland & Company, Inc., Publishers

Jefferson, North Carolina, and London

LIBRARY OF CONGRESS CATALOGUING-IN-PUBLICATION DATA

Play it again : baseball experts on what might have been /
    edited by Jim C. Bresnahan ; foreword by Pete Palmer.
        p.   cm.
    Includes bibliographical references and index.

    ISBN-13: 978-0-7864-2546-4
    ISBN-10: 0-7864-2546-6 (softcover : 50# alkaline papter) ∞

    1. Baseball—United States—History.   2. Baseball teams—United
States—History.   I. Bresnahan, James C., 1958–   II. Palmer, Pete.
    GV863.A1P59 2006
    796.357—dc22

                                        2006015609

British Library cataloguing data are available

©2006 Jim C. Bresnahan. All rights reserved

Cover art ©2006 Wood River Gallery

Manufactured in the United States of America

*McFarland & Company, Inc., Publishers
    Box 611, Jefferson, North Carolina 28640
    www.mcfarlandpub.com*

To my family: my mom and dad,
brothers and sister and my wife Mercy.
Thank for always being there!

Acknowledgments

This counterfactual baseball book would still be on the proverbial back burner, were it not for the expert commentary provided by my panelists through telephone interviews and written submissions. Thanks go out to all of the journalists, authors and historians who supplied their time, their talents and their invaluable input. I also want to express my gratitude to the former major leaguers who were willing to second-guess the past. It was a privilege and a joy to speak with each one of them.

The folks who took the time to read over the manuscript and offer input, including Bill Kramer, Pete Palmer, Steve Steinberg, and Thom Henninger, were a constant source of encouragement. I would like to thank several MLB teams and their personnel for furnishing photographs: I deeply appreciate the efforts of Jarrod Rollins and the Cincinnati Reds, Mark Langill and the Los Angeles Dodgers, Debbie Matson and the Boston Red Sox, and Curtis Danburg and the Cleveland Indians.

I am also indebted to my wife, Mercy, my mom and dad, my brothers Tim and Chris, and my sister Belinda. They kept me pointed in the right direction throughout the course of this project.

Contents

Foreword

Jim Bresnahan has entered into the world of a slightly different kind of fantasy baseball, not the Rotisserie kind, but the kind of alternate history which might have been. In doing so, he has also presented as background a fair amount of what actually happened in the early stages of the professional game, which might be unfamiliar to many of today's fans.

Jim's panel of experts included three dozen commentators and a dozen former players, who were free to expound on any subject on Jim's list that interested them. They gave their views of what might have happened at various turning points in the development of baseball. This includes eras through the Black Sox and World War II to the present with expansion, the DH and free agency. The experts also as well as analyzed decisions made in the World Series that are within the memory of most of us. Read about the stirring comeback made by Sandy Koufax after having the innovative surgery that now bears his name.

This nostalgic trip allows us to see what might have been. The experts do not always agree, and if any of the versions presented don't match your own, then you can make one up. After all, it is fantasy.

Pete Palmer

Preface

Babe Ruth leads the Boston Red Sox to several World Series titles in the Roaring Twenties. Carl Erskine relieves Don Newcombe in the decisive third game of the 1951 National League playoffs and slams the door on the New York Giants, allowing Brooklyn to advance to the World Series. A healthy Tony Conigliaro, serving as Boston's designated hitter, tops the American League in home runs in 1973. Fantasy headlines? I prefer to think of them as highlights from one of baseball's alternate timelines.

Let's face it, fans know the history of the game inside and out. They know what happened, when it happened and how it happened. My fascination lies with what *could have* happened, and this book gives historians, journalists and former players a chance to replay critical games, extend shortened careers and reverse ill-advised trades.

The possibilities are endless. Can you imagine Ty Cobb and Shoeless Joe Jackson side by side in Cleveland's outfield? What if integration had taken place in the majors before 1947? Who would have won the World Series in the strike-shortened season of 1994? Look for answers to those questions and more from the experts.

Our panel had free rein to second guess decision-makers and to make predictions about historical scenarios that never materialized, from the beginning of professional baseball in 1869 through the controversial 2003 playoffs. Each panelist has his own area of expertise, and multiple opinions on the same topic furnish the reader with a wide range of conclusions to consider. I must warn you that speculating about counterfactual history can be frustrating. Thanks to conflicting viewpoints, more arguments tend to get started than are settled.

Rarely do we get a chance to rewrite history. I think you will find the process entertaining and enlightening, so sit back and enjoy our version of fantasy baseball!

The Panel of
Baseball Experts

Jim Albright has written extensively on Japanese baseball history. He has done a great deal of research into comparing the majors and Japanese baseball and has calculated major league equivalents for current and past Japanese players. For a complete list of his articles, go to http://baseballguru. com/jalbright/

Maury Allen is the author of more than 30 books on baseball, including bestsellers on Joe DiMaggio and Casey Stengel. His latest book is *Brooklyn Remembered: The 1955 Days of the Dodgers*. He has been a working sportswriter for nearly half a century, with time as a columnist for the New York Post and the Gannett Journal News. Maury is also a member of several sports Halls of Fame including the Brooklyn Dodgers Hall of Fame.

David W. Anderson is a telecommunications executive living in Olathe, Kansas, Dave is the author of *More Than Merkle* and was a contributing author and team editor for the book, *Deadball Stars of the National League*. He has been a member of the Society for American Baseball Research since 1986.

Charlie Bevis is the author of two books on baseball history, *Sunday Baseball: The Major Leagues' Struggle to Play Baseball on the Lord's Day, 1876–1934* and *Mickey Cochrane: The Life of a Baseball Hall of Fame Catcher*. He was a 2003 recipient of the McFarland-SABR Baseball Research Award for his presentation "Evolution of the Sunday Doubleheader and Its Role in Elevating the Popularity of Baseball" given at the Cooperstown Symposium on Baseball and American Culture.

Gil Bogen is the author of *Tinker, Evers and Chance: A Triple Biography*, as well as an upcoming book on the Chicago Cubs catcher from the Deadball Era, Johnny Kling, Gil has been a member of SABR since 2000.

Marty Brennaman has been an announcer with the Cincinnati Reds for more than three decades. In 2000, he received the Ford C. Frick Award in ceremonies at the National Baseball Hall of Fame and merited induction into the National Sportscasters and Sportswriters Association Hall of Fame in 2005.

Darryl Brock is the author of the bestseller *If I Never Get Back*, and two other historical baseball novels, plus numerous articles on baseball history. He lives in Berkeley with his wife and daughter.

Steve Bullock is an assistant professor at the University of Nebraska at Omaha who specializes in sports history. He is the author of *Playing for Their Nation: Baseball and the American Military during World War II*.

Gene Carney is a native of Pittsburgh, and has been writing about baseball for more than 15 years. In that time, he has produced a historical baseball play, a number of short stories and a new book, *Burying the Black Sox: How Baseball's Cover-Up of the Fix of the 1919 Series Almost Succeeded*.

Bill Deane is a free-lance baseball researcher and writer stationed near Cooperstown, New York. He spent eight years as senior research associate for the National Baseball Library. He has written several books including biographies on Bob Gibson and Frank Thomas for young readers, and the book *Award Voting*, the winner of the Macmillan-SABR Baseball Research Award in 1988.

Jerry Eskenazi has written about sports for the *New York Times* for nearly half a century. He is the author or editor of more than a dozen books including *The Lip: A Biography of Leo Durocher* and *A Sports-Writer's Life*.

Sean Forman is an assistant professor of mathematics and computer science at Saint Joseph's University in Philadelphia, Sean created the on-line baseball encyclopedia, www.Baseball-Reference.com in 2000. Baseball Reference contains over 25,000 pages of baseball statistics and tools for answering important statistical questions.

Gary Gillette is the co-editor of the *2005 ESPN Baseball Encyclopedia*, a columnist for ESPN.com's MLB Insider, and a nationally known baseball author and analyst. Gary is also the co-chair of the Society for American Baseball Research's Business of Baseball Committee and was a featured panelist on the future of baseball at SABR's 2003 national convention.

Thom Henninger began his publishing career in New York in the 1980s and was commissioned to do editorial work for STATS Inc. in 1995. His involvement in the Publishing Department grew, and he formally joined the staff in 2000. Thom co-edited *The Scouting Notebook* by STATS, an annual publication that provides in-depth scouting and statistical reports on major leaguers and more than 300 minor league prospects.

Dan Holmes is the web manager for the National Baseball Hall of Fame and Museum, Dan is the author of *Ty Cobb: A Biography*. In his spare time, he maintains a personal web site dedicated to baseball history, www.thebaseballpage.com.

John Holway is the author of many books, mainly about the Negro Leagues, but also about baseball in Japan. His books include *The Baseball Astrologer*, *The Complete Book of the Negro Leagues* and *Josh and Satch*.

Rick Huhn is the author of *The Sizzler: George Sisler, Baseball's Forgotten Great*. An attorney and a member of SABR, Rick is currently writing a biography of Hall of Famer Eddie Collins.

Bill James is a premiere baseball analyst and is the author of a number of books including *The New Bill James Historical Baseball Abstract*. His other books include *The Bill James Guide to Baseball Managers* and *The Neyer/James Guide to Pitchers* with Rob Neyer.

Jeff Katz lives in Cooperstown with his wife and three sons. He has spent over two decades in financial trading, but is much happier talking and writing about baseball.

John Kuenster has been the executive editor of Century Publishing Company in Evanston, Illinois, since 1969. He is the editor of *Baseball Digest*, the nation's oldest baseball magazine, and is the author or co-author of several books including *Cobb to Catfish* and *Heartbreakers*.

Blair Lovern has written for magazines and newspapers most of his professional career. A member of SABR, Blair was also an editor at *Baseball America* magazine.

Bruce Markusen worked at the National Baseball Hall of Fame and Museum from 1994 through 2004 in education, research and programming. He now works as a free-lance writer and broadcaster in Cooperstown, New York. His books include *Baseball's Last Dynasty: Charley Finley's Oakland A's*, which won the 1999 Seymour Medal from SABR, and *Roberto Clemente: The Great One*.

Bill McNeil has been a Dodger fan since 1946; Bill is a baseball historian and the author of 12 baseball books including *The Dodgers Encyclopedia*, a 1997 finalist for the *Sporting News*–SABR Baseball Research Award. He is a member of SABR and a four-time recipient of the SABR Robert Peterson Recognition Award.

Rob Neyer is a senior writer and baseball columnist for ESPN.com. He is the author of *Rob Neyer's Big Book of Baseball Lineups* and *Feeding the Green Monster*. His website is www.robneyer.com.

Rob Rains has been writing about baseball in books, magazines and newspapers for more than 25 years. He is the author of more than 20 books including *Mark McGwire: Home Run Hero* and co-authored autobiographies of Jack Buck, Ozzie Smith and Red Schoendienst.

Mike Robbins is the author of *Ninety Feet from Fame: Close Calls with Baseball Immortality*; Mike is a member of SABR and a free-lance writer. His work has appeared in *ESPN: The Magazine* and the Forbes family of publications.

Bill Ryczek has written two books, *Blackguards and Red Stockings* and *When Johnny Came Sliding Home*, on the history of baseball in the 19th century. *Blackguards* won the 1993 Macmillan-SABR Award for best baseball history and *Johnny* was a runner-up for the Casey Award and a finalist for the Seymour Medal.

Gabriel Schechter has been a research associate at the Baseball Hall of Fame's A. Bartlett Giamatti Research Center since 2002, and is also the author of *Victory Faust: The Rube Who Saved McGraw's Giants*.

Alan Schwarz has covered baseball for more than 15 years, working for many of the most respected publications in sports media. Since 1991, he has been the senior writer of *Baseball America* magazine and has written a weekly in-season column for ESPN.com since 2001. Alan is the author of *The Numbers Game: Baseball's Lifelong Fascination with Statistics*.

David Shiner has written numerous articles and stories for sports magazines, research journals and literary publications, including *The National Pastime* and the *SABR Research Journal*. He is the author of *Baseball's Great-*

est Players: The Saga Continues and has been a member of the faculty and administration at Shimer College in Illinois since 1976.

Mike Sowell has been a sportswriter and columnist for two decades. Mike teaches journalism at Oklahoma State University and is the author of several books, including *The Pitch That Killed* and *One Pitch Away*.

Fred Stein was a dairy technologist and marketing specialist for the USDA before directing the first national study of the cost of cleaning up the nation's waterways for the Federal Water Pollution Control Administration. Since his retirement, he has written several books including *The History of the Baseball Fan, And the Skipper Bats Cleanup; Mel Ott: The Little Giant of Baseball;* and his latest, *The History of the Baseball Fan.*

Steve Steinberg is a baseball historian specializing in the early 20th century with a focus on St. Louis baseball and the New York Yankees. Steve is a member of SABR and maintains a baseball history web site, www.stevestein berg.net. He is the author of *Baseball in St. Louis: 1900–1925* and *The Genius of Hug,* a revealing book about Hall of Fame manager Miller Huggins.

Dean Sullivan is the editor of *Early Innings: A Documentary History of Baseball, 1825–1908; Middle Innings: A Documentary History of Baseball, 1900–1948;* and *Late Innings: A Documentary History of Baseball, 1945–1972.*

Jim Vail has written two books about the Hall of Fame selection process, *The Road to Cooperstown* and *Outrageous Fortune.* He is also the former Hall of Fame columnist for *Street & Smith's Baseball* magazine and currently serves as an occasional columnist and the staff baseball historian for the fantasy-related website, www.creativesports.com.

David Vincent is a former member of SABR's Board of Directors and recipient of SABR's highest honor, the Bob Davids Award. His books include *SABR Presents the Home Run Encyclopedia* and *The Midsummer Classic: A Complete History of Baseball's All-Star Game.* David is a well-known source for information on the history of the home run.

Marshall Wright has written several baseball books, including *19th Century Baseball; The American Association; The International League;* and *The National Association.* He won *The Sporting News*–SABR Baseball Research Award in 1998 for his book on the International League.

Fran Zimniuch is an award-winning journalist and columnist who has written for various newspapers and national magazines for more than two decades. He is the author of *Phillies: Where Have You Gone*; *Eagles: Where Have You Gone* and *Richie Ashburn Remembered*.

Former Players

Bobby Bolin pitched 13 seasons in the majors, including nine years with the San Francisco Giants. He recorded 88 victories and saved 50 games while compiling a lifetime ERA of 3.40. Bobby appeared in two games in the 1962 World Series.

Ron Cey was a long-time third baseman and hit 316 home runs in a career spanning 17 seasons. Ron played in six All-Star Games and shared Most Valuable Player honors in the 1981 World Series.

Bobby Doerr was the American League's Most Valuable Player in 1944 and knocked in over 100 runs six times in his career. Elected to the Hall of Fame in 1986, Bobby hit .409 and drove in three runs in his only World Series appearance, in 1946.

Carl Erskine pitched 12 seasons for the Dodgers, posting a record of 122–78. He played on six pennant winners, earned a world championship ring in both Brooklyn and Los Angeles, and pitched two no-hitters during his outstanding career. He is the author of *Carl Erskine's Tales from the Dodger Dugout*.

Bob Feller was elected to the Hall of Fame in 1962; Bob amassed 266 pitching victories in a career that began in 1936 and ended in 1956. Despite missing several seasons due to military service in World War II, Bob still chalked up 2,581 strikeouts during his 18 years in the majors.

Bob Friend won 197 games during his 16 seasons in the majors. The longtime Pittsburgh hurler had an earned run average of 3.58 for his career and won 22 games in 1958 to lead the National League.

Dick Groat was the Most Valuable Player of the National League in 1960, hitting .325 to help lead Pittsburgh to the World Series. A lifetime .286 hitter, Dick also hit .292 for St. Louis in 1964, as the Cardinals won the NL flag and beat the Yankees in the World Series.

Bill Lee is known as the "Spaceman," and won 119 games in a 14-year career. He won 17 games in three straight seasons for Boston between 1973 and 1975 and had 16 victories for Montreal in 1979.

Whitey Lockman started his career with the New York Giants in 1945. Whitey hit .279 in 15 seasons in the majors. He had a clutch double to drive in a run in the ninth inning of the deciding game of the 1951 NL play-offs.

Jim Northrup spent most of his 12-year major league career with Detroit. He helped the Tigers beat St. Louis in the 1968 World Series by hitting a grand slam in the sixth game and a triple off Bob Gibson to break a scoreless tie in Game seven.

Brooks Robinson was elected to the Hall of Fame in 1983, and spent an amazing 23 seasons in the majors, all with the Baltimore Orioles. Perhaps the greatest defensive third baseman of all time, Brooks won 16 straight Gold Gloves beginning in 1960, and used his glove and bat to lead Baltimore past Cincinnati in the 1970 World Series.

Frank Thomas has 286 home runs to his credit from his 16-year career. Frank played for eight different National League clubs. Acquired by the Phillies in the summer of 1964, Frank hit seven home runs in just 39 games, but his season ended abruptly when he broke his thumb.

1

Beginnings: 1869–1900

Historical Highlights

Thanks to baseball's evolution process during the second half of the 19th century, a social activity became the national pastime. Although amateurs dominated the scene in the 1840s and 1850s, baseball went professional in 1869; with the arrival of the 20th century, the game's popularity was ready to explore new heights.

There were no guarantees that baseball would climb as rapidly as it did. The first openly professional club, the Cincinnati Red Stockings, certainly achieved success on the field, but several issues had to be addressed before the game could legitimately label itself America's National Game. Who would be in charge, players or owners? Would there be one major league or several major leagues? Would there be enough paying customers to keep teams financially afloat?

Baseball in the 19th century provided some answers. Archaic practices vanished, league schedules expanded, and the introduction of unique statistics kept fans immersed in the game. When the National League, which arrived on the scene in 1876, chose to establish a reserve clause, to guarantee owners perpetual control of players and to clamp down on salaries, it became clear who would wield power. By 1892, the NL was the only major league still active, due to the disintegration of the Players' League in 1890, and the demise of the ten year old American Association in 1891.

With only one 12-team major league in existence in the 1890s, and attendance dwindling, baseball desperately cried out for competition. It would be a former sportswriter by the name of Ban Johnson who would revive the game, by turning a minor league into the American League in 1901.[1]

Playing for Pay

For nearly two-thirds of the 19th century, amateurs presided over baseball's landscape, playing mainly for social camaraderie and physical exercise.[2] However, in the 1860s, as attendance rose and talented players received compensation under the table, the game entered a new and potentially dangerous transition period.

It was time to see if professional baseball could be a financial success. The first all-professional team, the 1869 Cincinnati Red Stockings, paid each player a salary and sported a payroll of nearly $10,000.[3] One of the important figures in the venture, Cincinnati field general Harry Wright, had left New York in 1865 to join the Cincinnati Union Cricket Club. Wright eventually hooked up with the Cincinnati Baseball Club, the forerunner of the Red Stockings.[4]

The 1869 Red Stockings made it look easy, averaging more than 42 runs per game, en route to a perfect 57–0 record.[5] Harry Wright would go on to manage for several more decades, but his crowning achievement would be Cincinnati's perfect season, which paved the way for the first pro league, the National Association, in 1871.[6]

What if Harry Wright had not come to Cincinnati?
What if professional baseball had flopped in 1869?

DARRYL BROCK: After every war, a burst of sports activity has occurred in the U.S. as people celebrated an end to hardships. The Civil War spread the New York diamond-shaped game across the country, and afterward baseball was king; already it was called "the national game" and it was played everywhere. As high-caliber teams formed in Eastern cities to contest for the championship "whip pennant," not only star players but sometimes whole teams were paid clandestinely in various ways— given bogus jobs by private employers, carried on government payrolls (Boss Tweed's NY Mutuals received NY sanitation department funds), or simply handed shares of gate receipts.

By the late 1860s, the postwar blush had worn off and the game was falling into disrepute. Gambling, drunkenness and violence marked contests. Players jumped contracts from one to team to another ("revolved") and some teams, most notably the Troy Haymakers, geared their performances to betting odds ("hippodromed")— barely beating or even losing to a weak opponent, for example, to increase the odds against them versus a more powerful club they would then defeat. Middle-class individuals and families increasingly stopped attending games. By 1869 the future of the organized game was seriously in question (far more so than is today's steroids-challenged MLB) as it seemed that the old amateur framework had been profoundly corrupted. The sport was swiftly descending to a level occupied today by, say, mud wrestling.

Enter the 1869 Cincinnati Red Stockings. Taking advantage of a new rule permitting wholly professional (paid) clubs, they openly recruited and signed top Eastern players to contracts— the first club to do so. The theory was that if their salaries were guaranteed, the players would not be tempted by gamblers and raiding clubs; also, full-time baseball employment would go a long way toward insuring their fitness and sobriety. It was a radical, daring experiment, and quite controversial at the time. "They do nothing else," one critic sniffed, regarding the Red Stockings, "and are paid for it."

Cincinnati, the "Queen City of the West," represented the perfect venue for this new enterprise. The city was bursting with postwar prosperity and boasted several dozen millionaires. Although many affluent Cincinnatians still sent their sons off to Atlantic Seaboard schools, they were growing weary of Eastern supremacy— a sensibility dramatically reinforced by a baseball drubbing at the hands of the touring Washington Nationals, led by George Wright, in 1867. Following greater success in the 1868 season with a handful of imported pros, the Cincinnatis set out to raid Eastern ballclubs and obtain the very best ballplayers money could buy. They also lavished thousands on a state-of-the art, fenced-in ballpark with a shaded grandstand (known locally as the "Grand Duchess") to attract female spectators, whose presence would serve to "elevate" the game.

Just as no other venue in America existed at that time with such a fierce commitment to fielding a superb all-pro team, no better man than Harry Wright could have been found to lead it. A rare second-generation professional athlete, Wright was universally respected for his dedication and integrity. Playing center field — he would hit .493 and serve as the relief pitcher in 1869 — "Captain Harry" was equally skilled as a field tactician and a handler of men. He pioneered many tactics now accepted as fundamentals, such as shifting fielders, employing defensive signals, backups and cutoff men, and place hitting in order to advance runners.

Not least of Harry's many attributes was that he recruited his younger brother George, then the country's best player, to play for the Red Stockings. In the high-scoring 1869 season, George Wright would blast 49 home runs, bat .633 and average scoring six runs a game. Outstanding as a fielder and base runner, he was recognized as best shortstop of his era; at that position his wide range, athleticism, and strong arm enabled him play far deeper than competitors. Moreover, George was extremely popular with fans in Cincinnati and across the nation.

Exploding onto the national scene in 1869, the Red Stockings took on all comers and notched a gaudy undefeated record. Their sensational exploits galvanized baseballdom. Their snow-white knickers and crimson stockings changed uniforms forever. Capitalizing on advances in communication and transportation — the telegraph distributed their line scores; new engraving procedures in *Frank Leslie's Illustrated* and *Harper's Magazine* sent their images out to readers; and the recently completed Transcontinental Railroad carried them clear across the prairies and mountains to the Pacific — the Red Stockings literally took the game coast to coast, and became America's first national sports heroes. Moreover, their unprecedented financial success goaded rival cities to field top pro clubs; the Chicago White Stockings and others duly appeared the next season.

None of this, however, was foreordained or guaranteed. Had Harry Wright elected to stay in New York and succeed his father as the resident pro at the prestigious St. George Cricket Club (Harry worked winters as an engraver at Tiffany's), instead of relocating to Cincinnati, this pioneering professional team would not likely have appeared at all, much less achieved the triumph that launched the pro game on its course.

Similarly, had the 1869 Red Stocking team failed on the diamond, or split apart from its inner tensions (which definitely existed), or failed to draw paying fans, or put on shoddy exhibitions, professional baseball would have been set back for years, perhaps decades. At best, pro baseball, despite its difficulties, might have emerged before too long in other places, developed by different people — and perhaps with quite a different character. At worst, it might have followed the path of football, relegated to colleges and amateur clubs for nearly a century before the advent of a successful professional format.

Fortunately, thanks to the happy convergence of Harry Wright and the Cincinnati Baseball Club, neither of those alternatives came to pass.

BILL RYCZEK: Had Harry Wright not emigrated from New York to Cincinnati in 1866, many would say that Cincinnati would have found another prominent ball player to come to the city and organize a team, and that events would have followed much the same course as they had under Harry. Wright came to Cincinnati, however, not as a baseball player, but as a cricket professional. Had Harry not accepted the job with the Union Cricket Club, the position would probably have been filled by a cricketer with fewer ties to baseball.

Baseball clubs were springing up everywhere, and Harry Wright or not, some clubs would undoubtedly have appeared in Cincinnati, as they did in St. Louis and other Midwestern cities. Had Wright remained in New York, however, it is unlikely that Cincinnati would have fielded a nationally prominent nine. It was Wright's reputation, plus the stockholders' money, which drew top Eastern players to the Midwest.

In the early 19th century, Chicago was no more than a small village, dwarfed by the Queen City of Cincinnati. As Chicago grew, it exhibited the classic inferiority complex of the nouveau riche, which required that the city have the biggest and best of everything, including baseball clubs. If the Red Stockings brought fame and notoriety to Cincinnati, Chicago's White Stockings, organized in 1870, would bring even more fame and glory to their city. Had there been no champion Red Stockings to spur Chicago's envy, there may not have been any White Stockings.

William Hulbert, the Chicago businessman who initiated the formation of the National League, was introduced to baseball as a member of the management of the White Stockings. Had there been no White Stockings, Hulbert would most likely have remained a prosperous coal merchant with no connection with baseball.

Harry Wright begot the Red Stockings, who begot the White Stockings, who begot Hulbert, who begot the National League. If Wright had not established Cincinnati as a factor in baseball circles, and Hulbert not forged a connection with baseball, it is unlikely that Western teams would have had the temerity to challenge historically powerful clubs such as the Mutuals of New York and Athletics of Philadelphia to form the National League. The National Association, dominated by Eastern interests, would have continued in existence, or a new organization would have been formed by the Eastern clubs.

Hulbert's greatest contribution to professional baseball was the establishment of a league with integrity far greater than that exhibited in the loosely run National Association. If the chain of causality is no Harry Wright in Cincinnati, no Red Stockings, no White Stockings and no Hulbert, the worst case scenario is that the continued corruption of the National Association would have killed baseball. Baseball might have never become baseball. A less catastrophic, and more likely, scenario is that the corruption of the early 1870s would have gotten much worse before it got better.

Would a new league have arisen without Hulbert? Were the forces that led to the demise of the National Association so strong that a new organization would have arisen to fill the moral vacuum? That's possible, but who would have led the new league if not Hulbert? Had Wright remained in New York, and been active in baseball circles, he would have been a candidate. Yet, while personally above reproach, Wright showed little interest in initiating sweeping changes. He chose to mind his own shop, and toss off a stern rebuke now and then.

There were few other candidates. Crusading sportswriter Henry Chadwick was as upright as anyone, but Chadwick was a man of rhetoric, not action. Had Hulbert not set a course for reform, the National Association might have continued to drag the game down for years to come.

If Wright had never gone to Cincinnati, the world may never have heard of Albert Goodwill Spalding. Harry played a key role in Spalding's development, and if we assume Wright never captained a Cincinnati team, there is no reason to believe that another set of circumstances would have lifted Spalding to the heights he later reached. His ambition and ability would have undoubtedly resulted in his success in some endeavor, but would it have been baseball? Would it have included a sporting goods empire? Spalding's company eventually acquired the firm of Wright and Ditson, operated by Harry's brother George. Did Harry's move to Cincinnati deprive his brother of a nationwide sporting goods empire?

Fortunately for the future of baseball, Harry Wright went to Cincinnati, became marvelously successful and thus inflamed the jealousy of Chicago. Chicago produced the White Stockings and William Hulbert, who gave us the National League. Wright thereby spared us the continuing agony of the National Association and set baseball on its course to the present day.

The Reserve Clause

Chicago White Stockings owner William Hulbert has to rank as one of the most influential figures from 19th century baseball, as well as one of the most overlooked. Hulbert was instrumental in launching the National League in 1876; the NL would quickly develop into a league where owners wielded power and garnered profits.[7]

While Hulbert certainly strengthened the NL by hiring professional umpires and encouraging league-scheduled play, players could also thank him for a repressive restriction: the reserve clause. Enacted after the 1879 season, the clause allowed each owner to protect his top five players for life, thus reducing player mobility and salaries.[8] The reserve clause would soon be expanded to include every NL player.

What if NL owners had not employed a reserve clause?

BLAIR LOVERN: Because owners and players were and always have always been at odds, a clamp like the reserve clause was bound to happen. However, I think it is an interesting question. Baseball history is full of fascinating screw-ups, so what on earth would have taken its place? I'm not sure anything could have. Players certainly expected more freedom than they were given, which wasn't going to happen until there was a valid players union. Owners liked money a lot. They would not show the same affection for players unless forced, and even then, it is only because they are forced. So the only way to have balanced the tension between the players and owners back then, other than through a players union, would have been by inventing some sort of independent office, which may or may not have been like the commissioner's office. Nevertheless, there was no way that would happen, unless the game totally went down the toilet, which it almost did by 1919. If there had been no reserve clause, I'm sure baseball would have found that toilet, because it would have affected the major leagues and all rival leagues. A lot of history could have been changed. However, I don't know when the toilet would have been reached. For fun let me say May 17, 1898. No reasoning behind that.

The Players' League

John Montgomery Ward's distaste for the reserve clause ran so deep that the New York Giants shortstop helped establish baseball's first union, the Brotherhood of Professional Baseball Players. He was also swift to respond when National League owners tried to push through a new compensation system in 1889, aimed at reducing and then freezing players' salaries. Ward, and other players, arranged financial backing for a new league, the Players' League, to directly challenge the NL.[9]

With the National League and the American Association already on the scene, the question became a simple one: could baseball support three major leagues in 1890? The answer was a resounding no. All three leagues experienced financial problems, and despite the fact that the Players' League had surpassed its competitors in attendance, PL investors panicked and began to back out. After just one season, the Players' League was finished; with it went the Brotherhood and any hope of eliminating the reserve clause.[10]

What if the Players' League had successfully challenged the NL in 1890?

BLAIR LOVERN: If the Players' League had succeeded, baseball history would have been much different. However, once the Players' League fell apart, which it was bound to do because of its business structure, the National League took full advantage. Players eventually formally accepted the reserve clause and that was that. As with anything else in baseball (back then and today), there is never a major change unless owners are forced to make it. The Brotherhood had a chance, but it did not have a strong and lasting organization. Ward was undoubtedly the best person to have organized the Brotherhood, but I would argue that he was not the best man to lead it forward because it all fell apart under his guidance.

MARSHALL WRIGHT: Many stories have been told about the Players' League. Tales of how this social experiment took on the established baseball order, beating it at its own game — at least for a short while. What is not as widely known is that if a handful of key elements had fallen in just the right way, the story of the Players' League would have had a very different ending.

Baseball in the mid 1880s was a game dominated by the owners. These moguls set salaries, finalizing rosters, even to the extent of "reserving" players for subsequent years above and beyond the natural duration of their contracts. In short, players had little say. If a player cried foul over some perceived inequity, the miscreant was immediately slapped down with the threat of blacklisting.

In 1885, a step was taken by the players to alleviate the pressure. Under the leadership of John Montgomery Ward, a veteran pitcher/infielder who was also a lawyer, the "Brotherhood of Professional Baseball Players" was formed. In essence, this nascent organization served the function of baseball's first players union. Although the Brotherhood did not blunt many of the egregious practices of the owners, the owners still felt threatened.

To counter the perceived threat, baseball administrators put in a defacto salary cap following the 1888 season. Called the Brush Classification system, after the Indianapolis owner who had pushed it through, the onerous plan was conveniently announced when Ward was out of the country, participating in a World Baseball Tour. Under the plan, players would be grouped in a category based upon their "habits, earnestness and special qualifications." The categories with their respective salaries ranged from A ($2,500) to E ($1,500). To the outraged Ward and the Brotherhood, organized baseball had crossed the line.

During the summer of 1889, Ward and the Brotherhood approached several wealthy businessmen, seeking backing for a third Major League circuit. One of the businessmen, Albert Johnson of Cleveland, was convinced of the soundness of the idea. During the season, as visiting teams came to Cleveland, Johnson and his cohorts waylaid many, talking with them about the new league and signing several to contracts. All this was done under the noses of the existing National League hierarchy, who only fully realized the extent of the Brotherhood's plan when their "reserved" players refused contracts for the upcoming 1890 season. Plans continued, and backing was found in seven other cities: Boston, Philadelphia, Brooklyn, New York, Chicago, Pittsburgh and Buffalo. By the spring of 1890, the eight-team circuit — the Players' League — was ready to launch.

The rules governing the Players' League contained some novel ideas. Firstly, the dreaded reserve clause was banished. Other rules allowed multi-year contracts (unheard of in organized baseball at the time) and forbade the releasing of players until the end of the season. Teams were to be run by a governing board, elected by the players. Finally, the league constitution had a clause that outlined a profit sharing scheme in which the players and financial backers shared equally.

The defections from organized baseball were numerous. Over 100 players fled the National League, while another 20 jumped from the American Association. Especially hard hit were the New York Giants, who lost their entire starting lineup (save OF Mike Tiernan) to the Brotherhood. Virtually all of the stars of the game (Dan Brouthers, Pete Browning, Roger Connor, etc.) jumped to the new league. One of the only players of note to remain put was Chicago slugger Cap Anson, captain of the White Sox nine. Anson felt loyalty to his owner, Albert Spalding, in addition to having a financial interest in the team himself.

The Players' League schedule often conflicted with the established leagues, as games were scheduled for the same city at the same time. This was especially true in New York, where both the National and Players' League parks shared the same property. Separated by only a fence at the Polo Grounds site, it was possible to see both games at once.

The National League did not stand idly by while its larder was being raided. Stung by the defections, League magnates bribed, cajoled and offered multi-year contracts of their own. Despite the temptations, the Brotherhood stood fast.

The first few games were well attended, but by mid-summer Players' League attendance was dropping. Also adversely affected were the two existing leagues. All three leagues padded attendance figures frequently. One apocryphal tale tells of one game in which a four-figure attendance was reported. A critic claimed this could not be true as he saw less than 100 people in the stands. The original reporter then declared in the stands to left of him there were 24 people — in the right 33 — creatively making a total of 2433!

As the season unfolded, the Boston Reds (81–48), playing in the new Congress St. Grounds in South Boston, outlasted the field, winning the flag by a half-dozen games over the Brooklyn Wonders (76–56). The New York Giants (74–57) and Chicago Pirates (75–62) rounded out the first division, while the second tier consisted of the Philadelphia Quakers (68–63), Pittsburgh Burghers

(60–68), Cleveland Infants (55–75) and Buffalo Bisons (36–96). Overall, Cleveland, behind the efforts of batting titlist Pete Browning (.373) had the best team batting average (.286) while Chicago, courtesy of ERA champion Silver King (2.69), posted the lowest team ERA (3.39). Last place Buffalo had the worst hitting (.260) and pitching (6.11), the latter nearly two full runs higher than any other club's ERA. Other individual honors were taken home by New York's Roger Connor, who poled the most home runs (14) and by Boston's Hardy Richardson with the most RBI (146). From the pitching box, Pirate hurler Mark Baldwin posted the most wins (34) and struck out the most batters (211).

Financially, the 1890 Players' League season was not a profitable one. The total losses of the league were estimated at $125,000. However, in a fact unknown to the Brotherhood, the National League was in worse shape — their losses exceeded $250,000. So, when peace negotiations between the two leagues in the fall of 1890 took place, the Players' League did not have all the facts at their disposal. In a prearranged meeting, three leading Players' owners met with National League representatives, ostensibly to discuss a merger between the two leagues. When the Brotherhood representatives outlined their losses from the proceeding season, their National League counterparts remained coy about their massive debits and seized the advantage. The merger talks soon developed into complete Players' League acquiescence. In reminiscing about the events, National League leader Albert Spalding wrote that the Players' League greedily accepted his terms for unconditional surrender. In the end, the Boston, Brooklyn, Pittsburgh and New York franchises merged with their National League counterparts. The Chicago club was sold to Spalding, while the backers of the Philadelphia team bought the city's American Association franchise. The Buffalo and Cleveland clubs were left to twist in the wind. And with that, the short history of the Players' League ended.

However, what if events in the fall of 1890 had unfolded differently? Instead of capitulating, what if the Brotherhood had pushed back — nudging the National League to the brink of insolvency? If they had, baseball history in the 1890s and beyond would have certainly had a different slant. All it would have taken is for one key piece of knowledge to appear at the right time.

Let us suppose for a minute that the Players' League representatives in the fall of 1890 had full knowledge of the National League's shaky finances. If that were the case, negotiations would have taken a different turn, if they had happened at all. Let's continue this scenario and say that is exactly what took place. Let's speculate that Players' League backers, although on shaky financial footing themselves, were emboldened by the National League's plight and decided to not negotiate a truce in the fall of 1890. What might have happened next?

In actuality, before the negotiations took place following the 1890 season, the Cincinnati National League club was planning to join the Players' League, most likely taking the place of the Buffalo club. Faced with only a seven-team circuit, the National League most likely would have turned to the American Association. The Association had barely survived the 1890 season, recruiting several members (Columbus, Rochester, Toledo, etc.) just to fill out the league. In past seasons, the Association had seen franchises lured away (Pittsburgh) by the National League and with a second season of Players' League competition facing them, Spalding and his cohorts most likely would have done the same. The most likely candidate would have been the St. Louis club — for years one of the Association's strongest members. With that, in all likelihood, the Association would have quietly folded, one year ahead of when it actually did. (Probably the strongest reason it did survive in 1891 was because of the Boston Players' team, which had moved there after the demise of the Players' League. In our scenario, that did not happen.) Two years of three-league baseball would have been simply too much for the Association, especially with the loss of its strongest (St. Louis) team.

With these speculations in place, the lineup of Players' and National League clubs in 1891 most likely would have looked like this:

Players'	*National*
Boston	Boston
New York	New York
Brooklyn	Brooklyn
Philadelphia	Philadelphia
Cincinnati	St. Louis
Pittsburgh	Pittsburgh
Cleveland	Cleveland
Chicago	Chicago

Once again, the two leagues would have gone head to head in almost every location. Each team would likely have been stronger with all of the disbanded Association players thrown into the mix. The Players' League, with its multi-year contracts, certainly would have garnered its share of the orphans. However, the Nationals themselves actually waved around multi-year enticements in 1890, so they probably would have done the same in 1891 if forced to. Even if the Association players had been evenly divided between the two, the Players' would have come out on top talent wise because of their earlier advantage. Also, Spalding most likely would have tried to get the old National League players back in the fold, but because of the plethora of multi-year contracts already inked by the Brotherhood, that plan certainly would have failed.

In this scenario, the 1891 season could have been played out in the following fashion. Just as in 1890, baseball fans would have had their choice of major league teams in seven cities. Once again, competition would have been fierce, with each league fighting for the paying public's attention. Because of the quality of the product (i.e. better players), the Players' League would have come out on top. The National League might not have even finished the league intact. Its Pittsburgh franchise was woefully weak — it had barely survived the 1890 campaign. If it had folded during the 1891 season, an interim club probably would have replaced it in one of the stronger Association locales — maybe Baltimore.

At the conclusion of this mythical 1891 season, the Players' League once again held the stronger hand. Most likely, Boston would have finished again on top. (The same team actually won handily the American Association race in 1891.) The Players' League had most of the best players and a boatload of confidence after competing successfully with the established league two years running. Despite Spalding's strong leadership, it is doubtful that the remaining National League owners would have wanted to incur further losses. Thus, it would have been highly probable that the senior circuit would have sued for peace and a possible merger following the 1891 campaign. For them, it would have not gone well.

In actuality, the American Association folded after the 1891 campaign. Four of its franchises (Baltimore, Washington, Louisville and St. Louis) joined the National League. Although these were not the strongest Association clubs, the National League was careful not to create further competition — none of the four had any National neighbors in their locales. If the Players' and National had tried a similar tactic, it would not have worked. Neither party wanted competition — and the Players', with the upper hand, would not have tolerated any plan which would have allowed a rival's team to remain operational in one of its cities. So, in all likelihood, the weaker party — in this case the National League — would have been forced to capitulate, ending its 16-year existence.

As we continue the tale, an eight-team Players' League would have dominated the baseball world for at least several years. There may have been some franchise shifts, which would have added St. Louis into the mix. There is no doubt that the forceful presence of Al Spalding would have surfaced — maybe even as an owner. This brings up another point. Although formed with a very socialist slant, the Players' League soon had to adapt to the times. (During its short tenure, several of its original tenets, mostly involving profit sharing, actually were altered.) In theory, the ideas of group ownership and player profit sharing were noble. However, it was still difficult to shoehorn these concepts into the times. In American history, this was the era of big business—and baseball was a business just like any other. To succeed, the Players' League would have had to become as good a business as it could, even if it meant leaving some if not most of its ideology behind. The Players' League would have had a different name than the league it replaced—business-wise, it would have been largely indistinguishable from the Nationals.

During the 1890s, with only eight major league teams (instead of the actual 12) there would have been some wiggle room for a rival league in several of the former major league cities. So an entity like the American League likely would have formed, maybe even sooner than it did, although probably not for the same reasons. In actuality, the American League was formed partly in contrast to the out-of-control rowdy practices of the National League, practices the constitution of the Players' League forbade. In our scenario, a rival like the American League would have formed simply because there was room to do so and because they thought they could make a go of it, just as the Players' League had done a few years earlier.

Continuing the story into the 20th century, rival leagues like the Federal League (1914) and the major Pacific Coast League (1946) might have been emboldened by previous "rebel" successes and tried to stick it out longer. Today's baseball scene might have a very different look if they had succeeded.

As outlined by the above scenario, if the Players' League had been aware of the financial problems of the National League following the 1890 season, baseball's history might well have been rewritten. For instance, the original National League most likely would have died in the early 1890s. Rival leagues, spurred by the success of the Brotherhood, would have sprung up, perhaps several. In any event, the Players' League might well have continued to this day, serving as a bastion of baseball stability much as the National League has—the league the Brotherhood nearly toppled.

The American Association

The American Association, formed in 1882, posed the most consistent threat to National League dominance. The differences between the two leagues were crystal clear: the AA allowed games to be played on Sundays, its ballparks sold liquor, and league tickets cost just 25 cents, compared to the NL's price of 50 cents.[11]

A peace accord between the two leagues, known as the National Agreement, was hammered out early in 1883; the American Association responded by drawing more than a million fans in its second season, outpacing the National League by approximately 400,000. The AA's success was short-lived. Attendance numbers began to slide in 1888 and the brief appearance of the Players' League in 1890 further eroded the AA's fan base.[12]

When the American Association withdrew from the National Agreement before the 1891 season, the AA and the NL were officially at war. Although AA attendance rose by more than 300,000 in 1891, the NL turned in even better numbers. The older league then absorbed four AA franchises during the offseason, dooming the American Association to the junk heap of failed organizations.[13] The National League now had a monopoly on major league competition.

What if the American Association had survived beyond 1891?

CHARLIE BEVIS: Having a competitive two-league structure in the 1890s would certainly have changed the face of major league baseball, since it is unlikely that the American League would have come into existence in 1901.

Since the American Association was on shaky legs in 1890 and 1891, and well on its way to oblivion at that point, the real question is: would the American Association have survived if Brooklyn and Cincinnati hadn't jumped to the National League after the 1889 season? As it turns out, half of the teams in the 1890 National League were expatriates of the American Association — Pittsburgh and Cleveland that jumped after the 1886 and 1888 seasons, respectively, and Brooklyn and Cincinnati (which the NL made room for by dumping Washington and Indianapolis). So the National League had pretty much eviscerated the American Association by 1890.

If Brooklyn and Cincinnati had stayed in the American Association, the league could have remained viable competition to the National League throughout the 1890s and beyond. Having a strong East Coast presence was essential for the Association, since critics derided it for its low-brow spectator base with 25 cent admissions (vs. 50 cents in the NL), liquor sales in Midwestern cities of St. Louis and Louisville, and allowing games on Sunday. Brooklyn and Cincinnati left the Association when local law officials took action to prohibit Sunday games in those cities (Brooklyn avoided strait-laced Kings County officials by playing in more tolerant Queens County at Ridgewood Park just across the county line).

What would have been different in the future?

1. New York and Philadelphia would have been the only two-team cities in major league baseball. Chicago, Boston, and St. Louis would have remained

one-team cities since there would have been no need to introduce competition in these three cities, as the American League did 1901–1902, nor the need to invade New York in 1903 to establish a beachhead there. Just think, there would have been no rivalry between the Boston Red Sox and the New York Yankees.

2. More cities would have been represented at the major league level, which would have changed the development of the minor leagues. In the American Association, Louisville, Kansas City, and Columbus would have been in the majors as would have Indianapolis in the National League. The existence of Kansas City as a continuous member of the major leagues just might have encouraged more team relocations to Western cities earlier than 1955 (when the Philadelphia Athletics relocated west of St. Louis). All four teams were charter members of the minor league American Association in 1902; if they had been major league teams, how would have minor league baseball developed? Would the Pacific Coast League have come to dominate the minors instead?

3. A more robust postseason World Series would have been continued between the NL and AA, dating the origin of this competition to 1884, not 1903 as is currently accepted to be the inaugural series.

4. The National League may have been the less powerful of the two leagues, because it would have taken more years to adopt Sunday baseball to embrace spectators of the working classes. The NL only okayed Sunday games for the 1892 season due to the merger with the AA; Chicago would not have under Sunday games in 1893 without the AA merger.

Strengthening the NL

With the American Association extinct, the National League opted for expansion, going with a 12-team league in 1892. In order to create postseason competition, NL officials initially used a split-season format, pairing the winners of each half in a championship series. Starting in 1894, fans could look forward to four years of postseason excitement, such as it was, from the Temple Cup series, which matched the NL's first place and second place teams.

The NL stuck with the 12-team approach throughout the 1890s, finally contracting to eight teams in 1900. Perhaps by splitting the league into two six-team divisions earlier in the decade, with the division winners then squaring off in the postseason, more fans might have flocked to NL ballparks. Future organizations seeking major league status, such as the American League, might have had a much more difficult time making headway against a stronger, redesigned National League.

What if the National League had used a two-division approach in the 1890s?

CHARLIE BEVIS: A divisional format in the monopolistic National League in the 1890s, with a meaningful postseason championship series rather than the Temple Cup series between first and second place finishers, would have forestalled the formation of the American League in 1901 and likely continued its monopoly for several decades. Unfortunately, I'm not sure the NL ever considered a divisional format, although it did experiment with a split-season format in 1892, with first and second halves, with the winners meeting for a postseason title. That experiment was unpopular.

Certainly the NL of 1892 could have easily been split into eastern and western divisions, since the league did so anyway for scheduling purposes (for example, the six Eastern teams would all take road trips west at the same time to play the Western cities). These six-team divisions could easily have been expanded to eight teams, with these four additional teams likely representing other major cities in the country to expand the major league footprint beyond the larger cities. Alas, the NL owners hated the four AA teams adopted in the merger, and thus weren't inclined to consider a divisional set-up.

It's not likely that the postseason format would have morphed into today's playoff structure any sooner than it did. The minor leagues only adopted a multi-team playoff pattern in 1933, based on the NHL's Stanley Cup format that was put into place in 1926.

Changing the Rules

Those seeking to tackle the Mount Everest of baseball should take a stab at cataloging the various rule changes of the 19th century. Alexander Joy Cartwright's New York Knickerbockers, one of the first established clubs, laid out the rules for the New York Game in the 1840s. Pitchers threw underhand, runners were retired by being tagged or thrown out, and the game was played on a diamond shaped infield with recognized foul lines.[14]

Adjustments to the Knickerbocker rules came fast and furious. Changes in the 1850s placed bases 90 feet apart and gave umpires the power to call strikes.[15] Newspaperman Henry Chadwick, a native of Great Britain, further shaped the game by creating scorekeeping practices and statistics and by making sure that tie games would be settled through the use of extra innings.[16]

Additional changes in rules and equipment, during the final two decades of the 19th century, inched the game closer to where it is today. Players started wearing padded gloves in 1882 while catchers added chest protectors in 1885.[17] Starting in 1884, NL pitchers were given the opportunity to throw overhand and the mound was placed 60 feet, 6 inches from home plate in 1893.[18] The infield fly rule made its first appearance in 1895 and home plate took on a new look in 1900, changing from a 12-inch square to a five-sided shape that was 17 inches wide.[19]

What was the most important change in baseball during the 19th century?

CHARLIE BEVIS: Moving the pitcher farther back from the batter in 1893 to a distance of 60 feet, 6 inches was the most important rule change.

At this pitching distance, the game produced more offensive action to create more spectator interest, something the previous 50-foot distance discouraged. Without the increased hitting and scoring, baseball would not have become such a popular game.

The distance change also introduced the pitching rubber, to replace the former pitcher's box formed by lines on the diamond. Before 1893, it was literally possible to score many runs "to knock the pitcher from the box" in favor of a substitute pitcher. Today, such a term is only metaphorical.

BLAIR LOVERN: Among the non-playing rules, the reserve clause was a doozie. No, it was The King of Doozies. And it was created partly because of George Wright. In 1876, Harry and George Wright were part of an uncomfortable contract dispute between George and the Boston Red Stockings. Harry was the manager and one of the directors of the club and George was the shortstop. Boston's directors in August of 1875 drew up a contract for George to sign for the seasons of 1876, 1877 and 1878. For 1876, Boston and George had agreed for George to be paid according to the terms in the contract. But George had never signed it. It was still a verbal agreement. In fact, by February of 1877, George still hadn't signed. He was considering going to another club.

All NL teams were then put on notice that the Red Stockings, and only the Red Stockings, would employ George Wright from the 15th of March to the 15th of November in 1876, 1877 and 1878. He also had to agree "to comport himself in a quiet, temperate, and gentlemanly manner at all times." If he did not adhere to the terms of the contract, Boston said George would "nullify and destroy the whole of the said Association." George must have been thrilled. Unfortunately for him, he had no choice.

Guess what happened as soon as George's contract with the Red Stockings ended in 1878? He bolted. He managed his first team in Providence in 1879 and won the championship after a pennant race against Harry's Red

Stockings. Boston owners were so absolutely steamed that they led the way in the off-season for the creation in the NL bylaws of the Screw George Clause. (Seriously, it's the reserve clause.) And that's the rule that would bind players to their club for their whole careers for about the next 100 years. George didn't sign with Providence in 1880, and the reserve clause forced him to sit out all but one game of that season and all but seven games of 1881. In the meantime, Boston management, not the same group as when the Wrights first arrived there, didn't want Harry to manage. Both Wrights signed with Providence in 1882, Harry as manager and George as shortstop. After the season, George retired. Harry stayed on for another year but didn't like the city, and in 1884 he went to manage his final franchise in Philadelphia.

Regarding playing rules, there were so many changes in the 19th century that it's hard to pick just one. You had rules for batters that sound so silly today. For example, batters in the earliest days were allowed to ask for a ball pitched in a certain place, a walk was nine balls in 1879, pitchers had certain restrictions on their delivery until 1884. In 1876 the lone umpire on the field could stroll over to the stands after a play and ask something like, "Listen, I feel like an idiot, but did any of you guys happen to see if he was out?" The major leagues have officially been around since 1876. (I and many others would argue it should go back to 1871 with the creation of the National Association.) However, it really wasn't until 1903 when the AL became equal to the NL that everything pretty much settled into what we would consider modern baseball. If I were to pick important 19th century rule changes, relative to what we have today, among them would be the fly out on one bounce eliminated in 1864, and the ball size and weight regulated in 1872 and still the same today. (According to MLB current rules, the ball "shall weigh not less than five nor more than 5¼ ounces avoirdupois and measure not less than nine nor more than 9¼ inches in circumference.") Overhand pitching was allowed in 1884, and four balls became a walk and three strikes became an out starting in 1889. Player substitutions became unlimited in 1891 and the pitching distance went to 60.5 feet in 1893. There were so many 19th century rule changes that I can't mentally keep track of them all. That's a job for my bookshelves.

The Bullpen View

Baseball could have developed in a number of different directions in the 19th century. However, as the new century beckoned, amateurs had given way to paid professionals, owners had used the reserve clause to subjugate players, and the game had a revamped rulebook.

Harry Wright displayed in 1869 that professional baseball was financially viable, but Darryl Brock pointed out that Wright could have easily remained in New York and never ventured to Cincinnati. Had that happened, Brock speculated that the birth of pro baseball might have occurred much later or, at the very least, the professional game might have assumed a totally different character.

There was also the matter of which league would reign supreme. Both the American Association and the Players' League had opportunities to topple the National League. If the AA had supplanted the NL, Charlie Bevis theorized that more cities would have had major league clubs. He also claimed that westward expansion might have occurred sooner, if Brooklyn and Cincinnati had not jumped from the American Association to the NL in 1890, and the AA had found a way to survive. Meanwhile, under Marshall Wright's interesting scenario, the Players' League might have forced the National League to agree to a merger, if the PL could have kept a tight lid on its financial situation and continued to operate. Wright also hypothesized that the Players' League might have eventually wrecked the NL altogether, resulting in an earlier appearance by the American League, and improving the odds of survival for future organizations like the Federal League.

Today's fans would have had a difficult time recognizing baseball in 1870, but new rules and new equipment moved the game closer toward the modern age. Our panelists spotlighted several important revisions, including the 1893 rule that established 60 feet, 6 inches as the distance between pitcher and hitter.

Professional baseball had survived its beginnings. Various changes on the field, combined with the birth of the American League, would serve to boost the game's standing in America as the 20th century unfolded.

2

Deadball Days:
1901–1918

Historical Highlights

With only the National League operating as a major league between 1892 and 1900, and no postseason interleague competition since 1890, baseball had become stagnant. The game urgently needed a jump-start and got one from the American League in 1901. The former minor league declared itself a major league, lured away several stars from the NL, and forced the senior circuit to settle for a truce. Baseball's popularity was ready to skyrocket.[1]

Although the NL-AL war was technically over, there were still plenty of growing pains. The Boston Americans won the first modern World Series in 1903, but never got a chance to repeat as world champions. New York Giants manager John McGraw and team owner John Brush belittled the new league and declined to meet the AL champion in the 1904 postseason.[2]

While the opening decade of the 20th century featured low-scoring games and conservative offensive strategies, the Deadball Era also included some of greatest pennant races in baseball history. Look at 1908, when Detroit slipped by Cleveland to win the AL title, and Chicago outlasted New York for the NL flag, taking the pennant after beating the Giants in a makeup game. That extra game became necessary when an earlier Giants-Cubs tilt was ruled a tie due to the failure of New York's Fred Merkle to touch second base, after an apparent game-winning hit for the Giants.

One of the period's strongest dynasties, Connie Mack's Philadelphia Athletics, grabbed four AL titles and three World Series championships between 1910 and 1914 before financial problems forced Mack to dismantle his club. The era's top batsmen included Honus Wagner, Nap Lajoie and Detroit's talented outfielder Ty Cobb. Cleveland passed on a chance to pick up the fiery Cobb in exchange for veteran outfielder Elmer Flick. Cobb would rank as one of the AL's top hitters for two more decades; Flick would last only a few more seasons.[3]

The question of whether baseball could support three major leagues re-emerged in 1914 with the birth of the Federal League. After just two seasons in operation, the owners of the new league agreed to a peace treaty with organized baseball. While the FL's brief existence led to a temporary pay increase for major league ballplayers, salaries fell sharply when the Federal League folded.[4]

The American League

A new threat to National League supremacy surfaced in 1901, in the form of an established minor league known as the Western League, which began calling itself the American League. Intent on attaining major league status, AL president Ban Johnson tried to attract fans by cleaning up play on the field. The new league also placed franchises in some of the nation's largest cities and recruited several of the NL's top stars, including Philadelphia second baseman Nap Lajoie and pitching great Cy Young.[5]

Johnson's tactics worked. The NL and AL agreed to a peace treaty, the National Agreement, which recognized each league as separate but equal, and guaranteed that each would respect the other's contracts.[6]

What if the American League had never materialized or had been unable to survive?

BILL JAMES: Baseball was in a bad way in the 1890s. The National League was in a sort of free fall. Attendance wasn't very good, ladies didn't go to games for the most part, and there was a lot of violence on the field. The development of the American League redirected baseball in very profound ways that were beneficial for a number of years. The American League, which was much better managed, showed the National League how to conduct their business properly. Absent the example of a disciplined competitor, the National League would have continued to drift aimlessly for several more years until the situation got so bad that the league either failed completely, or faced a crisis. Thus, salaries would quite certainly have continued to fall because the revenues of the league would have continued to fall and there would have been no competition for players' services.

MIKE ROBBINS: Would major league history have been different if the American League had not challenged the National League? Probably. However, the National League was destined to face a successful challenge from some league at some point. Even with *both* the American League and National League in operation, the Federal League gave it a go in 1914 and 1915. Additional would-be major leagues known as the United States League and the Columbian League began and quickly failed in 1912. In addition, there had been an attempt to revive the American Association in 1900. True, none of these leagues lasted, but if the AL hadn't existed, there likely would have been enough pent-up demand for some league to last against the NL.

One could argue that future well-timed expansions by the National League might have preempted the need for a new league, but this isn't as straightforward as it might seem. Expanding into *new* cities wasn't the core of the American League's approach — the AL succeeded in large part by taking on the NL on its own turf. The National League wasn't likely to add additional teams in New York and Chicago.

Still, there is at least one reason why it matters that it was the American League that successfully challenged the National, and not some other circuit: Ban Johnson. Johnson helped make baseball respectable, reducing the amount of alcohol in the stands and umpire-tormenting and fighting on the field. In doing so, he played a significant role in cementing baseball's status as America's national pastime.

JIM VAIL: It was probably inevitable that some new baseball circuit would challenge the National League's monopoly during the first decade of the 20th century, well in advance of the Federal League's formation as a third major in 1914. The impetus for a new league's formation was evident by 1901, whether or not Ban Johnson and his Western League challenged the senior circuit that season. If Johnson had not done it, then someone else would have very soon — as there already was about as much historical tradition for two major leagues as for one. The NL began play in 1876. Beginning in 1882, there had been at least two "majors" in every year through 1891, with three big leagues operating (if not with stability for each) in the 1884 and 1890 seasons. Then the senior circuit absorbed the remnants of the defunct American Association in 1892, expanding from eight teams to 12, and retained that format through 1899. But the NL downsized for 1900, keeping only the eight franchises— Boston, Brooklyn, Chicago, Cincinnati, New York, Philadelphia, Pittsburgh and St. Louis— that, despite some relocations in the 1950s, comprised the senior circuit through its first modern expansion in 1962. The NL reduction of 1900 also meant there was a surplus of bona fide big leaguers available to any new circuit.

As evidenced by the population table below, the NL downsizing also left several legitimately "major-league" cities out in the cold, notably Baltimore, Cleveland and (to a lesser extent) Washington, each of which had been in the 12-team NL of the 1890s, plus Detroit (an NL member during 1881–88) and Buffalo (NL of 1879–85). Beyond that, during various seasons of the American Association's tenure (1882–91) there had been teams in both the NL and AA representing New York, Philadelphia, St. Louis and Brooklyn. Nature, at least as it applied to the public demand for top-level baseball, abhorred that vacuum; by the turn of the century the depression that plagued America during the middle 1890s (probably the worst in U. S. history before 1929) was over, making a new league economically viable.

The list below shows the top American cities, ranked by population, according to the 1900 U. S. Decennial Census. The National League's eight cities of 1901 are italicized. The populations are given in millions, to three decimal places. Note that New York City's overall population, including Brooklyn (which is subtracted from the rest of the city below), was 3.427 million. Given the rankings below, it was probably inevitable that, at minimum, top ten cities like Baltimore and Cleveland — both dropped from the NL after 1899 — would have clamored for a new team before long.

Rank	City	Pop	Rank	City	Pop
1	*New York*	2.260	11	*Cincinnati*	0.326
2	*Chicago*	1.699	12	*Pittsburgh*	0.322
3	*Philadelphia*	1.294	13	New Orleans	0.287
4	*Brooklyn*	1.167	14	Detroit	0.286
5	*St. Louis*	0.575	15	Milwaukee	0.285
6	*Boston*	0.561	16	Washington	0.279
7	Baltimore	0.509	17	Newark	0.246
8	Cleveland	0.382	18	Jersey City	0.206
9	Buffalo	0.352	19	Louisville	0.205
10	San Francisco	0.343	20	Minneapolis	0.203

It also seems likely that, in order to be credible, any new league during the first decade of the 20th century would have had to do exactly what the American League did — place teams in competition with the senior-circuit franchises in the nation's three largest cities, New York, Chicago and Philadelphia. Granted, the AL's incursion into New York City didn't occur until the Baltimore club (last place in 1902) moved there in 1903. But it was a sound move with regard to long-term perspective and prosperity nonetheless. Given that the AL's original Milwaukee franchise (last place in 1901) moved to St. Louis the following season, it's a bit surprising in hindsight that Ban Johnson and the AL owners didn't make the move to the Big Apple a year sooner.

In comparison, however, it seems a little odd that — almost from the start — the AL chose to go head-to-head with the NL in Boston and St. Louis too. Given what we now know and take for granted about the degree to which relative urban-area populations impact the economic success of modern baseball franchises, the populations of both of those cities (compared to those of the big four of 1901) were anything but a guarantee that either municipality could support two teams. In the long haul, predictably, one of the two clubs in each of those cities— the NL Braves in Boston and the AL Browns in St. Louis— became perpetual second fiddles in terms of on-field success and attendance. In turn, it gradually became inevitable that the Braves and Browns were the first of baseball's 16 franchises to change cities after 1903, the Braves moving to Milwaukee in 1953 and the Browns to Baltimore the next year (followed closely by the Philadelphia A's to Kansas City in 1955). But on the whole, it's also rather impressive that the two clubs managed to stay in Boston and St. Louis as long as they did, as no present-day franchise would spend anything close to 50 years in a town that didn't support it for much of that period.

Based on the populations listed above, the big loser in all of this seems to have been Buffalo. Among the nation's 15 largest cities of 1900, travel considerations obviously prevented San Francisco and New Orleans from consideration by the fledgling AL. But you would think that Buffalo, with seven prior seasons in the senior circuit and relatively near all of the American League's charter franchises except Milwaukee and Chicago, might have been a member of the new circuit — especially as its population was about one-third larger than Detroit, Milwaukee or Washington. The "Nickel City" did get a team in the Federal League, but that was little consolation for the AL's snub. In hindsight, it seems that placing what became the AL's Milwaukee-St. Louis franchise in Buffalo might have made more long-term sense in 1901.

I don't feel qualified to discuss the historical effects of the AL's formation on player salaries, but would like to examine the new league's impact on talent distribution. In that light, it's important to keep in mind that the junior circuit existed as the minor Western League in 1900, so it didn't spring to adulthood full-grown, like Aphrodite emerging from the sea foam. The Western circuit of 1900 included eight clubs in Buffalo, Chicago, Cleveland, Detroit, Indianapolis, Kansas City, Milwaukee and Minneapolis. Using the rosters provided in Marshall Wright's *Nineteenth Century Baseball*, a total of 200 men played in the Western League at some time that season. A handful of them also spent time on senior circuit rosters that year.

Turning to Neft and Cohen's *Sports Encyclopedia Baseball*, 184 men played in the American League at some time during the 1901 season. Among them, 63 (34.2 percent) were holdovers from the Western League of 1900 and 48 (26.1 percent) came from the previous year's NL. In comparison, National League teams employed 199 players during 1901. Among them, 106 (53.3 percent) had also played in the senior circuit during 1900, and 23 (11.6 percent) were crossovers from the Western League. Overall, 11 men played in both leagues in 1901. The bottom line to all of this is that almost 40 percent of the players in each league in 1901 were not on the rosters of either circuit at any time during the previous season.

At first, that number seems surprisingly high. However, it makes perfect sense if you think about it. Fearful that a new league might cause salary inflation as both circuits competed for talent, management of teams in both leagues jettisoned — no doubt prematurely in some cases — a lot of seasoned players who could command more money but who might be nearing the end of their usefulness. At the same time, given a choice between signing someone similarly cut adrift by another club or a young guy with no big-league experience, more often than not they opted for the lower-priced youth.

The National League of 1900 included 28 men who have since become Hall of Famers. In contrast, Ban Johnson's not-yet-major Western circuit had just one that season — Rube Waddell, who pitched 15 games for Milwaukee in addition to 29 for senior-circuit Pittsburgh (no doubt chasing fire engines in both cities).

By comparison, in 1901 American League rosters included ten future Hall of Famers, one of whom was Eddie Plank, a major-league rookie at 25. The other nine were lured from the older circuit. So the AL siphoned off a little more than one-third of the older league's theoretically biggest stars for its first season as a major. In that light, there's no real doubt that talent-wise, the National League was the stronger of the two circuits in 1901, because the senior league retained most of its biggest stars and had a slightly higher percentage of men who had played at the top rungs of baseball the previous season.

But over the next couple of seasons the junior circuit stole nine more future Hall of Famers from NL rosters (although one of them, George Davis, went back to the NL for a year in 1903). So, by 1903 the number of future Hall of Famers who had been in the majors two seasons earlier was split almost evenly between both leagues, and it's likely that the same relative balance was reflected among the descending levels of sub-Cooperstown talent in both circuits. As a result, the two leagues were relatively equal by 1903. Boston's victory in the first World Series that year should not have shocked anyone who closely followed the back-and-forth drift of talent during the AL's first three seasons.

The Fall Classic

With an AL-NL peace agreement in place, the Fall Classic made its first appearance in 1903 when Pittsburgh owner Barney Dreyfuss arranged to have his NL champions take on the AL pennant winners, the Boston Pilgrims.[7] Boston pitchers Bill Dinneen and Cy Young combined to win five games, as the Pilgrims took the best-of-nine postseason series five games to three, giving the AL bragging rights in the first modern World Series.

What if Pittsburgh and Boston had not initiated the World Series in 1903?

BILL JAMES: There are two possibilities. One is that the competition between the two leagues was inevitable, in which case it would have developed anyway. Another is that it was not inevitable, in which case the game would have been much the poorer.

It seems to me vastly more likely that the competition between the two leagues was inevitable. It is hard to envision two competing leagues playing out their schedules without resolving their differences, rather like envisioning an archway without a keystone. The natural desire to resolve the issue would have to assert itself, wouldn't you think? I note that postseason series had developed in the 19th century, even when there were not two leagues. Even in the 1890s when there was only one league, and one might think that the ultimate championship would be resolved by league games, playoffs were arranged between first-half champions and second-half champions, between first and second place teams. In all sports, there is a mechanism in place to resolve (often unsatisfactorily) the ultimate champion between the leagues. It was inevitable that it would soon have developed in this situation as well.

GABRIEL SCHECHTER: It was inevitable that the World Series would come into existence. There had been a version of it in the 1880s; even in the 1890s, with only the National League flourishing, there had been a championship series. Therefore, with two viable leagues, it would be common sense to have a championship series. Once "peace" was made between the leagues, there was no reason not to have a World Series. At the very latest, it would have begun in 1906 when the two Chicago teams won the pennants. They would not have been satisfied to call their traditional postseason meeting a "city series" if they were both already champions.

DAVID W. ANDERSON: The World Series would have come about eventually. After all, the old NL had tried a championship tourney in the 1890s. However, Pirates owner Barney Dreyfuss was visionary in his notion. The "war" between the AL and NL was counterproductive and expensive for owners. Dreyfuss' proposal was the step needed to end the warfare between the leagues and end player raids.

On the flip side, the Dreyfuss notion reinstituted the concept of the reserve clause, keeping players from selling to the highest bidder. So while the World Series increased interest in the game, it also helped the owners achieve financial stability.

The Giants Refuse

The NL and the AL may have had a peace treaty in place, but someone obviously forgot to mention that fact to New York Giants owner John Brush and his manager, John McGraw. Brush and McGraw disliked Ban Johnson, whom they had feuded with in the past; consequently, the Giants refused to participate in a 1904 postseason series with the AL champions from Boston.[8] The World Series would re appear in 1905, and would remain a fixture through 1994, but there would be no definitive world champions in 1904.

What if the Giants had agreed to play Boston in the 1904 postseason?

BILL JAMES: The odds are 2-to-1 that the Giants would have won. The Giants were 105–47 and the Red Sox were 95–59. Assuming that the quality of the leagues was even, a 105–47 team will beat a 95–59 team 58% of the time head to head. This edge doubles in a seven-game series. Thus, the 58% edge would double to 66%, actually a little over 66%. The Red Sox *could* have won, but the odds are pretty strongly against them.

DEAN SULLIVAN: To answer this we would have to know the mind of New York manager John McGraw. If he cared as little for this series as he and others in the 1890s cared about the Temple Cup series, anything could happen, but Boston would most likely win in a walk. If McGraw tried his best, the 1904 World Series would be closer, but the defending World Series champions, led by Cy Young, manager/third baseman Jimmy Collins, and the rowdiest fans in the majors, would probably prevail. Wouldn't it be fun to watch a Cy Young-Christy Mathewson matchup?

It's more fun to contemplate the results of a Giants-New York Highlanders series, had the Highlanders won the American League, instead of finishing one and a half games behind Boston. A primary reason McGraw and Giants owner John Brush refused to play the Series is their fear that their AL city rivals, led by Jack Chesbro, might defeat them. It would have been the original Subway Series, and the hatred on the field between the clubs would have produced some interesting baseball.

Cobb for Flick

Detroit's Ty Cobb for Cleveland's Elmer Flick. With the benefit of hindsight, it's easy to recognize that this trade would have ranked as one of the worst one-for-one deals of all time. However, following the 1907 season, the potential transaction looked inviting to both teams.

There was no disputing the talent of the 22-year-old Cobb. Even so, Detroit manager Hughie Jennings must have doubted whether the hot-tempered Cobb would ever get along with his teammates on and off the field.[9] Cleveland outfielder Elmer Flick seemed to be the safer bet, having already hit .300 or better eight times in his career, including a .302 average in 1907. Deciding that Flick would cause fewer headaches, Cleveland owner Charles Somers turned down Detroit's offer of Cobb for Flick.[10]

Talk about colossal blunders. Cobb hit .324 in 1908 and went on to collect 4,189 hits in a career that ran through the 1928 season. Cobb was destined for greatness; Flick was destined for early retirement, after developing a mysterious stomach ailment in 1908.[11] Had the Cobb-Flick deal gone through, an offense boasting Cobb, Nap Lajoie and Shoeless Joe Jackson might have brought several AL titles to Cleveland's doorstep.

What if Detroit had traded Ty Cobb to Cleveland in 1907?

DAN HOLMES: I don't know if the loss of Cobb would have prevented the Tigers from reaching the 1908 World Series but it is possible. Long term, I don't think it matters where Cobb played. Whether in Detroit or Cleveland, he still would have been a great player. It would have been interesting for Cobb and Nap Lajoie to be teammates. Flick and Lajoie didn't get along very well. One rumor was Lajoie had made fun of Flick. Flick wasn't known to be very sophisticated and Lajoie and some other teammates made fun of him and his sort of backward ways. Cobb and Lajoie might have had the strained relationship in Cleveland that Crawford and Cobb did in Detroit. Cobb would have had the same type of career numbers had he played in Cleveland. He might have hit for a bit less power because he would have been in a little larger park.

The trade would have been a real bust as far as the Tigers were concerned. With Cobb in Cleveland, Shoeless Joe Jackson might have stayed

Can you picture Ty Cobb in a Cleveland uniform? (Library of Congress.)

in Cleveland due to the influence of Cobb, another southerner. With Jackson in Cleveland, he would have missed the Black Sox World Series scandal of 1919. In fact, we might not have seen the fix in the Series, since Chick Gandil said that without Joe Jackson the White Sox could not have thrown Series games. The ringleaders of the fix could have approached Cicotte, Williams, Felsch and Weaver but it's no slam-dunk that the fix would have moved forward. They may have needed Eddie Collins and there was no way he was going to do it.

DEAN SULLIVAN: Cobb's statistics wouldn't have changed much, but he might have become part of one of the greatest outfields in history, and perhaps the greatest stain in baseball history might have been avoided.

Within a few years of Cobb's arrival in Cleveland, Joe Jackson would have joined him. Cleveland, with Cobb, Nap Lajoie and Addie Joss, would have won the 1908 pennant, and probably would have beaten the Cubs in the World Series that year, and possibly would have beaten Honus Wagner and the Pirates in 1909. Maybe with the success those two would have brought, Jackson might not have been traded to the Chicago White Sox during the 1915 season. Then they would have greeted new teammate Tris Speaker in 1916. Could Cleveland have lost with such an outfield? Meanwhile, the White Sox, without Jackson, would have been an excellent team but perhaps not good enough to make the 1919 Series. Even if they had won another pennant, they would have been such underdogs to the Reds that gamblers wouldn't have bothered with trying to throw the Series.

Merkle's Mistake

You learn the fundamentals at an early age. Hit the ball, run, and touch all of the bases. Fred Merkle should have remembered the basics.

In the midst of one of the greatest pennant races in baseball history, the events of September 23, 1908 irrevocably stained Merkle's otherwise solid career. It was on that day that the Giants hosted the Cubs in a crucial battle between National League pennant contenders. With the game tied and two Giants on base, Moose McCormick singled home what appeared to be the winning run, and fans at the Polo Grounds erupted into a raucous celebration. There was just one problem. The runner on first, Fred Merkle, failed to touch second base after McCormick's hit, veering off instead in the direction of the clubhouse in an effort to avoid the rowdy New York fans. Chicago second baseman Johnny Evers grabbed a ball—we'll never know for sure if it was the actual game ball—touched second, and then demanded that umpire Hank O'Day call Merkle out. Several sportswriters would later note that while the touching-second-base rule was on the books, many umpires had ignored it in the past. The Cubs had also experienced a similar play against Pittsburgh nearly three weeks earlier; on that occasion, O'Day had ruled against the Cubs and allowed Pittsburgh's winning run to score.[12] This time O'Day's decision pleased the Cubs: he called Merkle out on a force play and pronounced the game to be a tie. NL president Harry Pulliam upheld O'Day's actions and ordered a replay of the game on October 8, if necessary.[13]

When the Cubs and Giants finished the regular season tied at 98–55, the stage was set for a rerun of the disputed September 23 affair. Three Finger Brown's excellent relief work, and timely hitting by Joe Tinker and Frank Chance, carried Chicago to a 4–2 road victory, giving the Cubs their third straight NL pennant.

The AL boasted a tight race of its own in 1908, with Detroit finishing a half-game in front of Cleveland. The Tigers were not required to make up an earlier rainout with Washington, and the ensuing controversy led both leagues to require the re-scheduling of all rainouts and ties, if the games had a bearing on a pennant race.[14]

Fans would never forget the thrilling pennant races of 1908 or the events of September 23. Castigated by the New York press and bombarded with hate mail, Harry Pulliam suffered a nervous breakdown and committed suicide in 1909.[15] And although Fred Merkle would collect nearly 1,600 hits in a 16-year career, he would forever be remembered for his failure to touch second base, a mistake that may have cost his team a World Series title.

What if Merkle had touched second base during the September 23 game against the Cubs? What if Detroit had played a full schedule of games in the AL pennant race of 1908?

GABRIEL SCHECHTER: It's obvious that the Giants would have made the World Series. They still had plenty of games to play after September 23, so if they had won just one more game during that time, no replay of the September 23 game would have been necessary. Mathewson would have been fully rested for the Series, and he would have had no trouble shutting down the Tigers, so I'm sure the Giants would have won the Series.

If the Tigers had been forced to make up that unplayed game, at worst they would have wound up tied with Cleveland. Detroit had the better team, so unless Addie Joss had shut them out, the Tigers would have won a playoff game and made it to the Series. However, it seems ridiculous from our vantage point nearly 100 years later to think that they were not required to make up that game. Why should Cleveland have been penalized for being able to finish their schedule?

ROB NEYER: We'll never know for sure what the Giants would have done in the following games, had Merkle touched second base or had the umpire decided not to make the call he did. If the Giants had won the game, and the rest of the games went as they did in real life, the Giants win the NL pennant. It's Detroit and New York in the 1908 World Series and the Giants beat Detroit in the World Series. The Cubs wound up beating the Tigers in the 1908 World Series, four games to one, and it's pretty clear that the National League was the stronger league at that time, as the Cubs had swept the Tigers in 1907.

DAVID W. ANDERSON: Who's to say whether the Giants wouldn't have found another way to lose the pennant or that the 1908 Cubs, one of the toughest clutch teams in baseball history, wouldn't have run the table and still won the pennant?

As for the Tigers, the makeup game would have involved Washington. Although Washington finished seventh, this team would have been difficult to defeat because of one person, Walter Johnson. A Detroit victory would

Fred Merkle at bat. His life would never be the same after September 23, 1908. (Library of Congress.)

have been by no means certain had Johnson started. If the game had been played, I am certain Johnson would start because there had been reports of the Washington Nationals laying down, not playing to win, against Detroit.

MIKE ROBBINS: Whatever the outcome of the season, the implications for Merkle certainly would have been profound. Fans hounded Merkle over the incident for the rest of his career and beyond. Without the ruling, he would have had a much happier — if less memorable — life.

Oddly, if not for *another* player's crucial mistake, Merkle might even be remembered as a hero. The 1912 World Series was the first truly down-to-the-wire World Series ever played, and for a few minutes, the much-ridiculed Merkle appeared likely to be its star. In the top of the tenth inning of the seventh game (technically it was the eighth game, since an earlier game had ended in a tie) Merkle singled home the tie breaking run against Boston. Unfortunately for Merkle, the Giants blew the lead and lost the Series in the bottom of the tenth, thanks in part to Fred Snodgrass' famous "$30,000 muff."[16]

The Federal League

Past efforts to compete against existing major leagues had fizzled rather quickly. Both the Union Association, unveiled in 1884, and the Players' League, which debuted in 1890, had shut down after only one season. In 1914, the Federal League took its shot.

Operating as a minor league in 1913, the FL featured franchises in eight cities, such as Baltimore, Buffalo and Chicago. Several major league stars were also drawn to the new league, including shortstop Joe Tinker and pitcher Three Finger Brown in 1914, and pitchers Eddie Plank and Chief Bender in 1915.

Financial problems, however, forced FL owners to capitulate after the 1915 season.[17] Poor timing was another factor, with the baseball world in the throes of a recession brought on by World War I, a downturn that wound up burying a number of minor leagues, not just the Federal League.[18]

By way of a complicated settlement, the FL sold its stars back to AL and NL teams, which assumed responsibility for unsettled Federal League contracts. FL owners in Chicago and St. Louis were also allowed to purchase the Chicago Cubs and the St. Louis Browns, respectively.[19]

What if the Federal League had succeeded in becoming a third major league?

GIL BOGEN: If the Federal League had succeeded, player salaries would have been much larger than they were, especially for the stars. In addition, the Fraternity of Professional Baseball Players would have remained and the players union could have been established earlier, with player representation.

I expect that the reserve clause and the policy of blacklisting rebellious players could have been done away with. And who knows! The end result could have been a decision by the court whereby these practices by organized baseball would have been seen as a restraint of trade and in violation of the antitrust laws. Had this happened, baseball would be far different today.

As it turned out, Ban Johnson did not live up to what he had agreed to and there was nobody who could do anything about it. The players continued to be as powerless as before. This would not have happened had the Federal League remained afloat.

If the Federal League had been started earlier or later, they would have needed sufficient funds to keep the new league going, regardless of the attendance at the league's new ballparks. Owners in the other leagues were hurt financially due to the drop in attendance at their parks. What if they had hung on and three leagues had developed? Could the city of Chicago, for example, support three teams? If the Federal League had survived and we now had three leagues rather than two leagues, how would that have shaped baseball? We can only fantasize. However, if free agency had remained, those contracts that the players signed would have changed many careers.

STEVE STEINBERG: Competition would have continued to create player movement and salary increases. But financial losses in all three leagues would have continued, exacerbated by World War I. Something would have had to give, and the owners of organized ball would have settled, just as the NL had done with the AL more than a decade earlier. Ultimately, the team owners of the rival leagues would have realized they had more in common with each other than with their employees, the players.

Free agency would not have happened, or at least it would not have lasted very long. Some kind of settlement would have emerged. Rather than just two Federal League owners buying major league teams, a few more Federal League teams would have survived and joined the established leagues.

Perhaps the AL and the NL would have become ten-team leagues. Likely survivors from the Federal League would have included the Chicago, Baltimore and Kansas City franchises, as well as perhaps the Newark and Pittsburgh teams.

Mack's First Dynasty

Baseball's most dominant franchise between 1910 and 1914 was Connie Mack's Philadelphia Athletics, winners of the World Series in 1910, 1911 and 1913. Despite being heavy favorites to win another World Series title in 1914, Mack's club was shocked by Boston, as the Miracle Braves swept Philadelphia in four games.

In the wake of the Athletics' embarrassing defeat, and plagued by financial losses, Mack dismantled his dynasty, requesting waivers on veteran pitchers Chief Bender, Eddie Plank and Jack Coombs. The White Sox acquired second baseman Eddie Collins for $50,000.[20] A lack of funds also prevented Mack from purchasing Babe Ruth from Baltimore of the International League in 1914.[21] With the Athletics foundering midway through the 1915 season, Mack's fire sale continued. Shortstop Jack Barry went to the Red Sox, and the Yankees acquired pitcher Bob Shawkey and Frank "Home Run" Baker.

In getting rid of his stars, Mack claimed his team could remain competitive by relying on younger, more inexpensive players.[22] He was sorely mistaken. The Athletics, winners of 99 games in 1914, would claim just 79 victories over the course of 1915–1916, and would not climb over the .500 mark again until 1925.

What if Connie Mack had not broken up the Athletics' dynasty of 1910–1914?

BILL JAMES: Mack broke up the team not because he chose to but because he couldn't afford to pay them. If he had not chosen to sell off his players, it is overwhelmingly likely that the key players would have skipped to the Federal League, so the team would have broken apart anyway. The Federal League, being poorly financed, would have folded anyway, so nothing really would have changed. Connie Mack was a very good team builder and he could have kept his dynasty going strong for at least a few more years if he hadn't run into financial problems. The Athletics dynasty of the teens could have dominated the American League through 1920.

Connie Mack: architect and destroyer of two powerful dynasties. (Library of Congress.)

STEVE STEINBERG: The Athletics were still a very young team following the loss to the Boston Braves in the 1914 World Series. Home Run Baker was only 28. Catcher Wally Schang had just turned 25. Eddie Collins and Stuffy McInnis were both in their mid 20s and Mack had good young pitching talent in Joe Bush, Herb Pennock and Bob Shawkey. All three of those pitchers later wound up with the New York Yankees in the 1920s. The Athletics had a good mixture of youth and veterans and would have competed for the American League pennant for several more seasons. They would have been right there in the late teens with the Red Sox and the White Sox. Philadelphia would have grabbed at least one additional American League pennant.

GABRIEL SCHECHTER: Things definitely would have been much tighter in the AL for the rest of that decade. Mack's team was talented and still very young. They had only one regular, Rube Oldring, who was as old as 30, and only two pitchers, Bender and Plank, over the age of 30. Herb Pennock was just coming up, Collins was only 27, Baker only 28, and McInnis just 23. Pennock, Bush, and Shawkey could have anchored the staff for many years. Therefore, it was a shame that Mack allowed competition from the doomed Federal League to scare him into dismantling his franchise.

The Bullpen View

Competition is good. National League owners probably would not have agreed with that assessment in 1901, but baseball needed a second major league to provide a spark, and the American League turned out to be just what the doctor ordered.

Most of our experts agreed that the National League was bound to face stiff competition eventually. Bill James maintained that the AL served as a good role model for the NL and boosted baseball at a time when attendance was lagging. Mike Robbins added that the efforts of AL president Ban Johnson helped to solidify the game's status as America's national pastime.

While the AL arrived on the scene at a most opportune time, the bid by the Federal League to become a third major league occurred during tough economic times. Had the FL succeeded, higher salaries for players probably would have remained in place. That was the prediction from Gil Bogen, who concluded that a players union might have developed much earlier, possibly ending the reserve clause.

The modern World Series certainly experienced its share of trials and tribulations in its early days, as John Brush and John McGraw spurned a meeting with the AL champions in 1904. Bill James stated that McGraw's

Giants probably would have defeated the Boston Pilgrims, while Dean Sullivan suggested that a Highlanders-Giants match-up would have been even more intriguing.

1908 was the year that Fred Merkle's decision to bypass second base resulted in lasting notoriety for the New York Giants infielder. Rob Neyer and Gabriel Schechter asserted that the Giants probably would have won the NL title and the World Series, if Merkle had taken the time to complete his journey to second base. If nothing else, as Mike Robbins pointed out, Merkle's life would have turned out to be much more uneventful.

How about Cleveland's decision to turn down an opportunity to pick up Ty Cobb from Detroit? Can you imagine an outfield consisting of Cobb, Shoeless Joe Jackson and Tris Speaker? Had the trade gone through, Dan Holmes theorized that Cleveland might have decided against trading Jackson to the White Sox. By avoiding the 1919 World Series scandal, Shoeless Joe would undoubtedly be in the Hall of Fame today.

3

Between the Wars: 1919–1941

Historical Highlights

Offensive production had certainly lagged during the early stages of the 20th century, but big changes were in the offing. The move to keep clean balls in play, the abolition of the spitball, and the introduction of a new cushioned cork center baseball in 1925 led to a spike in scoring during the Roaring Twenties.[1] Sluggers like Babe Ruth, Lou Gehrig, Jimmy Foxx and Hack Wilson captivated the public's attention with their ability to crush baseballs and clear fences.

Several important events changed the complexion of the game, including the 1919 World Series. Eight members of the Chicago White Sox were accused of throwing the series. Although the players were acquitted in the courts, all eight were banned for life, wiping out any hopes that the White Sox dynasty would continue. Meanwhile, fans in Boston could blame owner Harry Frazee for ruining the Red Sox and assisting in the construction of a new powerhouse in New York. To finance his theatrical interests, Frazee sold and traded several of Boston's best players to the Yankees, including Babe Ruth and top-flight pitchers like Waite Hoyt, Joe Bush and Herb Pennock. The result was twofold: Boston faded into oblivion and the Yankees rose to prominence.

Several talented players also had their careers cut short in the years between World War I and World War II. Tragedy descended on Cleveland on August 16, 1920 when a pitched ball killed Indians shortstop Ray Chapman, fueling efforts to make the game safer by introducing a greater number of clean, white balls into games. One of baseball's top pitchers in the 1930s, St. Louis' Dizzy Dean, suffered a broken toe in the 1937 All-Star Game. In trying to recover from the injury, the Cardinals' right-hander changed his throwing motion and ruined his arm in the process.[2]

The 1919 Series

Heading into the 1919 postseason, AL teams had totally dominated their NL counterparts during the decade, winning eight of nine World Series matchups, and many experts expected that trend to continue. Despite the fact that the NL champions, the Cincinnati Reds, had amassed 96 victories, many still viewed the AL pennant winners, the Chicago White Sox, as the team to beat.

The experts had no way of knowing that gamblers had promised payments to several Chicago players to throw the series. One of the conspirators, pitcher Eddie Cicotte, was bombed in the opener 9–1; Lefty Williams, another White Sox hurler in on the fix, lost the second game by a 4–2 count. Chicago's Dickie Kerr blanked the Reds on three hits in Game 3, and after the two teams split the next four games, the Reds' advantage stood at 4–3. Just when it looked like the White Sox might rally to win the series, the Reds blasted Lefty Williams in Game 8. Throwing nothing but fast balls, Williams never escaped the first inning, surrendering three runs as the Reds won 10–5 and took the series 5–3.[3] One year later, baseball commissioner Kenesaw Mountain Landis slapped lifetime bans on eight of the White Sox, for participating in or knowing about the fix.

The absence of eventual Hall of Fame pitcher Red Faber, who was unable to play due to a sore ankle, further reduced the odds of a White Sox victory in the series. Faber had won three games against the New York Giants in the 1917 World Series, and White Sox catcher Ray Schalk later asserted that the Black Sox scandal might never have transpired, had Faber pitched against the Reds.[4]

What if the Black Sox had played to win throughout the 1919 World Series? What if Red Faber had pitched for Chicago in the series?

DAVID SHINER: Red Faber was not part of the Chick Gandil group, which was at the core of the effort to throw the 1919 World Series. Faber had been the star of the 1917 World Series, winning three games. If he had been healthy in 1919, then the emphasis on the importance of Eddie Cicotte and Lefty

Williams would have been much less. The gamblers and most of the White Sox didn't have a lot of faith in Dickie Kerr's ability, and no one else on the Sox staff was a go-to guy. Without Faber, it came down to Cicotte and Williams and it was much easier to rig the series when essentially you only had to deal with two pitchers. If Faber were available, you would have to guess he starts either the first or the second game and the situation is completely different.

It's difficult to say who would have won the series if both teams had played it straight up. The Pirates' win over the Yanks in 1960 was kind of a poster child for throwing predictions out the window. There has been a fair amount of revisionist scholarship recently that says the Reds would have won the 1919 series even if it had been on the level. I tend to doubt that. The Reds had a deeper pitching staff, given the injury to Faber, but a deep staff doesn't necessarily help you in a short series. If you look at each team position by position, the White Sox were clearly the better club. The Reds had a better regular-season record, but the AL was a much stronger league than the NL. The AL had been dominant in the World Series for the entire decade coming up to 1919. The White Sox had defeated the Giants in 1917 and that New York team was at least as good as the 1919 Reds.

DAVID W. ANDERSON: The 1919 Reds were a fine ball club and a White Sox victory was far from a foregone conclusion even if some of the Chicago players hadn't thrown the series. The idea that the 1919 Chicago White Sox was one of the greatest teams ever is a myth. The reality was Chicago was thin on pitching and there was little, if any, team chemistry.

The 1919 World Series also was not going to be halted due to rumors of the fix. The owners needed the World Series to restore profitability after the 1918 season and World Series, which had been adversely impacted by World War I. That was one reason why the fix was so devastating to the game and why Judge Landis' arbitrary actions against the fixers were accepted.

There had also been rumors of fixes in the 1903, 1914, 1917 and 1918 fall classics. Nothing was proven because baseball governance was completely unwilling to face up to the issue. In my book, *More Than Merkle*, there is an account of an attempt to bribe the umpires in the final Cubs-Giants game of the season. Other than banning the New York team physician from baseball for life, nothing significant came of the National League investigation of the matter. I conclude that baseball did not want to do anything about gambling until forced.

GENE CARNEY: We can never be completely sure as to how many games were thrown and the degree to which players threw games. I think all eight of the players banned from baseball were somehow involved but certainly not to the same degree. If the series had been played straight up, it was not going to be a clear-cut White Sox victory as some people have assumed.

Game 1 was a key game as was Game 4. Many people think Game 4 was one of the fixed games but I don't think it was. The first two games were tampered with. It's hard to look back and say who would have won those games and the series if the White Sox had been playing to win. The Reds shouldn't have been that much of an underdog, thanks mainly to their pitching.

The White Sox might have been able to match up better if Chicago had Red Faber healthy. The White Sox had three quality pitchers available in October, Eddie Cicotte, Lefty Williams and Dickie Kerr. When you look at the other pitchers available to Chicago, you have to wonder how the White Sox made it to the World Series. The Reds had a much deeper pitching staff and many people, including Christy Mathewson, gave the Reds the edge in pitching. Had Faber been available, Kerr might not have received his two starts and he pitched pretty well. Let's not forget the Sox were trying to win both of those games. Sometimes people think Kerr won those games by himself with five or six players behind trying to throw the game and that wasn't the case. With Faber, Chicago would have had a few more options. White Sox manager Kid Gleason, who I think knew about the fix early on, could have managed differently with Faber healthy.

I know there had been suspicions raised about other series games being fixed before 1919. Hugh Fullerton, one of the main whistleblowers of the 1919 Series, was convinced several other series results might be tainted but he never really went on record detailing specific series, teams or players. Several years come up in conversation when you start talking about suspicious series, including 1914 and 1918. I know in the first series, in 1903, Boston catcher Lou Criger was offered thousands of dollars to throw a game. Gambling was big in the first two decades of the 20th century and even in 1919, the World Series was a huge event, comparable to the Final Four or the Super Bowl today.

JIM VAIL: Prior to the 1919 World Series, except for the Miracle Braves sweep of Philadelphia in 1914, the American League champs had won every fall classic during the period 1910–18. Even including that sweep, AL clubs had won 32 of the 49 World Series games played during those years, for a winning percentage (.653) that was higher than the average regular-season mark (.646) posted during that period by the junior circuit winners as a group. Three of those overall series victories (the A's of 1913, plus the Red Sox of 1916 and 1918) also came against National League clubs with better regular-season records. Therefore, it was not intimidating to AL faithful that Cincinnati entered the 1919 series with a season mark of 96–44 (.686), while Chicago won the AL with an 88–52 (.629) ledger.

The White Sox roster included three future Hall of Famers (Eddie Collins, Ray Schalk and Red Faber) plus two other players (Joe Jackson and Eddie Cicotte) who—I believe—would also be in Cooperstown absent their roles in the series fix. In comparison, the Reds included just one Hall of Famer (Edd Roush) and three guys at most (Jake Daubert, Dolf Luque and Heinie Groh) with marginal HOF credentials.

When you combine all that with Chicago manager Kid Gleason's adamancy that the 1919 White Sox were the best team he had ever seen in a big-league career that dated to 1888, there's an unavoidable tendency to conclude that the White Sox deserved to be prohibitive favorites against Cincinnati. In turn, Eliot Asinof reports that the betting odds on the series, which favored Chicago, were 8–5—indicating a 61.5-percent expectation of Pale Hose victory—the day before the professional gambling community got wind of the nefarious doings and started to bet on Cincy.

Despite all that, even without the fix, it's my own view that the Chisox team chemistry was so poisoned by the start of that series that they would have been hard-pressed to win it anyway. It's been fairly well documented that a substantial portion of Chicago's less-educated lineup regulars was resentful of college boy Eddie Collins, and had been for some time. The same seems true, albeit to a lesser degree, with regard to Ray Schalk. Description of Schalk's combative, cheerleader personality read like a cross between a Leo Durocher/Eddie Stanky type and a rah-rah "Atta Boy!" guy like Tommy Lasorda—in other words, more than enough to get on almost anyone's nerves. Add to that Eddie Cicotte's reputed disappointment over losing out on a chance to win 30 games and a bonus promised by owner Charles Comiskey, and it's clear the White Sox were anything but a group of happy campers. When you toss in the fact that midway through the series the eight conspirators were squabbling with each other about who had been paid off with how much, and who hadn't been paid at all, it's quite evident that the 1919 Black Sox were not the Fightin' Oakland A's of the early 1970s—a club that could duke it out between victories and then leave all their personal animosities in the locker room each time they played.

Beyond that, it's also evident that first baseman Chick Gandil, instigator of the fix among the Chicago players, and his conjoined-at-the-wallet Siamese twin Swede Risberg were both slick enough (and resentful enough towards Comiskey) to have sought out, absent the compliance of players like Cicotte, Jackson and Lefty Williams, some kind of bet(s) in which they laid down—perhaps to lose a game or two—in order to make some side money of their own. Granted, it would have been far more difficult for a first sacker or a shortstop to throw any contest than a pitcher, but such an effort was still within their apparently amoral provinces. If they had succeeded just once or twice, that still could have made the team's over-all effort an uphill struggle.

One should also note that the Reds, not the White Sox, were the hotter team going into the series. They won the NL flag going away, increasing their regular-season record from 28 games above .500 on August 1 to 52 above at season's end. In contrast, Chicago was at +24 on the first of August, and finished at +36. So Cincinnati gained twice as much ground on their circuit as a whole in the last two months as the Chisox did on theirs.

There's no doubt that the absence of Red Faber, who won three games in the 1917 World Series, hurt Chicago as well. Faber was 16–13 during 1917, but just 11–9 two years later. Cicotte and Williams were still the Chisox aces in both seasons, going 28–12 and 17–8 respectively in 1917, then 29–7 and 23–11 in 1919. Chicago's other 1919 starter, Dickie Kerr, won an inordinate amount of recognition for his two victories against Cincinnati, but he was still a rookie with a regular-season mark of 13–8. Faber's record for 1919 doesn't justify unqualified confidence that he would have been as dominant in the 1919 series as he was two years earlier; and, if Faber had been available in 1919, then Kerr would certainly not have gotten the two starts he won. Any way you approach it, Faber's presence was no guarantee of Chicago victory.

Baseball's hierarchy, which at the time included league presidents Ban Johnson (AL) and John Heydler (NL) plus National Commission chairman Garry Herrmann (who was owner of the Reds), was not about the halt the series of 1919 or any other year because of rumors about the fix. It's clear from Asinof and the much broader history written by Harold Seymour that official baseball's compulsion at the time was to sweep such allegations under the rug and keep them hidden for as long as possible, preferably forever. As is, although the Gleason-to-Comiskey-to-Johnson communication of a possible fix occurred during the series itself, it was not until late in the 1920 season that the full exposé of what had happened reached the nation's papers—evidence that the obfuscation by baseball's moguls was relatively successful for nearly a year.

Given all of the above, it's my own view that, absent the fix and even with Faber available, Cincinnati would have won the series in nine games anyway. Such a victory should not be seen as anything more surprising than the 1990 Reds sweeping the heavily favored Oakland A's—a club which, like the Black Sox, seemed to have talent and destiny on its side.

The Black Sox

Landis' decision to issue a lifetime ban against the eight Black Sox barred the road to Cooperstown for several star players, including Shoeless Joe Jackson and Eddie Cicotte. Jackson left the game with a lifetime batting average of .356; Cicotte finished with 209 victories and a career ERA of 2.38. Three other Black Sox, infielder Buck Weaver, outfielder Happy Felsch and pitcher Lefty Williams, were just beginning to put together impressive numbers on a consistent basis. Williams had won 45 games in 1919–1920, Felsch had hit .300 or better in 1916, 1917 and 1920, and Weaver had hit .300 in 1918 and .331 in 1920.

The scandal also decimated one of the AL's strongest clubs. With the White Sox trailing first place Cleveland by just a half-game in the 1920 pennant race, a grand jury indicted the eight Black Sox for conspiring to throw the 1919 World Series. White Sox owner Charles Comiskey suspended those Black Sox still active, Chicago dropped two of its final three games, and Cleveland won the pennant by two games.[5] Without stars like Jackson, Weaver, Felsch, Cicotte and Williams, the White Sox finished a distant seventh in the AL in 1921, a whopping 36½ games behind the first place Yankees.

If the Black Sox don't throw the 1919 World Series, which Chicago players wind up in the Hall of Fame?

BILL DEANE: Jackson hit .382 in his final season of 1920 before being banned. Jackson was banished from the game just as baseball was entering a heavy hitting era. Jackson had plenty of baseball left in him. He played amateur ball until the mid–1930s so I believe Jackson could have continued in the majors for perhaps another decade. Some Hall of Famers who were nearly the same age as Jackson, Ty Cobb, Eddie Collins and Tris Speaker, all put up good offensive numbers in the '20s. Both Speaker and Collins actually had higher batting averages after 1920 than they did before 1920 although they were older, and Cobb "slumped" to .360. Those players took advantage of the improved hitting conditions in the '20s and I have no doubt Jackson would have done the same. I have projected that Jackson would have finished his career with over 3,000 hits and a lifetime batting average of over .350. Those are sure Hall of Fame numbers.

I think Eddie Cicotte was also headed for the Hall of Fame. He nearly had Hall of Fame credentials as it was, looking at his pitching numbers through 1920. Cicotte racked up 210 wins and was outstanding in 1917, 1919 and 1920 with nearly 80 victories in those three seasons. I believe Cicotte would have remained effective for several more seasons and would have

What if Shoeless Joe Jackson had avoided the Black Sox scandal of 1919? (Library of Congress.)

approached the 300-win mark and he would have been a Hall of Famer. It's difficult to say whether Lefty Williams, Buck Weaver or Happy Felsch might have had Hall of Fame careers. None of them played even ten years in the majors and Weaver and Felsch were just starting to put together good offensive seasons. Williams was a good young pitcher who had just put together a couple of 20 win seasons. He may well have developed into an outstanding pitcher in the 1920s. He had 62 lifetime wins so it's difficult to say whether he would have been able to put together Hall of Fame numbers by the end of his career.

DAVID SHINER: The only clear Hall of Famer among the banned players was Joe Jackson. He was only 31 when his career ended and had played roughly ten full seasons. Jackson's accomplishments, however, were such that he had a chance at the Hall of Fame even if he had simply retired then (like Ken Griffey, Junior, if he had retired rather than accepting the trade to the Reds a few years ago). Given that Jackson probably would have played another five to ten years, there would have been no question about his making the Hall of Fame.

Eddie Cicotte was on the verge of Hall of Fame qualifications based on what he did through 1920. Most of the pitchers with his credentials are not in the Hall but some are. He won 50 games in his last two seasons, in 1919 and 1920. One or two more seasons, even with records along the lines of 13–11, would have left no doubt.

The older a player is when he leaves the game, the easier it is to project their career numbers. Therefore, it's easier to make predictions for Buck Weaver than Happy Felsch. Felsch had only been in the majors for about six years. Weaver had been in the majors for nine seasons. When you try to project a player's future career, you look at his possible decline phase and players comparable to him in the era. The most comparable player to Weaver in baseball history, ironically, was Heine Groh, the third baseman for the Reds in the 1919 World Series. That was pretty well known at the time. People were saying these were the two best 3B in baseball in 1919. Groh was a very good third baseman but not a Hall of Fame caliber player. That's probably the best guess we can make about Buck Weaver, had he been able to finish out his career. He probably would not have been in the Hall of Fame but he would be remembered as a good player and one of the best at his position when he played. Felsch was a very good defensive center fielder who had started to put together some solid offensive seasons when he was banned following the 1920 season. He could have become a Hall of Famer but it's hard to make that projection based on his numbers through 1920. He was probably at the peak of his career in 1919–1920. He probably would have had a 12–15 year career, but would have started to decline a bit soon after 1920. He certainly wasn't in the class of a Tris Speaker or an Edd Roush, the Hall of Fame center fielders of that time. Felsch would have had to improve but he wasn't that far away from All-Star type status.

GENE CARNEY: Joe Jackson and Eddie Cicotte would be in the Hall of Fame today had they played to win in the 1919 World Series and not been banished from baseball. Jackson could have put together some amazing career numbers with another five years in the majors, with the lively ball being used. Jackson might have swung more for the fences rather than the gaps and might have developed into a true power hitter. Cicotte would have continued to throw some of his trick pitches, like his shine ball. I think he might have gotten into the Hall of Fame just based on his statistics through 1920. If fact, if you go to the Hall of Fame, you'll find Cicotte's name on a plaque for one of the lowest earned run averages and Jackson's name for the third highest batting average of all time. The names are there. They just don't have the bronze plaque. Buck Weaver was just starting to come into his own. He would have needed several more seasons to earn a spot in the Hall. He had a great reputation and was certainly headed in the right direction.

BILL MCNEIL: 'Shoeless Joe' Jackson was a Hall of Fame baseball player when he was banned from the game by Commissioner Kenesaw Mountain Landis for no good reason. He didn't participate in throwing the 1919 World Series. He tried to notify Charles Comiskey about the plot prior to the Series but was rebuffed by the White Sox owner. He went on to lead all hitters in the Series with an average of .375, hit the only home run of the Series and played flawlessly in the field. The commissioner made him a scapegoat.

At the time of his banishment, his 13-year batting average stood at .356, the third highest average of all time, behind Ty Cobb and Rogers Hornsby. In addition to his hitting prowess, he was an outstanding base runner and an excellent defensive outfielder with a strong, accurate throwing arm. If he had been allowed to continue his career, he would have accumulated over 3,000 base hits and still hit well over .350. He may even have improved on his career numbers during the beginning of the lively ball era. He had one of his best seasons in 1920, pounding the ball at a .382 clip with 42 doubles, a league-leading 20 triples, 12 home runs, 105 runs scored, and 121 runs batted in. Jackson was one of the greatest hitters the game has yet produced, and his smooth swing was copied by some of the superb hitters that followed him, including Babe Ruth. Today there is a furor about admitting Pete Rose to the HOF but before that is given consideration, Shoeless Joe should be admitted first. He was persecuted and treated unfairly by the baseball establishment, and his vindication is long overdue.

What if the White Sox had remained intact for the 1921 season and beyond?

STEVE STEINBERG: Offense was starting to explode in the majors in 1920, and several members of the White Sox, including Joe Jackson and Buck Weaver, put up some impressive numbers in 1920. Along with Hap Felsch and a pitching staff that included Lefty Williams, Red Faber, Dickie Kerr and veteran Eddie Cicotte, the White Sox would have presented a serious challenge to the Yankees' dynasty of the early 1920s. With the economy booming and baseball attendance soaring, the White Sox owner, Charles Comiskey, probably would have been inclined to keep this team together for several seasons.

DEAN SULLIVAN: Given that many of the best players were still in their prime, I think that the Sox could have dominated the AL well into the 1920s. Although the Yankees won pennants in 1921–23 behind historic years by Babe Ruth, they were not the juggernaut they would soon become, and Chicago, with Joe Jackson enjoying the fruits of the lively ball, could well have led the Sox to multiple pennants during this period. If so, it could have delayed or affected the construction of Yankee Stadium, since the Yankees would have not had the pennant to advertise their status as an elite team and to draw additional fans. Nevertheless, the popularity of Ruth and the unwillingness of the Giants to continue to share the Polo Grounds would have required the building of a stadium soon.

DAVID SHINER: Had the White Sox stayed together in the 1920s, it seems likely Chicago would have won additional AL pennants. Even with rumors that the White Sox were throwing crucial games during the 1920 season, Chicago narrowly missed winning the AL flag. The banned Black Sox were not permitted to play the final series of the season against the St. Louis Browns. If those players were available, Chicago might well have swept St. Louis.

The White Sox and Red Sox had dominated the AL in the period 1915–1919. Thanks to the Red Sox trades, New York was the franchise on the rise in the AL heading into the '20s. The White Sox of 1920 were still a relatively young club. They may not have been a dominant dynasty in the '20s but they would have been able to compete very strongly with the Yankees. I could easily see the White Sox winning five to six AL pennants over a ten-year period, starting in 1917.

Frazee's Deals

It was the biggest transaction in baseball history. Theatrical producer Harry Frazee, owner of the Boston Red Sox since 1917, sold outfielder Babe Ruth, his best player, to the New York Yankees in 1919 for cash and a

$300,000 loan, secured by a mortgage on Fenway Park.[6] As a hitter, Ruth slugged 29 homers for the Red Sox in 1919; as a pitcher, he won 65 games between 1915 and 1917.

The Yankees actually received several gifts from the benevolent Frazee. A number of talented Boston pitchers found their way to New York between 1919 and 1923, including Carl Mays, Waite Hoyt, Joe Bush, Sam Jones, and Herb Pennock. The Yankees also picked up infielders Joe Dugan and Everett Scott and catcher Wally Schang from the Red Sox. While the trades helped the Yankees become a dynasty, Boston struggled to recover from Frazee's dubious deals. The Red Sox, winners of five of the first 15 World Series, would not make another postseason appearance until 1946.

What if Boston had not traded Babe Ruth and several star pitchers to the New York Yankees?

BILL DEANE: The Red Sox in the first few decades of the 20th century dealt away Babe Ruth, Tris Speaker, Waite Hoyt and Herb Pennock. The owner of the Red Sox, Harry Frazee, had other financial priorities beyond owning a successful Red Sox club. Most people tend to focus on the Ruth deal, and there's no question that really hurt the Red Sox, but people tend to overlook the other pitchers that Boston traded away. Hall Of Famers Hoyt, Pennock and Red Ruffing in 1930 all went from Boston to the New York Yankees. So while the Red Sox were going down in talent, Boston's ownership was boosting a league rival, the Yankees, at the same time.

Babe Ruth could have actually landed in Philadelphia before he went to the Red Sox, possibly with the Phillies or the Athletics. If the Phillies had signed Ruth, think of the numbers that he would have had playing his home games in Baker Bowl. The Phillies used Baker Bowl from 1915 through 1938. It was the Coors Field of the 1920s and 1930s. We're talking about a park where it was 280 feet to the right-center field power alley. There was a tall fence in place there, but any good hitter could easily rattle drives off the fence or pop flies over it. For example, a guy like Chuck Klein pretty much rode to the Hall of Fame based on his hitting in Baker Bowl. Klein hit .397 lifetime at Baker Bowl and .277 in the other parks. I think if Ruth had played most of his career in Baker Bowl, he would still be the all-time home run leader and the modern stars would still be shooting at several of his records. If Ruth had played 15 seasons in Baker Bowl, with his road numbers, he could have hit 70 to 80 homers, hit .400 in several different seasons, and hit over 800 homers for his career. Major League owners aren't always known for their foresight. Before we start criticizing the Phillies or the Athletics for not signing Ruth, we have to remember that Ruth was regarded as a pitcher and possibly be difficult to handle. When the Red Sox traded Ruth to the Yankees, many baseball people thought New York was taking a gamble.

STEVE STEINBERG: Boston won the World Series four times in the teens, in 1912, 1915, 1916 and 1918. The Red Sox had the makings of a dynasty capable of extending well into the '20s, with outfielders Babe Ruth and Tris Speaker (Speaker was traded to Cleveland), and pitchers like Herb Pennock, Joe Bush, Sam Jones, Carl Mays and Waite Hoyt (all of whom went to the Yankees). Those five pitchers eventually won hundreds of games for the Yankees. I would argue that the Yankees could have more easily replaced Babe Ruth than all the pitching that they acquired from the Red Sox. They could not have replaced Ruth's hitting with just one person. They would have needed two or three bats but they were out there. The Yankees would have been more hard-pressed to replace the pitching arms than Ruth's offense. There were a lot of good hitters in the '20s but good pitching was hard to find. Mays, Hoyt, Bush, Jones, Pennock and George Pipgras won more than 600 games for the Yankees, more than 500 of them in the 1920s. Even with the fat wallet of the Yankees owners, such pitching talent would have been virtually irreplaceable. Great pitchers were such a rare commodity in the lively ball era of the 1920s.

If the Red Sox had kept the players they traded, especially all those pitchers, Boston's dynasty might have been extended for another ten years. Certainly one key for the Yankees was ownership's ability to pay for players. The secret was that their owner, Col. Ruppert, did not draw out profits from the club. He also took the risk of building a spectacular new ballpark. Yankee Stadium opened in 1923 and quickly generated much revenue. There weren't too many dynasties that were able to dominate in back-to-back decades. The Red Sox might have been able to accomplish that feat in the teens and '20s, just as the Athletics might have been able to do, had Connie Mack not been forced to break up his club after 1914.

DAVID VINCENT: Yankee Stadium was perfect for the left-handed Ruth. Had Ruth stayed with Boston and played his entire career with the Red Sox, he would have had different career numbers. Fenway Park is not favorable to left-handed power hitters. Yastrzemski talked about that throughout his career in Boston. Yankee Stadium was literally built for Ruth. The dimensions to right field were made so the Babe could hit plenty of homers. Had Ruth played his entire career in Fenway, he never would have had the career numbers he put together. He certainly would not have surpassed the 700 home run mark and he probably wouldn't have had the high season totals he had in New York. Ruth had a short porch in right in Yankee Stadium.

Would Babe Ruth have made the Red Sox the team to beat in the 1920s? (Library of Congress.)

In Fenway Park, right field was even deeper in the 1920s than it is now, because the bullpens weren't there in the '20s. The bullpens were added later to give Ted Williams a shorter distance to hit home runs.

Ray Chapman

In addition to being one of the game's top shortstops in 1920, Cleveland's Ray Chapman was also one of the most popular players in baseball. On August 16, in the thick of the AL pennant race, New York's Carl Mays fired a pitch that struck the 29-year-old Chapman on the left temple. Chapman, a right-handed hitter who liked to crowd the plate, never regained consciousness and died the following morning from a fractured skull.[7]

Although Cleveland slumped for a time following the tragedy, the Indians had the good fortune to acquire future Hall of Famer Joe Sewell from the minors. Sewell hit .329 in 22 games, and Cleveland rebounded to win the AL pennant and the 1920 World Series.

Chapman's death stunned the baseball world. It also greatly accelerated the implementation of safety measures. Before the incident, new clean balls rarely found their way into games. The year after Chapman's death, the use of clean baseballs greatly increased, making the game safer and expanding offensive production as well.[8]

What if the fatal beaning of Ray Chapman had not occurred in 1920?

BILL JAMES: Ray Chapman would have been a Hall of Famer if he had not been killed. There were three outstanding shortstops, other than Chapman, who were born in 1891: Rabbit Maranville, Dave Bancroft and Roger Peckinpaugh. If you compare Chapman with those three players up through 1920, Chapman was clearly the best of the group. Since two of those three made it to the Hall, I think you would have to say Chapman would have made it to the Hall of Fame as well.

ALAN SCHWARZ: Chapman was hit at a time when baseball was cracking down on the spitball. At the time, baseballs were used over and over, so as the game progressed, you wound up with balls that were dingy and brown and not particularly easy for the batter to pick up, especially from a submarining pitcher like Carl Mays. It is quite likely that Chapman never even saw the ball. Due to the nature of the incident and Chapman's popularity, there was an immediate crackdown on the use of dirty baseballs. Umpires were instructed to regularly introduce into a game new and unused baseballs as soon as they felt a ball might be difficult to see. The immediate impact of this, at a time when Babe Ruth was showing people that power hitting was important, was a huge spike in runs scored. Babe Ruth certainly showed baseball how valuable power could be as opposed to the speed, sacrifice and station-to-station game. A batter's ability to see the baseball had to be a factor in the explosion of the offensive numbers in baseball. Whether we are talking about Rogers Hornsby or George Sisler or others, a number of players saw their offensive numbers greatly increase following Chapman's death and the decision to steer clear of dirty, hard-to-see baseballs.

JIM VAIL: There are actually two Hall of Fame–related questions involved in the fatal Ray Chapman beaning of 1920. One, of course, involves whether or not — had Chapman survived and returned to his previous skill level — he would have posted good enough numbers for election to Cooperstown. The other, which gets overlooked in emphasis on the victim of the incident, is whether or not — without the beaning — pitcher Carl Mays would have been enshrined on the merits of his full career.

Between the two, and given only the reality of their careers as actually happened, there is no doubt that Mays is by far the better candidate. In the final ratings for my book, *Outrageous Fortune*, which measured the relative Hall of Fame credentials of the roughly 2,300 players who had met Cooperstown's ten-year, major-league minimum-service requirement for eligibility during the period 1876–1994, Mays ranked — based on regular-season career statistics alone — as the 22nd best-qualified pitcher eligible for Cooperstown through the 2000 voting. Among the pitchers not yet enshrined at that point in time, only Bert Blyleven and Dennis Eckersley (who was elected in 2004) scored higher, and Mays ranked above 38 of the 58 pitchers already on the Hall of Fame roster.

The method used for those rankings involved using Z Scores, which measure a player's individual achievement in a given statistic against the mean for a specific group, to show — in standard deviations above or below the norm — how that performance compares to the group as a whole. The rankings were then derived by averaging the individual Z Scores obtained for 26 different career-performance statistics for pitchers (and 30 for non-pitchers) among three separate measurements (for players from the same era, players at the same position (starters and relievers, with respect to pitchers), and among all eligible players as a whole) to produce a final average Z Score indicative of each man's relative non-subjective (i.e., statistical-only) credentials for Cooperstown.

Some of Mays' statistical credentials include a career won-lost mark of 208–126, for a winning percentage of .623. He posted a career ERA of

2.92, and was also a five-time 20-game winner, who led the American League with 27 victories for the pennant-winning Yankees of 1921, topping the circuit in winning percentage as well as games and innings pitched that season. He also was a two-time league leader in both complete games and shutouts, and led his circuit in saves on one occasion. Mays played for four pennant winners, posting a World Series record of 3–4 with a postseason ERA of 2.20 that included one fall classic shutout for the Red Sox in 1916. Although Carl's career victory total is larger than only 11 of the pitchers enshrined to date, his winning percentage is better than all but 15 of the pitchers currently in the Hall.

Despite all that, and although he was eligible from the start of Cooperstown voting in 1936, Mays received a total of just six votes from Hall of Fame electors, all in 1958. The obvious reasons for his lack of support are his role in the Chapman beaning and the fact that he has long been regarded as one of the surliest players in major-league history, at least outwardly defining the term "mean SOB." As a result, and much like Ty Cobb, Mays made few friends among teammates or competitors during his career, and it's obvious he acquired no more than a half-dozen admirers among the scribes who vote in Cooperstown elections, belated ones at that. In fact, Mays was so disliked that — with many assuming he had beaned Chapman on purpose — there were calls for the pitcher's banishment from baseball after the shortstop died. It's possible that Mays' career was saved only because witnesses agreed that Chapman, who crowded the plate as a matter of habit, had leaned in too close on a pitch in or near the strike zone.

As for Chapman, his nine-year career was too brief to qualify for Cooperstown eligibility under the current standards. However, that did not matter in the voting prior to 1960, and Chapman received a token vote for the Hall in 1938. Beyond that, three other shortstops— Ross Barnes (whose career spanned 1871–81, but included only four seasons in what are now considered "major" leagues), Joe Boley (1927–32) and Charley Gelbert (nine MLB seasons during 1929–40)— also received votes prior to 1960 for careers of less than ten years.

Chapman was well-liked by players and fans alike, so there's no reason to suspect that — like Mays— he would have suffered any lack of support from Hall of Fame voters for reasons involving his personality. As a result, the question really comes down to whether or not the stats he accumulated for his nine years in the majors project to something Cooperstown-worthy over a career of greater duration. To answer that question for this book, I did another Z-Score comparison, albeit simpler than the one in my own.

First, I made a rough estimate of Chapman's likely stats for an 18-year career (the average career length among the 20 shortstops currently in the

Hall) for each of the eight traditional batting statistics which are, by and large, the best predictors of Hall of Fame voting support — including (in no particular order) games played, hits, home runs, total bases, runs scored and RBI, plus batting and slugging average. I ignored Sabermetric measures, like runs created and win shares, because they were not available during the years (roughly 1936–60) when Chapman would have been eligible for election by the baseball writers. The methodology for the estimate, too long-winded to describe here, attempted to account very simply for likely changes in Chapman's production due to offensive context and advancing age. The result, shown below, is a nonscientific, but quick and easy "ballpark" estimate of Chapman's likely production over 18 seasons (the Sample Means and Standard Deviation numbers are explained below).

Player	GP	H	HR	TB	R	RBI	BA	SLG
Ray Chapman	2087	2087	35	2832	1330	730	.278	.377
Sample Means (n=34)	1568	1505	37	1998	730	625	.265	.349
Standard Deviation	490	606	40	888	346	333	.024	.054

Next, I compared Chapman's stats above to the career numbers in each category for the 33 other shortstops who played ten major league seasons and whose careers would have been contemporary with or overlapped Chapman's during the years 1912–29 (the period encompassed by his hypothetical, 18-year career). As a group, these shortstops included eight of the 20 men from that position elected to Cooperstown to date (Dave Bancroft, Joe Cronin, Travis Jackson, Rabbit Maranville, Joe Sewell, Joe Tinker, Honus Wagner and Bobby Wallace), plus several others with varied, but relatively competitive HOF credentials (notably Dick Bartell, Art Fletcher, Red Kress, Roger Peckinpaugh and Glenn Wright). The sample means and standard deviations for the 34-man group as a whole are given beneath Chapman's projected stats above.

Using that data, I then developed Z Scores for each player in each of the eight statistical categories above, and then averaged them into one score, reflecting each man's overall career credentials for the statistics used, relative to the rest as a whole. The top 20 among the sample are listed below, with current Hall of Famers italicized.

Rank	Player	ZAvg	Rank	Player	ZAvg
1	*Honus Wagner*	2.69	11	Roger Peckinpaugh	0.36
2	*Joe Cronin*	1.88	12	Glenn Wright	0.35
3	*Joe Sewell*	1.11	13	*Joe Tinker*	0.19
4	*Travis Jackson*	0.95	14	Art Fletcher	0.09

Rank	Player	ZAvg	Rank	Player	ZAvg
5	*Rabbit Maranville*	0.91	15	Donie Bush	0.03
6	Dick Bartell	0.89	16	Woody English	-0.03
7	*Bobby Wallace*	0.86	17	Lyn Lary	-0.10
8	Ray Chapman	0.75	18	Ivy Olson	-0.24
9t	*Dave Bancroft*	0.45	19	Mark Koenig	-0.27
9t	Red Kress	0.45	20	Everett Scott	-0.32

The results above imply that, given an 18-year career, Chapman probably would have been among the top 25 percent (eighth out of 34) of his shortstop contemporaries, with primary Hall of Fame credentials about 0.75 standard deviations above the norm for the group as a whole. Among the sample measured, his average projected career numbers would have been better, overall, than at least two of the shortstops of his relative era who have been elected to the Hall.

On the whole, that evidence makes it very doubtful that Chapman would have been elected to Cooperstown by the baseball writers. Among the men above, only Wagner, Cronin and Maranville were enshrined by the scribes, with the other five shortstops entering Cooperstown via the old-timers or veterans committees. In all, the five shortstops elected by the VC plus Bartell, Kress, Peckinpaugh and Wright received a total of 585 Hall of Fame votes on 74 different ballots, for an average of just 7.9 votes per ballot — with well over half of those votes going to either Tinker (228) or Bancroft (172). Although stranger things have happened in HOF voting, the fact that at least one unelected shortstop (Bartell) ranks ahead of Chapman above also seems to diminish the likelihood that Chapman would have been enshrined by the VC.

As for Carl Mays, one suspects that — even without the Chapman beaning — he made enough enemies on and off the field during his career to prevent his election to baseball's shrine by either voting process, and it's especially doubtful he could have ever had enough supporters on the old Veterans Committee to carry his election by that body. Whether or not his absence from Cooperstown represents baseball "justice" is a matter of opinion, but I think he is more deserving of election based on career performance alone than several contemporary pitchers who made it — notably Waite Hoyt, Jesse Haines and Rube Marquard.

MIKE SOWELL: Chapman would have led the Indians to the 1920 pennant and World Series title that they won with Joe Sewell at shortstop. At the time of the beaning, Chapman was batting .303, the third time in the past four seasons he batted .300. Considering that 1920 was the first year of the live ball, and league batting averages were up across the board, it is reasonable to assume that Chapman would have continued to hit at least .300, if not higher. He already had 41 sacrifice hits, so he would have finished with 50 to 60, close to his major league record of 67 in 1917. He scored 97 runs in 111 games, so he probably would have finished the season with at least 125 runs scored. Chapman was also having an outstanding season in the field. His fielding average of .959 was 15 points higher than the league average for shortstops, and he had great range.

Having helped the Indians win their first pennant and World Series title, Chapman probably would have reconsidered his decision to retire. I believe he would have played three more seasons, retiring at age 32.

With Chapman still at shortstop when the Indians met for spring training in 1921, the question becomes what would have happened to Joe Sewell, an outstanding young hitter and fielder, as he proved when given the opportunity. I don't believe Cleveland manager Tris Speaker would have wasted Sewell's talent in the minors once it became apparent he was ready for the big leagues. Larry Gardner, entrenched at third base, would bat .300 in 1921, and Bill Wambsganss was an outstanding fielder and adequate hitter at second. I think Sewell probably would have spent the 1921 season as a valuable utility player who filled in at second, short and third. With Sewell's bat and Chapman still in the lineup, Cleveland would have improved on its 94–60 record and won 100 games in 1921, beating out the Yankees for the AL pennant. Cleveland was in first place in the AL as late as September that season and having Chapman could have made the difference. An argument can be made that Sewell did just what Chapman might have done. Sewell hit .318 with 93 runs batted in but Chapman was a much better fielder than Sewell. They would have gone on to beat the New York Giants in the 1921 World Series.

Cleveland's pitching faltered in 1922 so this likely would have been the Indians' last pennant until 1948. However, Chapman's presence in the lineup would have given Cleveland back-to-back titles and delayed the Yankees' dynasty by one season.

Chapman also would have benefited from three more seasons of hitting against the live ball, raising his career numbers high enough to earn him a spot in the Hall of Fame. Sewell also would have played out his Hall of Fame career, leaving both men in Cooperstown.

The final twist is that Carl Mays would not have pitched in the 1921 World Series, when New York Yankees manager Miller Huggins suspected him of throwing a game. That would have removed two stigmas from Mays' record: the fatal beaning of a player and suspicions over his World Series game. Relieved of this, he also would have been voted into the Hall, as he deserves to be based on his record.

STEVE STEINBERG: As tragic as Chapman's death was and as famous as the incident became, it really had little impact on the game and its players, with one major exception.

1. The popular Chapman was on track for a possible Hall of Fame career (though the Hall didn't exist at the time). However, though he was only 29 at the time, Chapman had already decided to retire at the end of the season to spend more time with his expectant wife and their child.

2. The 1920 Cleveland Indians rallied after the tragedy, won the AL pennant, and went onto win the World Series.

3. The man who settled in as Chapman's replacement at shortstop, Joe Sewell, went on to a Hall of Fame career and hit .312 for his career.

4. The man who threw the pitch that killed Chapman, Carl Mays, had a reputation as a "head hunter." Ironically, while Mays used the "beanball" as a weapon of intimidation when he was with the Boston Red Sox, the Chapman beaning was most likely an accident. No punitive action was taken against him, and Mays didn't let the incident bother him: he led the league with 27 wins in 1921. He ended his career with 208 victories and only 126 losses, a borderline Hall of Famer. Did the Chapman tragedy keep Mays out of the Hall of Fame? Baseball historian Fred Lieb felt it was rumors and suspicions of Mays "throwing" a 1921 World Series game (never proven), not the beaning of Chapman, which kept the pitcher out.

5. Protective headgear was not adopted for many years. Chicago Cubs player-manager Frank Chance, the victim of many serious beanings, had a helmet designed a decade earlier, but it was not accepted. Other serious beanings would occur, including the near fatal one of Detroit's player-manager Mickey Cochrane in 1937, but no one else would be killed.

6. Replacing dirty and darkened baseballs with clean and white balls throughout a ballgame was a result of Ray Chapman's death. It had a significant impact on the game and it jumpstarted the lively ball era as much as any other factor. In the deadball era, pitching had the upper hand. In a typical game, only a handful of balls was used, with a ball staying in play for many innings. As the ball became discolored and even misshapen — a process helped along by pitchers, who spat on the ball and rubbed it with dirt — the batter had a hard time seeing it and an even harder time sending it very far. Before the start of the 1920 season, baseball owners instituted changes to encourage more scoring. They banned "freak" pitches, including the spitball, although 17 spitball pitchers were "grandfathered" and allowed to continue using the pitch. A little known fact is that the owners also gave umpires instructions to introduce new balls into games at that time. But as the season progressed, they backed off. Owners had complained

of the increased cost of using so many balls in a game. It took the Chapman beaning for clean white balls to become a regular part of the game. A number of observers felt that Chapman, who always crowded the plate when at bat, simply never picked up the ball coming from Mays' submarine delivery. After Chapman's death, a constant flow of bright and firm balls made for a much more inviting target for the batter.

George Sisler

New York's acquisition of Babe Ruth had transformed the Yankees into a legitimate pennant contender for the 1921 season. Now the Yankees went hunting for another offensive star, offering the St. Louis Browns $200,000 for first baseman George Sisler, in what was believed to be the largest cash offer for a single player up until that point in time.[9] St. Louis owner Phil Ball rejected New York's overture and Sisler, a career .340 hitter, stayed with the Browns.

What if the Browns had traded George Sisler to the New York Yankees in 1921?

RICK HUHN: What baseball fan is not intrigued by the story of Lou Gehrig subbing at first base for Wally Pipp, a long-time New York Yankees regular who took a day off due to a headache? Once on the field Gehrig never relinquished the job. In taking the field in May 1925, the Iron Horse joined Babe Ruth to form the foundation of Murderer's Row and a 1927 Yankees team generally acknowledged as the sports' finest. In 1920, long before Gehrig was on their radar, Yankees ownership sought the purchase of George Sisler of the Browns, then baseball's best fielding and hitting first sacker and a base stealer supreme. If that high-priced sale is consummated, Lou Gehrig plies his trade elsewhere, and baseball history is significantly altered.

In 1921 Sisler batted .371 (12 HRs, 104 RBIs, and 35 SBs). In 1922 he hit .420 (8 HRs, 105 RBIs, and 51 SBs). A serious eye problem destroyed his 1923 season and negatively impacted his return to action in 1924. Still, his superstar status, above-average skills, and cost to the team likely would have kept Gehrig, who played only 23 games in 1923–24 combined, on the bench. Given Lou's obvious potential he was prime trade bait, long gone by 1928 when Sisler's skills diminished.

A secondary issue is the effect of Sisler's presence on a Yankees team that won pennants without him in both 1921 and 1922. Based on his actual performance, Sisler at first, instead of Pipp, would have added 75 points in batting average in 1921 and 90 in 1922. While comparisons with Pipp in HRs and RBIs are essentially a wash, Sisler stole an additional 65 bases over the two years. In addition, his 19 HRs in 1920 were second in baseball only to Ruth. It is likely many, if not all, of Sisler's batting statistics significantly rise hitting in front of the prodigious Ruth, even though "Gorgeous George" disdained the walk. It is arguable then that instead of losing the 1921 and 1922 Fall Classics to the Giants, the Sisler-fortified Yanks rule the roost in those two seasons, as well as in 1923 when they bested their cross-town rivals in six games.

The Browns' Opportunity

With George Sisler still a member of the Browns, St. Louis nearly grabbed the franchise's first AL flag in 1922. The Browns went into August with a slight lead over the Yankees, but ran into problems when Sisler severely strained his deltoid muscle in a game against the Tigers on September 11. In a crucial late season series in St. Louis, the Yankees took two out of three from the Browns, as New York held on to win the pennant by a single game. It would be another 22 years before the long-suffering Browns made their first and only appearance in the World Series.[10]

What if the Browns had captured the A.L. pennant in 1922?

STEVE STEINBERG: The Browns were really the more popular team in St. Louis for many of the first 25 years of the 20th century. The Cardinals were not as strong a team or as popular as the Browns. In their inaugural season of 1902, the Browns had raided the Cardinals and signed most of their stars. It was a battle from which the Cardinals didn't recover for years. They were in desperate financial shape in 1918 and 1919. If the Cardinals hadn't persuaded the owner of the Browns to rent the Browns' stadium, Sportsmans' Park, to the Cardinals, its quite possible the Cardinals might have left St. Louis. The Cardinals' field was a ballpark that was falling apart. By convincing the Browns ownership to lease Sportsman's Park to the Cards, the Cardinals were able to sell their park and the adjacent land, get a lot of money and pay down the club's debt. The Cardinals were also able to use the remaining money to finance their farm system. Without the ability to use Sportsman's Park, its quite possible that St. Louis today would be Brown rather than Cardinal red. The Cardinals grew to be a powerful team in the NL in the mid to late '20s while the Browns just missed out on an AL pennant in 1922. Had the Browns won the pennant, their popularity would have been fueled to new heights in St. Louis.

The 1922 Browns had great hitters, led by George Sisler who hit over .400 in 1920 and 1922. Their offense also included an outfield of Ken Williams, Jack Tobin and Baby Doll Jacobson. From 1919 through 1925, all three of those outfielders hit over .300 with the exception of Tobin, who missed by one hit in 1924. The 1922 Browns led the league in batting but they also led the majors in ERA in 1922. One of their top pitchers was Urban Shocker, who died of heart disease in the late '20s. You could argue that Shocker deserves to be in the Hall of Fame or that he might have been able to find his way to the Hall had he pitched a few more seasons. As a spitball pitcher, Shocker could have pitched into his 40s, just as Red Faber and Burleigh Grimes, two Hall of Fame pitchers, did. If Shocker had pitched several additional seasons, he would have reached 250 wins and that's probably a Hall of Fame career.

RICK HUHN: If we assume that the Browns won the pennant in 1922 by besting the Yankees in the "Little World Series" despite George Sisler's injured shoulder, little would have changed in the short run beyond that fact. Given the extent of his injury, it is unlikely Sisler would have recovered enough by World Series time to be truly effective, to turn the Browns into the dangerous team they were before his injury. The 1922 New York Giants of Frankie Frisch, Heinie Groh, George Kelly, Irish Meusel, Art Nehf and others, under the tutelage of John McGraw, were more than enough for a healthy Yankees team which lost in four games(with one tie). The Browns, saddled with a lame star, were no match either. In 1923, the Yankees returned the favor, besting the Giants in six. The Browns, however, without Sisler that entire season due to an eye problem, finished fifth, a poor 74–78. After that, one dismal season followed another until 1944 when they played an intra-city World Series with the Cardinals. By then it was too late; much of the original fan base had eroded and the team was soon gone.

On the other hand, since we are merely speculating, we can take the long view. Historically, at least until 1926 when the Cardinals won it all, the Browns were the favored franchise in St. Louis. By winning a pennant in 1922, they would have drawn first blood, permanently endearing the team to their fans. That fact alone might have kept the embers burning a little longer, and might have provided high enough attendance figures to finance the development of more teams capable of playing a "Little World Series." Perhaps then in 1995 Cal Ripken, Jr. is a St. Louis Brown, not a Baltimore Oriole, when he breaks Lou Gehrig's all-time record for consecutive games played. A couple more wins by the Browns in 1922 is all it would have taken.

Connie's Second Dynasty

Connie Mack could build and dismantle championship ballclubs with the best of them. Mack's first dynasty, the Philadelphia Athletics of 1910–1914, won three World Series crowns before Mack razed the club due to pressure from the Federal League, salary demands, and a general lack of funds. It took Mack more than a decade to rebuild, but one could argue that his second powerhouse was even stronger than his first. With an offense led by first baseman Jimmy Foxx, outfielder Al Simmons and catcher Mickey Cochrane, and Lefty Grove, Rube Walberg and George Earnshaw supplying the pitching, Mack won back-to-back world championships in 1929 and 1930.

Financial problems surfaced again in the midst of the Depression, and Mack's best players soon found themselves on other teams. Al Simmons, third baseman Jimmy Dykes and outfielder Mule Haas went to the White Sox for $150,000 after the 1932 season; Detroit got Mickey Cochrane for $100,000 following the 1933 season.[11] The Red Sox then picked up Grove, Walberg and second baseman Max Bishop for $125,000 and landed Jimmy Foxx for $150,000.[12]

After nine straight winning seasons from 1925 through 1933, the Athletics finished 68–82 in 1934 and dead last in 1935. Mack's club would not experience another winning season until 1947.

What if Connie Mack had not broken up his second dynasty in the 1930s?

SEAN FORMAN: Many of the players Mack let go were sold without the Athletics getting very much in return. Many of the players were still young in 1932. Cochrane was 29, Foxx was only 24 and Simmons was 30. Grove was 32 but still had several good years left in him. The Athletics finished second in 1932, and third in 1933, but with the proper supporting cast they could have gone on to win another pennant or two. Mack had a good eye for finding talent and probably could have found some talent to work into the lineup to combine with his veterans. Mack just couldn't come up with the resources to pay his star players.

Mack was over 70 years old. Perhaps by this time, Mack had accomplished all that he was looking to accomplish as a manager. It might have made more sense for Mack to sell the team. If he had done that, and the Athletics had found an owner who was interested in spending a little money, Philadelphia might still have the Athletics.

BILL JAMES: Mack was a very good team builder, and he could have kept both of his dynasties going strong for at least a few more years if he hadn't run into financial problems. I think his second dynasty probably only had a couple of good years remaining.

By 1935, Connie Mack was getting behind the curve. The other franchises were building farm teams and front offices. Mack wasn't. The other teams were developing marketing strategies that were really changing the game. Mack was a brilliant man at the game he had played, but was not forward looking enough, at that point of his life, to keep the A's competitive — with or without better financing. The only way that the Athletics could have remained strong after 1938 would be if Mack had sold the club.

FRED STEIN: I don't believe the Athletics were a dynasty on the decline at all. Al Simmons, Lefty Grove and Jimmy Foxx had several good seasons left, as did Mickey Cochrane. Foxx had nearly ten years left and Cochrane was going strong until he was beaned in 1937. Lefty Grove remained an excellent pitcher through the 1930s. Grove started out as a power pitcher but he was a classic example of a pitcher who learned how to pitch effectively later in his career without relying too much on throwing at high speeds. With other stars like Mike Higgins and Bob Johnson being added in the 1930s, I believe the Athletics could have been very competitive with the Yankees for the rest of the decade. Connie Mack simply had to sell his players to stay afloat financially.

GARY GILLETTE: It would have been interesting to watch the A's challenge the Yankees in the 1930s, if Connie Mack had kept his veteran stars from the American League pennant-winners of 1929–1931 and mixed them together with some promising young players. There was a big statue of Connie Mack outside of Veterans Stadium in Philadelphia and when I saw it, I always thought it was ironic that they had a bronze statue of this tall, patrician-looking man — as if he should be honored. As I see it, Mack steadfastly refused to integrate his team when other teams were integrating. When the Athletics finally integrated, it wasn't done with much enthusiasm. It was token integration and Mack has to bear a lot of responsibility for that. Mack also destroyed American League baseball in Philadelphia. After he broke apart his second dynasty, the A's finished last or next to last for roughly two decades. It was a cynical attempt to make money without taking any risk. In my view, Mack took advantage of the fans in Philadelphia. By the time the team moved to Kansas City, no one in Philadelphia cared about the A's. Whom can you blame but Connie Mack? I don't think you should put up statues to guys like that. There's no shame in taking a team of veterans and saying its players are past their prime, then trying to get good young talent in exchange for the veterans in an effort to rebuild. The problem with Mack was he never made an effort to rebuild. His philosophy was that the best team an owner could have was a team that contended for most of the year and then finished second or below. Fans would come all season and you would make money but, come contract-negotiating time, you wouldn't have to give the players raises because the team hadn't won the pennant. That kind of cynical manipulation of both your team and your fans is reprehensible.

Dizzy

Dizzy Dean's meteoric pitching career reversed course in 1937, thanks to a line drive off the bat of Cleveland outfielder Earl Averill at the All-Star game in Washington. Averill's liner broke Dean's left little toe, and in his comeback effort, the St. Louis pitcher wound up changing his throwing motion to favor the broken toe. By placing all of his weight on one foot, Dean eventually ruined his arm; although he pitched effectively as a spot starter in 1938 and 1939, Dean's career was over by 1941.[13]

From 1932 through 1936, there was no better pitcher in baseball: Dean recorded 120 victories over the five-year period. Even an abbreviated career could not stop a pitcher with Dean's talent. With 150 victories to his credit, and a lifetime earned run average of 3.02, Dean was elected to the Hall of Fame in 1953.

What if Earl Averill's line drive had not collided with Dizzy Dean in 1937?

GABRIEL SCHECHTER: Without a doubt, Dizzy Dean would have gone on to a terrific career. He was a dominating pitcher with big win and strike-out totals during his peak years and he had both the talent and the demeanor to continue for a long time. He was only 27 when he got hurt and he still won 150 games. I think Dean would have had a good shot at 300 victories if he had stayed healthy, especially if he had been able to play during the World War II years.

FRED STEIN: Dean's delivery after the injury was unnatural and certainly affected his performance. Instead of being a pitcher with tremendous power and speed, Dean had to depend on his expertise to get by. Dean was able to pitch for a few more seasons but he lost his effectiveness. It's difficult to say how long Dean might have lasted or what his final career numbers might have been, had he not suffered the injury. However, he was a great pitcher before the injury, a man who could back up his boasts. As a pitcher ages, he usually substitutes knowledge of how to pitch for the loss of sheer power. It's fairly unusual to have power pitchers like Nolan Ryan and Roger Clemens who seemed to throw as hard late in their careers as they did when they were younger.

DEAN SULLIVAN: If Dean had stayed healthy, he would have pitched into the early to mid–1940s (or until he was drafted), adding at least 100 victories to his total. The Cardinals would have won another pennant or two in the late 1930s, and the early 1940s club — already very talented — would have been perhaps one of the greatest teams in history. This might have eased tensions between Cardinals owner Sam Breadon and Branch Rickey, who ran the club's tremendously productive and profitable farm system. Rickey resigned from the Cardinals at the end of the 1942 season and joined the Brooklyn Dodgers, where he earned deserved fame for breaking baseball's color line with Jackie Robinson. If Rickey had stayed in St. Louis — a strongly segregated Southern city — he could not have signed Robinson, and it is unlikely anyone in Brooklyn or elsewhere would have. The integration of baseball would have been left to Bill Veeck, whose claims that he planned the integration of the Philadelphia Phillies in 1943 have been disproved, but whose sympathy regarding segregation is unquestioned.

Mickey's Passed Ball

Decades of futility ended for Brooklyn in 1941, as the Dodgers captured their first NL title since 1920. Although the Yankees grabbed two of the first three games of the World Series, the Dodgers appeared to be on the verge of drawing even when they took a 4–3 lead into the ninth inning of Game 4.

A single pitch changed everything. With two outs, Brooklyn reliever Hugh Casey kayoed Tommy Henrich with what should have been a game-ending strikeout. However, when Dodgers catcher Mickey Owen let the ball get away, Henrich raced to first base and the Yankees had new life. New York made Owen pay for his passed ball, scoring four times in the inning to win 7–4. Another victory in Game 5 gave the Yankees the championship, the first of six World Series titles that New York would grab in the '40s and '50s at the expense of the Dodgers.

What if Mickey Owen had held onto the third strike in Game 4 of the 1941 World Series?

MAURY ALLEN: Hugh Casey threw a hard breaking ball to Tommy Henrich and it got away from the catcher, Mickey Owen. It was either a curveball or a spitter but it slipped by Owen and he was charged with a passed ball. Casey's pitch may have been the most significant single pitch in the history of baseball. What it did was to turn around the entire history of the Dodgers. Who knows, there might still be a team in Brooklyn today. Had Mickey caught the ball, I think the Dodgers would have gone on to win the series in 1941 and may have dramatically changed their future course. Brooklyn was snake-bit until winning in 1955 their only World Series while in Brooklyn.

The Dodgers had a superb team in 1941 led by Dixie Walker, Pete Reiser, Pee Wee Reese and pitchers like Whitlow Wyatt. If Owen had caught the ball, the series would have been tied at two, and the momentum would have shifted to Brooklyn's favor. It would have given the Dodgers a great deal of confidence to finish off the Yankees in the 1941 World Series, and to come back after World War II to win additional titles in the late 1940s and into the 1950s.

DAVID SHINER: It is hard to look at the 1941 Dodgers and see a team that was truly competitive with the Yankees of the Joe McCarthy era. It was such a striking point, in that the game was over if Mickey Owen caught the ball. Momentum could have shifted if the final out had been recorded, but you are looking at a Yankee team that was superior to the Dodgers. If Owen makes the play, they are down to a three game series. Yes, the Dodgers could have won but it seems likely to me that the Yanks would have prevailed anyway.

Mickey Owen's passed ball may have prevented Brooklyn from winning the 1941 World Series. (Courtesy Los Angeles Dodgers, Inc.)

The Bullpen View

The Black Sox provide a multitude of "what ifs." If Chicago had played to win, would the White Sox have beaten Cincinnati in the 1919 World Series? According to David Shiner, position by position, the White Sox were the superior ballclub, although Jim Vail decided that Chicago's problems with team chemistry would have resulted in a Cincinnati triumph in nine games. When it comes to the individual Black Sox, Bill Deane and Bill McNeil declared that Shoeless Joe Jackson would have produced outstanding offensive numbers during the '20s and would have wound up in the Hall of Fame. Deane and Gene Carney foresaw an invitation to Cooperstown for Eddie Cicotte as well.

New York's acquisition of Babe Ruth and several dependable pitchers from Boston turned the Yankees into a perennial winner and ruined the Red Sox franchise for nearly two decades. Steve Steinberg contended that Boston could have dominated throughout the '20s, had Red Sox owner Harry Frazee not transferred so much talent to New York. From an individual standpoint, Babe Ruth hammered 714 home runs during his illustrious career, including 659 long balls for the Yankees. Had the Babe remained with the Red Sox, David Vincent envisioned a reduction in Ruth's power output, due to Fenway Park's size, and predicted that the Babe would have finished his career with less than 700 homers.

Ray Chapman's death in 1920 prompted the introduction of safety measures, including the increased use of clean, white balls, which served to jumpstart offenses, according to Alan Schwarz and Steve Steinberg. Chapman's death also cut short a potential Hall of Fame career. Both Bill James and Mike Sowell projected Hall of Fame status for the Cleveland shortstop, while Sowell added that Carl Mays might have landed an invitation to Cooperstown as well, had the tragic incident not occurred.

The Philadelphia Athletics of 1929–1931 won three straight AL pennants, and seemed capable of reeling in additional championships, until Connie Mack decided that he could no longer afford to pay his superstars. Sean Forman suggested that Philadelphia might still have the Athletics today, if Mack had sold the franchise to an owner willing to spend some money.

Thanks to popular players like Babe Ruth and Lou Gehrig, baseball had survived the Black Sox scandal of 1919. The decades of the 1940s and 1950s would bring war and peace, major league employment for African-Americans, and the relocation of several cherished franchises.

4

Careers Lost, Teams Lost: 1942–1959

Historical Highlights

December 7, 1941, changed the lives of nearly all Americans. The Japanese attack on Pearl Harbor thrust the United States into World War II, sending an entire generation of young Americans, including major league ballplayers, to fight overseas. The war itself dramatically reduced the career statistics for superstars like Bob Feller, Ted Williams and Hank Greenberg; many of those who departed for military service were never able to recapture their glory days upon their return from the conflict.

Jackie Robinson, Branch Rickey, and the Brooklyn Dodgers integrated the majors in 1947. Amidst unbelievable pressure, Robinson hit .297, won the Rookie of the Year award, and helped the Dodgers grab the NL pennant.

October produced several memorable World Series moments in the post-war years, including Enos Slaughter's mad dash for home in 1946 and Sandy Amoros' brilliant catch against the Yankees in 1955. At times, playoff games decided league titles, as was the case in 1951 when the Giants' Bobby Thomson inflicted an agonizing defeat on the Brooklyn Dodgers.

The 1950s also boasted geographical changes, as long-standing franchises found new homes. The Browns moved to Baltimore, the Athletics shifted to Kansas City, and the Braves relocated to Milwaukee. By 1958, the majors extended from coast to coast, as the Dodgers took up residence in Los Angeles, and the Giants transferred to San Francisco.

World War II

The Japanese attack on Pearl Harbor placed America squarely into World War II, sending hundreds of major leaguers and thousands of minor leaguers into the military.[1] Cleveland's Bob Feller, who joined the U.S. Navy in January of 1942 and served on the battleship Alabama, won five campaign ribbons and eight battle stars.[2] Ted Williams enlisted as a naval aviator in the spring of 1942 and missed three full seasons to the war, as well as nearly two seasons to the Korean War in the early '50s.[3] Several other stars had their career numbers reduced due to World War II, including Joe DiMaggio and Joe Gordon of the Yankees, Hank Greenberg of the Tigers and Dom DiMaggio of the Red Sox.

Many players were able to return from the conflict and regain their pre-war numbers, but such was not the case for Washington's Cecil Travis, who suffered frostbite while serving in Belgium.[4] In Travis' last season before the war, the 27-year-old shortstop hit .359; five years later, in 1946, he hit just .252. Travis would later claim that the four years he had spent away from the game cost him his timing, and with his average down to .216 in 1947, Travis decided to retire.[5] Travis, who had hit .317 or better seven times between 1934 and 1941, may have found a spot in Cooperstown if not for World War II.[6]

What if some of baseball's top stars had not missed several seasons due to World War II?

STEVE BULLOCK: Ted Williams was the best pure hitter who ever lived, and if you look at the nearly five years he missed due to World War II and Korea, he would have been very close to 700 homers and perhaps would have eclipsed that number. If he hadn't missed those years, Williams would hold the all-time RBI record.

If you look at 1940-1941, before he departed for the military, he had two outstanding seasons. Williams never put together back to back seasons that were as good after World War II. If you average out what Ted did before 1942, you might be talking about 35 homers a season. It's possible that if Ted hadn't missed those seasons to World War II and Korea, he might have retired sooner. It's also possible that if Williams is close to Ruth's all-time home run record, he plays a few more seasons, perhaps as a part-time player, and surpasses Ruth.

Hank Greenberg was one of the major stars that left early for the military, even before Pearl Harbor. He had been released from military duty right before the Japanese attack, due to his age. After Pearl Harbor, Greenberg decided to re-enlist. Consequently, he missed 1941–1944 and missed

most of 1945. Greenberg was able to play late in the 1945 season and helped the Tigers in the AL pennant run. Greenberg missed four and a half seasons due to World War II. Greenberg's numbers were very similar to Joe DiMaggio's. When people talk about the top five or ten offensive players in baseball history, they don't usually mention Greenberg. If you look at the numbers he was putting together before he departed for the military (40 homers and 150 runs batted in) and multiply them by four, you have some pretty serious numbers. You have a guy with more than 500 homers. His power numbers would be comparable to one of Greenberg's contemporaries, Mel Ott. You can make the claim that Hank Greenberg was indeed one of the top ten offensive players of all time.

When you ask people who is the top right handed pitcher of all time, Bob Feller usually winds up third or fourth on that list. He was 22 years old and already had over 100 victories. That's amazing. Here was a guy who probably wouldn't have been drafted into the military but decided it was his responsibility to enlist. Feller enlisted right after Pearl Harbor. Feller's dad had cancer so odds are Feller would not have been drafted. Because of Feller's decision to enlist, he missed 1942, 1943, 1944 and most of the 1945 season. Feller would have surpassed 300 victories had he not missed those years during World War II.

Joe Gordon missed two years to the war. If you look at his offensive and defensive numbers, he really does merit inclusion into the Hall of Fame. Gordon was invaluable to the Yankee championship teams of the 1930s and 1940s and to the Cleveland Indians in 1948. Compare Gordon to the guy he replaced at second base for New York, Tony Lazzeri. Gordon played on more championship teams than Lazzeri and had better power numbers. Bobby Doerr, a contemporary of Gordon, is in the Hall, and Doerr only played in one World Series.

Cecil Travis of the Senators was another guy whose career was hurt by World War II. Travis was a great offensive and defensive player. He was 27 when he left for the Army and was at the prime of his career. At the Battle of the Bulge, Travis had to hole up in a foxhole and wound up with frostbite in his feet. He had had quite a bit of speed as a player and Travis never regained his mobility.

There were others who had their careers negatively impacted by the war, including Washington outfielder Buddy Lewis. He was very fast and very good defensively. He hit close to or above the .300 mark from 1936 through 1941, missed 1942–1944 due to the war, and was never the same

Opposite: Just imagine Ted William's numbers, if he had not served in World War II and Korea. (Courtesy Boston Red Sox.)

when he returned. Larry French, a solid left-handed pitcher, had nearly 200 wins when he went into the military. His last season was 1942. He went into the Navy, decided to make the Navy his career, and never returned to the majors. French was a guy who was still pitching well at the age of 34. He conceivably could have won another 50–75 games and perhaps made it into the Hall of Fame.

FORMER BOSTON SECOND BASEMAN BOBBY DOERR: Washington's Cecil Travis had his feet frozen during the war and never could play again at the same level as before the war. Travis was a very good ballplayer and would have been a sure Hall of Famer. Dom DiMaggio lost three prime years to the war, and if he had played during those years, Dom would have been a Hall of Famer as well. Johnny Pesky lost several years to the war. Being moved from shortstop to third base later in his career also hurt him. He was never able to establish himself at just one position. Bob Feller lost several years to the war. Before the war, Feller was the best pitcher I saw. There's no telling how many more victories he would have had if he had not lost those years due to the war.

FORMER CLEVELAND PITCHER BOB FELLER: Winning World War II was the most important thing that happened in this country in the past century. It was a war we had to win. Otherwise, you and I wouldn't be here today. Sports are very insignificant when there's a war going on. I joined the Navy two days after Pearl Harbor and served on the battleship the U.S.S. Alabama on the anti-aircraft guns. I was aboard the Alabama for 34 months. I was proud to serve my country and lucky enough to survive and play 11 more years in the majors after the war. In the three years before I went into the Navy, I was averaging about 25 wins a season. I won 26 games in 1946, my first full season after returning from the war. It's certainly possible that I could have won another 80 to 100 games in the years I missed.

Several other players missed years to the war, including Cecil Travis of Washington, who should be in the Hall of Fame. Travis was a great shortstop, a very good hitter and excellent on defense, but he never recovered from his injuries from the Battle of the Bulge. Several others were injured during the war, including Lou Brissie, a very good pitcher who never quite could make a comeback. A lot of good ballplayers in the minor leagues also lost their lives in the war, fighting for freedom, and never had a chance at the majors.

BILL MCNEIL: Ted Williams' career was affected more than most because he lost three years to WW II and another two years to the Korean War. If he hadn't lost those five years (less 43 games), he might have hit another

Would Bob Feller rank as the greatest right-handed pitcher of all time, were it not for World War II? (Courtesy Cleveland Indians.)

172 home runs, giving him a career total of 693 home runs. He would also have established major league career records with 2,421 runs scored (126 more than Rickey Henderson) and 2,704 RBIs (a whopping 407 more than Hank Aaron). I saw Williams play many times and, although I am not a big Ted Williams fan, he may in fact have been the greatest all-around hitter in major league history. At the time of his induction into the U.S. Navy in

WW II, the 24-year-old "Splendid Splinter" was sporting a .356 career batting average and was still years away from his prime. After the war, American League teams began employing the famous Williams shift, leaving just one infielder and one outfielder to cover the left side of the field and stacking the right side with five players. The stubborn Williams refused to hit to left field, which obviously affected his batting percentage, but he maintained his home run average. The smooth-swinging Williams finished 23 points below Ty Cobb in the batting average race, but far above him in the power game and, considering the fact that he lost his three peak years, he may well have been the best all-around hitter ever.

Other players whose careers suffered because of military service included Bob Feller, Warren Spahn, Buddy Lewis, and Cecil Travis. Bob Feller lost almost four years to military service, costing him an estimated 95 victories and more than 1,200 strikeouts. His final career totals could well have included 361 victories and 3,800 strikeouts. Warren Spahn also lost almost four years during WW II, but they would have been his first four years in the major leagues, if he hadn't been farmed out for at least one of those years. If he had played in the majors all four years, he might have added another 52 victories to his career totals, giving him 415 victories, one of just three pitchers with more than 400 victories. He might also have accumulated another 500 strikeouts giving him about 3,100 strikeouts. Buddy Lewis was a 25-year-old hard-hitting outfielder for the Washington Senators when the war broke out. He had played in the major leagues for seven years with a .304 batting average. After four and a half years away from the game, he couldn't resurrect his career at the level he was used to, and he retired in 1949. Lewis probably wouldn't have become a Hall of Fame player, but then again he might have. If he had played until he was 40 years old without interruption, he could have finished his career with over 3,000 base hits and a .300 batting average, making him a definite HOF candidate. His teammate on the Senators, Cecil Travis, was another potential Hall of Famer who missed his chance because of the war. Travis was a good defensive shortstop and an outstanding hitter in the nine years he played in the major leagues before going into military service. When his career was interrupted, he carried one of the highest career batting averages for a shortstop at .327. Late in 1945, after missing almost four years, he returned to action, but couldn't recover his old form and he retired after playing only 221 games over two years. Cecil Travis was 28 years old in 1941. If he had played another 10-years, he might also have finished with more than 3,000 base hits, and he might have finished second to Honus Wagner for the highest career batting average by a shortstop. As it was, he is number three all-time, behind Wagner and Arky Vaughan.

BILL DEANE: I did some projections once to see how Ted Williams' final career numbers might look, had he not lost years to World War II and to Korea. My projections gave Ted 681 lifetime homers and a .345 career batting average. According to my numbers, Williams would have set the career records for runs scored with 2,392, for RBI with 2,409, and for bases on balls with 2,713. Another point to consider is the possibility that had Williams not missed seasons due to the two wars, he may have retired a lot earlier than he did. He retired at the end of the 1954 season, but a fan convinced Ted that if he retired at that point that his career numbers wouldn't measure up to the all-time greats and he wouldn't achieve his goal to be one of the greatest hitters who ever lived. As a result, Williams came back to play in 1955 and retired after the 1960 season. I think if Ted hadn't missed seasons in World War II and Korea, he wouldn't have had a reason to come back for the 1955 season and may have quit after 1954. Had he played during the war years but decided to retire after 1954, my projections give him 526 home runs and a .347 batting average, pretty close to the numbers he finished with.

JOHN HOLWAY: If Ted Williams had not missed years due to World War II and Korea, he would have easily surpassed 600 homers. He would have been close to what Willie Mays did, about 660 career home runs. The curse of the Red Sox was not Babe Ruth but rather World War II. The Red Sox may well have won the American League in 1942, 1943 and 1944. Ted Williams would have hit .400 at least one of those three years. Man for man, the Yankees were three to four years older than the Red Sox. Many of the Yankees were on the downside of their careers by the time World War II arrived. The Yankees were ready to be beaten and many of the Red Sox were just starting to hit their peak years. I think if the war hadn't sent so many players overseas, Boston would have exposed the Yankees for what they were and that was an older team past its glory.

Bob Feller also missed out on a number of victories due to World War II. For some reason, Feller was left off the All-Century team, which was a travesty. He missed his best years due to the war. If he had been able to pitch in those seasons, Feller would have broken Walter Johnson's strikeout record. He probably would have pitched one or two more no-hitters and his name would rank right up there with all the top pitchers in baseball history. You also have to realize that when Feller pitched, hitters were more difficult to strike out. Batters would choke up on the bat and punch the ball around. Today, hitters strike out twice as much as they did in the 1940s. Feller struck out 348 hitters in 1946. Today, he might strike out 700!

Slaughter's Mad Dash

St. Louis and Boston certainly gave fans their money's worth in the hotly contested seven-game World Series of 1946. In the eighth inning of the decisive seventh game in St. Louis, Boston center fielder Dom DiMaggio hit a two-run double off reliever Harry Brecheen that tied the game, but DiMaggio's hit came with a price. A twisted ankle forced Boston's defensive whiz out of the battle.[7]

With two outs in the bottom of the eighth, and Cardinals outfielder Enos Slaughter on first, Harry Walker dropped a short fly into center, over the head of Boston shortstop Johnny Pesky. Running with the pitch, Slaughter flew around second and sprinted for third while DiMaggio's replacement, Leon Culberson, bobbled the ball and then tossed a weak relay to Pesky. Whirling around third, Slaughter dashed for home and outraced Pesky's throw to the plate, giving St. Louis a 4–3 lead.[8] A tired Brecheen, who had pitched a complete game victory for the Cardinals just two days earlier, held off the Red Sox in the ninth, as St. Louis claimed its third world championship in five seasons.

Boston's loss would be the first of many disappointing defeats for the talented Red Sox over the next few years. Meanwhile, Red Sox outfielder Ted Williams, who hit just .200 in seven games against the Cardinals, had just made his first and last World Series appearance.[9]

What if Enos Slaughter had not tried to score from first base in Game 7? What if Dom DiMaggio had not suffered his injury in Game 7?

Former Boston second baseman Bobby Doerr: You had to see the field for the seventh game. The grass was not smooth at all. It was very tough, and I think Leon Culberson probably got very conservative in playing the ball hit by Harry Walker, to guard against the ball taking a bad hop and going by him. Dom always said if he had been playing center field with Walker at bat, he would have been playing a shade toward left center, rather than straight away center field. I have talked with Dom quite a lot about this and I think Dom would have been more aggressive getting to the ball. Slaughter may still have tried to score. Slaughter always said he knew Culberson was out there in center, but I really think Slaughter's attempt to score from first base was a spontaneous thing. If Dom had been in center field, the play would have been a lot different. Dom had a good throwing arm. He didn't

Opposite: Boston's Hall of Fame second baseman Bobby Doerr. (Courtesy Boston Red Sox.)

have an overpowering arm but it was very accurate, and he would have been more aggressive in relaying the ball back to Johnny Pesky. The play would have been completely different. Folks have blamed Pesky over the years and some people ask why I didn't call out the play. With 33,000 people yelling, it's very difficult to be heard. I can't say for sure if I made a call on Slaughter's move around third to Pesky. I do remember seeing Slaughter make his turn at third base, so I have to think that I did call out the play, but I doubt Johnny would have ever heard it in the stadium that day.

People also talk about Ted Williams not having a good series. It's true that Ted got hit on the elbow right before the series, but every year in the fall Ted seemed to get a flu virus and he had a virus right around the 1946 Series. His body was run down more from that than anything else. The virus had more of an impact than being hit on the elbow before the series. I never heard him use that as an excuse. If it had happened during the regular season, he probably would have been out a couple of games because of it.

MIKE ROBBINS: Enos Slaughter said after the Series that if slick-fielding DiMaggio—rather than emergency replacement Leon Culberson—had been in center, he never would have tried to score. And indeed, it was Culberson who made the difference on the play. Though history blames Johnny Pesky for "holding the ball" as Slaughter streaked home, any hesitation on his part was brief. The real trouble was that Culberson bobbled the ball briefly, then made a weak toss to Pesky at short.

And what if Slaughter had held at third? The odds seem better than average that the Red Sox would have lost anyway. Remember, Slaughter's run wasn't the *tying* run in a Series the Sox were about to win, it was the *go-ahead* run in a Series that was still very much up for grabs. The situation is somewhat analogous to the famed Buckner error in the 1986 Series. The Mets had already tied the game up before that ball rolled through Bill Buckner's legs. Thus, the error didn't really cost the Sox the win, just the opportunity to win. Considering the Sox were the visiting team for both the Slaughter game and the Buckner game, the odds of a Boston victory were probably a bit south of 50/50 in each case.

Had Slaughter stayed on third, the Cardinals would have had runners on second and third with two outs and Marty Marion at the plate facing Sox pitcher Earl Johnson. Marion had doubled off Johnson in Game 6, so perhaps he would have come through again and been remembered as the hero. Or maybe the Sox would have intentionally walked Marion—there was a base open and the pitcher was due up next—prompting the Cards to pinch hit for pitcher Harry Brecheen, perhaps with Dick Sisler or Erv Dusak.

If the pinch hitter failed to deliver the run, the game would have continued, perhaps into extra innings. If so, St. Louis had a full bullpen ready to hold the Sox down — except for Brecheen and game-seven starter Murry Dickson, the whole Card staff had at least three days rest. The Cardinals also had a full bench ready to pinch hit as needed — they had used only one reserve to that point, backup catcher Del Rice. The Sox, on the other hand, already had run through four pitchers and five players off their bench. They were not set up anywhere near as well for a long extra-inning game, had it come to that. Nothing is certain, of course, but the odds were with the Cards.

JOHN HOLWAY: I think Dom DiMaggio was the greatest defensive center fielder of his day. When the Cards came up in the last of the eighth inning, with lefties like Slaughter and Walker coming up, I would have called for a left-handed reliever, perhaps Earl Johnson or Mickey Harris. Instead, Boston manager Joe Cronin called for a right-handed reliever, Bob Klinger, and both lefties got hits. Slaughter was able to score from first off Walker's hit. Slaughter says he never would have tried to score if Dom had been in centerfield. Dom says he thinks he could have caught Slaughter at third base. I also think Boston shortstop Johnny Pesky gets a bum rap for allegedly holding the relay throw for a moment. There's no doubt in my mind that Pesky did not hold the ball. Pesky might be in Cooperstown today, if not for the belief by some people that he held onto the ball too long.

Integration

It should have happened much sooner, but major league baseball's color line was finally erased in 1947. The list of talented black ballplayers who never got a chance to play in the majors is a long one; many will never gain the full recognition they deserve.

Two brothers, Moses and Welday Walker became the first blacks to play in the majors when they took the field for Toledo of the American Association in 1884.[10] Resistance from established stars like Cap Anson abruptly ended any hopes of making integration a permanent fixture, leaving the barnstorming circuit as the only option available for black players for several decades.[11]

By the 1920s, a few more alternatives had become available, including the Negro National League and the Eastern Colored League. Although both leagues had collapsed by 1931, the Negro National League reappeared in 1933, and the Negro American League began play in 1937.[12]

With pressure mounting for the majors to integrate, 28-year-old Jackie

Robinson joined the Brooklyn Dodgers in 1947. The trailblazing Robinson would go on to hit .311 in ten seasons with the Dodgers and would earn a spot in the Hall of Fame in 1962.[13]

Unfortunately, a number of black players, like slugger Mule Suttles and pitcher Ray Brown, never received an opportunity to display their skills in the majors, leaving their talents largely forgotten.[14] One can only wonder how many of baseball's cherished records might have different owners today, if the game's color line had never existed in the first place.

What if integration had occurred in the majors before 1947?

JOHN HOLWAY: I think Josh Gibson and Mule Suttles both would have broken Babe Ruth's single season home run mark in the late 1930s if they had been allowed to play in the majors. Ruth won a number of consecutive home run titles in the 1920s and 1930s and I'm certain Suttles would have grabbed some of those titles.

Mule Suttles should be in the Hall of Fame. In fact, he should have been in the Hall decades ago.* Suttles and Gibson were rivals. Suttles came along a few years earlier than Josh did. They weren't one-dimensional players by any means. Both hit over .400 in the Negro Leagues. Josh died young; he possibly destroyed himself with drink and drugs because he was so broken-hearted that he didn't get to play in the majors. If Gibson had been allowed to play in the majors, he might not have died at such a young age. I'm not sure what kind of lifetime numbers Gibson might have had, but I'm positive he would have demolished Babe's single season home run record. If Roger Maris could break Ruth's record of 60, I'm certain Suttles and Gibson could have surpassed 60. Oscar Charleston probably would have hit .400 once or twice in the majors. Cool Papa Bell would have been a great player in the majors. He wasn't a great base-stealing champ in the Negro Leagues but there are different ways to use your speed, stealing bases being only one of them.

I know there was a move on in 1942 to open the majors to blacks. There were many names bandied about, like Roy Campanella and Sam Jethroe. The owner of the Washington Senators, Clark Griffith, in whose park the Homestead Grays played, was talking about signing up players like Josh Gibson, Ray Brown and Buck Leonard. The addition of a few players like Josh Gibson would have made Washington one of the better teams in the American League. The Senators already had players like Mickey Vernon, George Case, Dutch Leonard and Early Wynn. The Senators might still be in Washington.

Editor's note: Suttles was elected to the Hall of Fame in February, 2006.

The Pittsburgh Crawfords could have beaten the best in the majors in the mid–1930s. The Crawfords had stars like Oscar Charleston, Josh Gibson, Cool Papa Bell and pitcher Leroy Matlock, who won 26 in a row over two years in 1935–36. I think the Crawfords could have beaten the Yankees in 1936. In 1924, I would have taken the Kansas City Monarchs over the Washington Senators, the World Series champion. The Monarchs boasted Hall of Fame pitcher Bullet Joe Rogan. He was a little guy, about 5'6 but he was one of the greatest all-around players in baseball in 1924. Rogan could pitch and hit. He could hit .400 and hit with power. Kansas City also featured Heavy Johnson in the outfield and Dobie Moore at shortstop. They beat the Philadelphia Hilldales in the championship series 5–4. The Hilldales had the great left-handed pitcher Nip Winters, who drank himself out of baseball. Philadelphia also had Hall of Famer Judy Johnson at third base. Either one of those teams could have beaten the 1924 Senators.

GARY GILLETTE: It would have been a great thing for baseball if there had never been a color barrier to start with. There are those who say the Negro Leagues were the same caliber as major league baseball. I believe that's true because, in the sphere in which they were forced to operate, the Negro Leagues were the best in the business and had a lot of major league talent. That did not make every Negro League player a major league player, as some now claim. The greatest of the Negro Leaguers, Oscar Charleston, Josh Gibson, Cool Papa Bell, Martin Dihigo, Buck Leonard, Satchel Paige and several others, would have undoubtedly been superstars in the majors and they would be viewed the same way as DiMaggio, Cobb, Ruth, Johnson, Mathewson, etc., are. There are those who try to extrapolate from the incomplete stats they compile what the top Negro League stars would have done had they played their careers in the major leagues. They try to use the head-to-head records from the games in the off-season between the Negro Leaguers and the Major Leagues. We can't be sure what kind of career numbers the greatest stars of the Negro Leagues might have compiled had they played in the major leagues throughout their careers. We can say for sure that baseball would have been richer, and American history would have been better off, had blacks not been prevented from playing baseball up until 1947.

People like to think of 1947 as some sort of magical point where the color barrier was totally erased in baseball. That's not true. Although people don't remember it, the American League resisted true integration for at least a decade and a half. Many AL teams did not integrate until the mid to late 1950s. The Tigers and Red Sox were the final two teams to integrate. When you look at the percentage of black and Latin ballplayers in the American

League, compared to the National League, you can make an argument that the American League never really fully integrated until the late 1960s, perhaps even the early 1970s for the Red Sox.

DEAN SULLIVAN: As politically incorrect as this may seem, it would not have made much of a statistical difference. Let's take Babe Ruth's career as an example. If baseball was proportionately integrated during Ruth's career (and African Americans constituted roughly ten percent of the population), then blacks would have replaced about two to three white players per team. Half of those players would have been in the NL, where Ruth wouldn't have faced them at all. This means that about 15–20 black players would be on the seven other AL teams, maybe seven of whom would be pitchers. If you add another eight or so Negro League pitchers in the NL, you have about 15 black pitchers to consider. With the limited talent pool to draw from, the Negro Leagues did not have at any time during Ruth's career 15 superior pitchers who could have significantly reduced his statistics. There would not have been much of a talent difference between the lower levels of the ten percent of Negro League players to make the move, and the white players losing their jobs. Given the Yankees' advantage in money and baseball brains, they might have acquired some of the best Negro League pitchers to make sure Ruth didn't have to face them. In addition, it's possible that Ruth might have hit even Satchel Paige and Smokey Joe Williams quite well.

It's pure folly to predict the statistics of players like Paige and Josh Gibson, since aside from exhibition games, we don't know how they would have fared against major league teams, much less who they would have played for. In addition, the style of playing was different. Paige wouldn't have pitched as much as he did in the Negro Leagues, and couldn't have used the illegal or trick pitches common in the Negro Leagues. Cool Papa Bell wouldn't have been permitted to steal at every opportunity — steal totals in the majors throughout the entire Negro League era were very low. The introduction of Negro Leaguers would have liberalized the playing style somewhat, but not dramatically. I'll guess that Paige would win about 250–300 games, Bell might steal around 350 bases and Gibson would slug 475 home runs, more if he switched from catcher several years before retirement.

Baseball couldn't have integrated much later than it did — societal and economic pressures were too great. Recent research has revealed that the extra revenues brought into southern towns by black fans desperate to see African American players helped change laws and attitudes toward strict segregation in baseball. The rapid failure of the minor leagues in the 1950s, due to over-expansion in the post-war era, and the competition posed by television, made baseball's financial future even more precarious. Segregation would not have survived much into the 1950s, and therefore the prospects of early black players like Mays, Aaron and Banks wouldn't have changed much.

BILL MCNEIL: Between 1962 and 2000, 58 players were elected to the Hall of Fame by the Baseball Writers of America. Of that total 17, or 29%, were black. Before 1962, 147 players, all white, were elected to the Hall. If the percentage of black players to white players deserving election into the Hall was the same, both before and after 1962, there should have been 43 black players elected to the Hall between 1936 and 2000.

In my book, *Baseball's Other All-Stars,* I developed formulas for predicting how Negro League players, who never had an opportunity to play in the major leagues, would have performed in the Big Show if given the chance. The formulas were based on actual statistics of the dozens of former Negro League players who went on to successful major league careers. According to my formulas, Josh Gibson would have hit a solid .312 with an astonishing 61 homers for every 550 at-bats. That compares to Mark McGwire's 52 homers for every 550 at-bats, Babe Ruth's 47, and Barry Bonds' 42. Some of the other outstanding Negro League players who would have excelled in the major leagues include Dobie Moore who was predicted to hit .317, Oscar Charleston at .300, Jud Wilson at .300, and John Beckwith at .306. Mule Suttles would have hit .279 with 43 homers. Turkey Stearnes would have hit .302 with 38 homers, and Edgar Wesley would have hit .274 with 36 homers.

There is no question that fans missed seeing some of the greatest players in history play the game because of the heinous major league segregation agreement. The records speak for themselves. Barry Bonds holds the single season home run record (73), Hank Aaron holds the career records for home runs (755), RBIs (2,297), and total bases (6,856). We can only imagine what records players like Josh Gibson and Mule Suttles would have set.

JIM VAIL: The Walker brothers did not make their brief big-league appearances until 1884, and then in a season when there were three recognized major circuits and an above-normal number of roster spots available. As a result, I believe it's fair to argue historically that — even if no color barrier had been adopted in the late 1880s — real integration on any meaningful level would not have occurred in the majors until after 1900 at the earliest, and may have taken as long as the advent of the Great Depression to achieve.

The basis for that viewpoint is multifold, but simple and obvious. First, it took eight seasons before the first two African-Americans were allowed even token participation in the majors. Second, throughout 1876–1930 there was simply too much institutional racism in all other aspects of American society for an entity like baseball to effectively challenge, if it had the nerve to do so. Major league integration would not have prevented or diminished the deep resentments in the South against post–Civil War Reconstruction, and it could not have stopped the production of influential racist films like D. W. Griffith's *Birth of a Nation* or the Stepin Fetchit cultural stereotypes presented by the entertainment industry as a whole. Third, at least three of the majors' cities— St. Louis, Cincinnati and Washington — were, by proximity, highly susceptible to the Southern form of racism and its economic impact on attendance, and the more industrialized cities of the North all had their own deeply rooted, if different, kinds of social segregation. Fourth, it was not until the administration of Franklin Roosevelt, beginning in 1933, that any meaningful effort was made on a federal level to oppose the cultural-bigotry status quo (and even then, much of the effort was lip service).

In that light, it seems likely that the first (probably small) influx of Afro-American players in the majors would have come during the initial decade or so of the 20th Century, a period when John McGraw is known to have tried to sneak one or two light-skinned men of color onto his roster by spurious means. The first two decades of that century, coinciding with the majors' deadball period, was also the first era from which one can find public statements in meaningful number by white baseball players and officials openly praising the skills of dark-skinned counterparts. True integration, as it gradually evolved from 1947 to roughly the mid 1960s, would probably not have occurred until the Great Depression, at which point, absent the color barrier, almost every big league team would have encountered numerous economic motives to expand their talent and marketing bases. Even then, however, one suspects that individual clubs run by overtly racist owners would have resisted such change despite the depression; and it's not unlikely that every team would have agreed to some kind of quota system limiting the number of dark-skinned players on each roster.

Given all that, it seems improbable that the men who became Negro Leaguers (primarily Afro-Americans and dark-skinned Cubans) would have made much impact on the majors prior to the 1930s. Granted, there would have been a cadre of Hall of Fame-caliber players prior to that time (beginning with Rube Foster and Pop Lloyd in the first decade of the 20th century), and players like Oscar Charleston surely would have ranked among the very best of their era, both subjectively and statistically. But, due to small numbers, their impact on the standings would probably have been minimal, depending upon the relative closeness of given pennant races and whether or not the major league clubs they played for were perennial contenders or perpetual also-rans.

As a result of all of the above, and beyond the socio-cultural impact, the most meaningful difference integration might have made in baseball is the variation it would have imposed upon the current roster of Hall of Famers enshrined at Cooperstown. As is, none of the Negro Leaguers were elected to the Hall until establishment of a special committee for that purpose in the early 1970s. But with integration from the start of major league history, many Negro League players presumably would have been eligible from the start of HOF voting in 1936.

At present, there are 18 men in Cooperstown who were elected for their Negro League careers, the most recent being pitcher Hilton Smith, tabbed by the old Veterans Committee in 2001. *The chronological list below gives each man's name, primary playing position and approximate career (inclusive dates of Negro League service, including time as manager, coach or executive, if any).

Player	Pos	Career	Player	Pos	Career
Rube Foster	sp	1902–26	Martin Dihigo	2b-p	1923–45
Pop Lloyd	ss	1905–32	Willie Wells	ss	1924–54
Joe Williams	sp	1905–34	Satchel Paige	sp	1926–55
Oscar Charleston	of	1915–54	Josh Gibson	c	1928–46
Bullet Joe Rogan	sp	1917–46	Hilton Smith	sp	1932–48
Judy Johnson	3b	1918–38	Ray Dandridge	3b	1933–49
Turkey Stearnes	of	1920–42	Buck Leonard	1b	1933–50
Cool Papa Bell	of	1922–46	Leon Day	sp	1934–50
Bill Foster	sp	1923–37	Monte Irvin	of	1937–48

I have absolutely no doubt that, had they played in the majors for anything resembling the durations of their Negro League careers, each of the men above would have demonstrated ample talent and achievement to justify their Hall of Fame elections. Absent the color barrier, and barring any application of unacknowledged racial quotas over time, I also believe that an equal, perhaps larger number of those who played in the Negro circuits would have compiled similar big-league credentials meriting either Cooperstown election or inclusion among the upper echelon of players (Bill

*Editor's note: Several former Negro League players were elected to the Hall of Fame in 2006, including Mule Suttles, Biz Mackey, Ray Brown, Willard Brown, Andy Cooper, Cristobal Torriente and Jud Wilson as well as 5 pre–Negro Leaguers, Frank Grant, Pete Hill, Jose Mendez, Louis Santop and Ben Taylor.

Dahlen, Carl Mays, Wes Ferrell, Joe Gordon, Gil Hodges, Maury Wills, Ron Santo, Joe Torre and Dick Allen, to name a few) often cited as having been unfairly overlooked to date.

But beyond any list of likely Hall of Famers and near misses, it's equally interesting to speculate about which current members of the Hall would never have been added to the Cooperstown roster if they had played against integrated competition. Given that the voting baseball writers have long been limited to listing a maximum of ten names on their ballots, it's a given that many, perhaps most votes cast for otherwise Negro Leaguers since 1936 would have taken support away from other candidates, possibly several who were elected by slim margins.

During the period 1936–62 (the latter date coinciding with Jackie Robinson's HOF election), there were 14 players elected by the writers with less than 80 percent support. They included Cy Young (elected in 1937), Eddie Collins and Willie Keeler (1939), Rogers Hornsby (1942), Mickey Cochrane and Lefty Grove (1947), Herb Pennock and Pie Traynor (1948), Jimmie Foxx (1951), Dizzy Dean and Al Simmons (1953), Bill Terry (1954), Gabby Hartnett (1955) and Joe Cronin (1956). Given the legendary (or near so) status of many of those players, it's safe to argue that most of them would have been enshrined anyway — whether by the scribes or one of the early veterans committees. Among them, however, it is possible to argue with some merit that the elections of Pennock, Traynor, Dean, Terry and Hartnett (at least) all might have been delayed if those men had faced ballot competition from the likes of Rube Foster and Oscar Charleston with big-league credentials.

But the most likely changes in the Hall of Fame roster resulting from early integration would clearly have involved the players elected by Cooperstown's veterans committees. In that light, and given proportional representation for Afro-Americans on those panels themselves (a debatable assumption in its own right), it's possible to imagine that the Hall of Fame roster might not now include people like Dave Bancroft, Johnny Evers, Rick Ferrell, Chick Hafey, Jesse Haines, George Kelly, Fred Lindstrom, Rube Marquard, Phil Rizzuto, Ray Schalk, Joe Tinker, Bobby Wallace, Lloyd Waner and Ross Youngs, among numerous other players who are often cited as Cooperstown's most blatant errors of selection. If that were the case, there would also be much less argument than there is at present about the number of players who have been unfairly overlooked. Beyond the obvious justice involved and the socio-cultural advantages of early integration, such an outcome might be the most positive result engendered had there never been a color barrier in the first place.

McCarthy's Surprise

The battle for the AL title in 1948 has to rank as one of the most exciting pennant races in league history. In early August, Boston, Cleveland, New York and Philadelphia found themselves competing for the top spot; by September 23, the Indians, Yankees and Red Sox were in a dead heat for first place.[15] When the smoke had cleared at the end of the regular season, Boston and Cleveland were tied at 96–58, forcing the two teams to stage a one-game playoff at Fenway Park to determine the fate of the championship.

For the first playoff game in AL history, Indians' player-manager Lou Boudreau named rookie Gene Bearden his starting pitcher. Boston manager Joe McCarthy countered with 36-year-old right-hander Denny Galehouse, who had spent most of the year in the bullpen, finishing with a record of 8–8 with an ERA of 4.00.[16] McCarthy certainly had other options: rookie southpaw Mel Parnell had won 15 games during the season while right-hander Ellis Kinder was a 10-game winner.

Behind Bearden's strong pitching and two home runs from Boudreau, Cleveland toppled the Red Sox 8–3 and went on to defeat the Boston Braves in six games in the 1948 World Series.[17] Frustrated Red Sox fans were left to ponder whether an all-Boston World Series might have occurred, if McCarthy had used a different starting pitcher in the playoff game with Cleveland.

What if Joe McCarthy had chosen another starting pitcher for the Red Sox in the 1948 AL playoff game?

FORMER RED SOX SECOND BASEMAN BOBBY DOERR: Galehouse starting the game was quite a surprise to all of us. Galehouse was a good pitcher but he hadn't pitched a whole lot in the latter stages of the 1948 season. Cleveland had us beat almost before we got started in that game. Mel Parnell was the one who should have been starting for us at pitcher. He was the most logical choice. Parnell might have allowed us to stay close early in the game and that might have made the difference. We felt we had a good advantage playing the game on our home field, but we fell behind early and couldn't catch up. Gene Bearden pitched a good game for Cleveland. He wasn't overpowering. He had that knuckleball that he used very effectively in 1948. His pitches broke out in front of the plate so we all moved up on the plate during the next season and we just about ran him out of the majors.

We had good teams in the late 1940s. In 1947, we lost Boo Ferris and Tex Hughson, our top pitchers from 1946, with sore arms, and had to rebuild our pitching staff in 1948, 1949 and 1950. Mickey Harris pitched well in 1946 and got a sore arm after that season. It makes you wonder whether

What if Joe McCarthy had selected Mel Parnell to be his starting pitcher in the 1948 AL playoff game with Cleveland? (Courtesy Boston Red Sox.)

they were overpitched in 1946. If we had just one of those pitchers healthy, like they were in 1946, we probably would have won three American League pennants and maybe one World Series. If management had just gone out and picked up one more pitcher for 1948, 1949 and 1950, we might have won the American League. Our manager, Joe McCarthy didn't want to do that. He thought he had a good enough pitching staff and it was a poor judgement by the team's management not to get another good pitcher for us.

We lost the playoff in 1948, and then in 1949 we went into the final weekend against New York with a one game lead and lost two games to the Yankees. Those two seasons were very disappointing to us. We lost several games in 1948, 1949 and 1950 in the late innings of ballgames. If we had a pitcher who could have relieved in those close games, we might have won the American League all three seasons.

JOHN HOLWAY: Mel Parnell could have started and would have pitched much better than Galehouse, who got his ears pinned back by the Indians. Parnell was the obvious choice to start. He was well rested. The Red Sox scored three runs against Cleveland's Gene Bearden. If Parnell had pitched, I think he had a good shot at holding Cleveland to two runs or fewer. The Red Sox then would have beaten the Boston Braves in the 1948 World Series.

The Red Sox didn't choke in the 1948 pennant race. Boston started the pennant drive several games behind Cleveland in the final few weeks, but the Red Sox won several big games and the Indians lost some important games in Detroit down the stretch. Boston came on strong and the Indians almost kicked away their chance at the American League pennant.

FORMER CLEVELAND PITCHER BOB FELLER: We were slightly surprised that Joe McCarthy started Denny Galehouse and not Mel Parnell. McCarthy felt that Galehouse could keep our right-handed hitters off balance with his slider, and could keep the ball away from our hitters so they wouldn't pull the ball off the big left-field wall at Fenway Park in Boston. It's all second-guessing. Mel Parnell was one of the best pitchers in the American League for many years, but Denny Galehouse was a fine pitcher as well.

The 1948 Indians had improved rapidly because Bill Veeck bought the ballclub. We got Larry Doby and Bob Lemon, and Lou Boudreau had a great year too. To be successful, you need four or five players having career years, as well as a few pitchers winning plenty of ballgames. Our 1948 team was a better ballclub than the Cleveland team that won the American League in 1954. We had better leadership in 1948, we were more cohesive, and Lou Boudreau was a very good manager.

ROB NEYER: Joe McCarthy's decision to start Denny Galehouse was criticized at the time, and it's been criticized ever since. I won't say the criticism was or is unfair. I will say that McCarthy, during his long managerial career — a career that got him into the Hall of Fame — displayed an uncanny knack for deciding who should be his starting pitchers. For many years, McCarthy would have seven or eight pitchers who could start ballgames, and somehow he knew whom to start on a given day. I think McCarthy's judgement was almost unparalleled. It's hard to criticize McCarthy for his choice of Galehouse for the playoff game. His three best pitchers had started the previous three games, so it really came down to Galehouse, who had a 4.00 ERA that season, and Ellis Kinder, with a 3.74 ERA. So McCarthy's choices were limited. Galehouse didn't pitch well against the Indians, of course, and the Red Sox were able to score only three runs themselves. No matter whom McCarthy started, it's unlikely that Kinder or whoever would have given up three runs or fewer. Therefore, while McCarthy's decision obviously didn't work out, it has to rank pretty far down the list of stupid things that managers have done over the years.

Sending Abrams

Nail-biting pennant races were nothing new for the Brooklyn Dodgers. St. Louis had beaten Brooklyn in a best-of-three playoff in 1946 and the Dodgers had returned the favor by nipping the Cardinals by a single game in 1949. Led by sluggers Duke Snider, Roy Campanella and Gil Hodges, Brooklyn seemed to be a safe bet to repeat as NL champions in 1950, but a new threat had emerged in Philadelphia. A young Phillies club nicknamed the "Whiz Kids" featured offensive production from Del Ennis and Richie Ashburn, reliable starting pitching from Robin Roberts and Curt Simmons, and 33-year-old reliever Jim Konstanty.

The NL pennant race came down to the final game of the regular season as the Phillies, clinging to a one game lead, visited the second-place Dodgers. With the score tied at one in the bottom of the ninth, and with runners on first and second and none out, Duke Snider ripped a hard liner to center off Robin Roberts. Although Richie Ashburn fielded the ball quickly, Dodgers third base coach Milt Stock elected to send the runner on second, Cal Abrams, to the plate, instead of holding him at third. Ashburn's throw home nailed Abrams by 15 feet.[18] Brooklyn's excellent scoring opportunity vanished completely when Roberts intentionally walked Jackie Robinson and then retired the next two hitters.[19] Philadelphia had dodged a bullet, and Dick Sisler made Brooklyn pay with a game-winning, pennant-winning three-run homer in the top of the 10th inning.

What if the Dodgers had held Cal Abrams at third base, following Duke Snider's single against the Phillies?

FORMER BROOKLYN PITCHER CARL ERSKINE: The decision not to hold Abrams at third has been replayed repeatedly. Duke Snider was up with runners on first and second and none out. The Phillies were expecting Snider to bunt, to advance the runners. Duke was a .300 hitter and the decision was to let Snider swing away. The Phillies played a bit closer expecting the sacrifice and Ashburn, the Phillies center fielder, was playing a bit shallower than he usually would have been. Ashburn did not have a real strong arm. Snider hit a shot off Robin Roberts, a clothesline right up the middle. You usually hesitate on a shot like that if you are a base runner, to avoid being doubled up, so I'm sure Abrams didn't get a real good jump from second. Ashburn got to the ball quickly. The big mistake wasn't made by Cal Abrams but rather by the Dodgers third base coach Milt Stock. Abrams couldn't see where the ball was. He had his back to the play running from second base toward third base. The smart play is to hold the runner at third base with no outs in the inning. For some reason, Stock kept Abrams running, and Ashburn was able to throw the ball to the catcher and Abrams was out easily. Roberts got out of the inning and then Sisler homered for the Phillies and Philadelphia went to the World Series. I would have liked our chances with the bases loaded and no one out.

MAURY ALLEN: The Dodgers would have won the National League pennant if Abrams had not tried to score from second base. Third base coach Milt Stock sent Abrams home and Abrams took an incredibly wide turn around third base. It was ridiculous for Abrams to try to score. The situation would have been bases loaded and none out for the Dodgers, with the next two hitters being Carl Furillo and Jackie Robinson. Abrams did not have great speed and got a bad turn around third. You need a good turn around third base to have a chance at getting to the plate safely and Abrams went very wide around the base.

BILL MCNEIL: Two questions have been asked about the Dodger strategy in the fateful ninth inning. What if Abrams had been held at third base? And why wasn't a pinch runner put into the game for the slow-footed Abrams? If Abrams had been held at third, and both Furillo and Hodges, the next two batters, performed the same way they did in the game, Gil's long fly ball to right field would have scored the winning run, throwing the season into a flat-footed tie and necessitating a three-game playoff. On the other hand, if one of the Dodgers' reserves, such as the fleet-footed Eddie Miksis, the man who had scored the winning run in the famous Bill Bevens game in the 1947 Series, had pinch-run for Abrams, he would have scored easily on Snider's single, again necessitating a playoff.[20]

In either scenario, the Dodgers and the Phils would have met in a three-game playoff, matching Brooklyn's power of Gil Hodges (32 homers, 113 RBIs), Duke Snider (31, 107), Carl Furillo (18, 106), and Roy Campanella (31, 89) against the Whiz Kids' outstanding pitching staff of Robin Roberts (20–11), Curt Simmons (17–8) and Jim Konstanty (16–7 with 22 saves). And, as often happens in cases like this, the team that got the breaks would have won.

The Shot Heard Round The World

If Brooklyn fans thought the worst was behind them after Dick Sisler's pennant-winning blow for Philadelphia, they were sorely mistaken. As cruel as 1950 was, 1951 would be even worse.

By August, it looked like the Dodgers had overpowered the rest of the National League, as Brooklyn took a 13-game lead over New York, with a 15-game edge in the loss column.[21] The Giants then put together one of the greatest stretch runs ever, winning 37 of their remaining 44 games to finish the regular season tied with Brooklyn at 96–58, forcing a best-of-three playoff to determine the NL champion.[22]

After a split in the first two games, the series came down to the decisive third game on October 3, 1951, at the Giants' Polo Grounds. Brooklyn's prospects appeared to be bright with a 4–1 lead heading into the bottom of the ninth, but New York refused to quit. Brooklyn's fatigued starter, Don Newcombe, surrendered a single to Al Dark, and when Dodgers first baseman Gil Hodges surprised many observers by stationing himself close to the bag, lefty Don Mueller laced a single past Hodges into right field. New York now had runners on first and third. After Monte Irvin popped out, Whitey Lockman ripped a clutch double to left, reducing Brooklyn's lead to 4–2.

With one out, runners on second and third, and Bobby Thomson striding to the plate, it was decision time for Brooklyn manager Charlie Dressen. Would Dressen intentionally walk Thomson, in order to face the on-deck hitter, rookie Willie Mays? Dressen also had his pick of relievers. Would he choose Ralph Branca, a 13-game winner with an ERA of 3.26, or go instead with Carl Erskine, a 16-game winner with an ERA of 4.46? Upon hearing from bullpen coach Clyde Sukeforth that Erskine was bouncing his overhand curve, Dressen selected the 25-year-old Branca and instructed him to pitch to Thomson.[23]

Branca's first pitch to Thomson was a strike. Thomson hammered Branca's next offering into the left field stands for a miraculous three-run shot that gave New York an amazing 5–4 victory and the NL flag. For the second straight season, a pennant-winning home run by the opposition had crushed Brooklyn's title hopes.

What if Dressen had chosen Erskine, and not Branca, to pitch to Thomson? What if the Dodgers had walked Thomson and pitched to Mays instead?

DAVID SHINER: I assume that Chuck Dressen must have been aware that Ralph Branca had surrendered several homers to Bobby Thomson during the 1951 season but wasn't concerned about it. I think Carl Erskine had a better chance than Branca to get Thomson out.

Even these days, where baseball is much more specialized, we don't always see managers walking a right-handed hitter to get to another right-hander. Willie Mays had really come on as a hitter in August and September. Mays was also very fast; if they decided to walk Thomson to get to Mays, the Dodgers would have had a force at any base but Mays was unlikely hit into a double play. I do believe if Erskine had been brought in to relieve, it's likely the Dodgers would have faced the Yankees in the 1951 series.

FORMER DODGERS PITCHER CARL ERSKINE: I would like to think I would not have thrown the home run pitch that Ralph threw. I bounced a curveball while warming up in the bullpen and the decision was made to use Branca. I really don't know how I did against Thomson over my career, but I know the plan was to pitch Thomson up, using off-speed pitches and curves. He liked to hit fastballs, low and away. Branca's first pitch to Thomson was a low fastball right down the gut and we all just about fell off the bench. Thomson took that pitch for a strike. The next pitch was a fastball up and in, which is the best way to throw Thomson a fast ball. Thomson fought it off and hit it into the lower deck of the Polo Grounds for the game-winning home run.

One possible factor was that the Giants might have been stealing our signs. We always rather suspected that was happening, but we didn't know they had a buzzer system set up. A guy in center could see the catcher's signals through binoculars and signal, with a buzzer system, what the pitch was going to be to the bullpen. The hitter would then receive hand signals from the bullpen. Not all hitters take the signs. Some prefer to use their instincts as a hitter. Most good hitters don't want the signs. Thomson has been very coy over the years about whether he took the sign. He has only said the Giants were getting the signs, but never said whether he took the signs, or if he took the signs during the plate appearance when he hit the home run.

We certainly never thought about walking Thomson to get to Willie Mays. You just don't walk the winning run to pitch to Willie Mays, not even in his rookie season. Another possible factor in the loss was the decision to have Gil Hodges hold Al Dark on first base after Dark got a leadoff single. I don't think we ever had a meeting and talked about that later. It was rather hidden in all the excitement that took place.

The word bitter doesn't come close to describing the way I felt after the loss. Losing to our hated rivals, the New York Giants, was devastating to the players and to our fans. To our credit, we didn't fold because of the loss. We came back in 1952 and won the pennant, as we did in 1953, 1955 and 1956. A lesser team would not have been able to bounce back.

MAURY ALLEN: The Dodgers had their choice of relievers to face Thomson: Ralph Branca or Carl Erskine. Dodgers' manager Charlie Dressen spoke with the bullpen coach Clyde Sukeforth just as Erskine bounced a curveball while he was warming up. Erskine had a sinking curveball and they have a tendency to bounce in the bullpen. Consequently, Dressen chose Branca, which was a tremendous mistake. Branca had surrendered a home run to Thomson in the first game of the series. Willie Mays, a rookie, was on deck. Willie has always said he was surprised the Dodgers didn't intentionally walk Thomson to load the bases. Mays said he was very nervous and was afraid he would hit into a double play to end the series. I think it was a mistake pitching to Thomson, rather than pitching to Mays.

Another important play came earlier in the inning when lefty Don Mueller came to the plate with Al Dark on first base. Brooklyn first baseman Gil Hodges was told to stay on the bag and hold the runner. The move left a big gap between Hodges and second baseman Jackie Robinson for Mueller to aim at. With the Dodgers up by three runs, it made no sense to hold Dark. The key wasn't Dark at first base but getting outs. Dark's run wasn't that important. In this day and age, if Dark had tried to steal second, teams would allow him to steal without a throw. Mueller drove the ball to right field on the ground and Hodges narrowly missed the ball. If he had been playing where he should have been playing, I think Hodges would have gotten to the ball and at least gotten one out and possibly could have turned a double play. The Giants might have been looking at a situation where they have no one on base with two out, with Monte Irvin coming up, and Thomson may never have had a chance to bat in that final inning. Instead, the Giants had men on first and third with no one out. Dressen never explained why he had Hodges hold the runner on at first base. Perhaps he was looking for a double play by keeping Dark close to the bag and getting Mueller to hit the ball to the left side of the infield.

FORMER NEW YORK FIRST BASEMAN WHITEY LOCKMAN: I have reviewed the film of the game and noticed that Hodges was playing well off first base. At some point, I thought Hodges was holding Al Dark on first base, but he really wasn't that far out of position. Don Mueller just found a hole. We used to call him Mandrake the Magician because every ball he would hit seemed to have eyes and somehow would get between fielders. Hodges could not have played much further away from Dark because Alvin could have stolen second base. The Dodgers wanted to keep Dark somewhat close to first base to keep the double play in order.

I went to home plate realizing I was the tying run in the game. I was not a home run hitter, but you could hit short homers down the lines at the Polo Grounds so I thought about the possibilities of tying the game with a home run. The Dodgers felt the same way so they kept the ball away from me. The pitch that I hit for the double was probably a strike, but I hit the ball a lot to the opposite field anyway and hit this pitch down the left field line for a double.

I'm not sure things would have turned out differently if the Dodgers had used Carl Erskine rather than Ralph Branca. I know Bobby Thomson hit Branca well that season and had hit a home run off him in the first game of the playoffs. Brooklyn manager Charlie Dressen got word from their bullpen that Branca was throwing the ball the best. I can't second-guess the decision to use Branca. It would be easy to do because of the outcome of the game and Bobby's success against Branca. The odds were with Branca to get Bobby out. It was just God's intervention that things turned out as they did. The first pitch Branca threw was right down Broadway. I was on second base and got a good look at the ball going into home plate. I just cringed when Bobby took that pitch and didn't swing. I thought to myself that was the pitch for Bobby to hit. The next pitch Branca threw was up and in and I didn't have a good feeling about it. When Bobby hit the ball, I thought he got good wood on it, but I wasn't sure if it would get out of the park. I'm not sure I had ever seen a ball with that kind of trajectory, a line drive like that, go into the lower left field stands at the Polo Grounds. Somehow the ball went into the stands and the rest is history.

I'm sure the idea of walking Thomson to pitch to Mays entered Dressen's mind. He probably had never done something like that in his managerial career because in those days it was just something you didn't really do. I don't know how often we had intentional walks in 1951. To put the winning run on base was rather sacrilegious back then. Mays was not an easy out at that point, even though he was a rookie. I'm sure the Dodgers figured that Mays was pretty good and had good reflexes. The Dodgers were just hoping to get Bobby out and go on from there.

Amoros to the Rescue

Brooklyn fans must have begun to wonder if the Dodgers would ever win a Fall Classic. Heading into their 1955 showdown with New York, Brooklyn had lost all seven appearances in the World Series, with the Yankees responsible for five of those defeats.

In typical Yankees-Dodgers fashion, the '55 World Series was a nip and tuck affair that came down to a winner-take-all seventh game in Yankee Stadium. Brooklyn left-hander Johnny Podres, who had won just nine games during the regular season, squared off against New York southpaw Tommy

Byrne. Gil Hodges drove in two runs to give the Dodgers a 2–0 lead heading into the bottom of the sixth inning.[24] It was then that Brooklyn manager Walter Alston made a crucial defensive move, replacing Jim Gilliam in left field with Sandy Amoros, and shifting Gilliam to second base.

With two Yankees on base and left-hander Yogi Berra at the plate, Alston shifted the Brooklyn outfield around to the right.[25] Berra took dead aim at tying the game by driving the ball the opposite way, forcing the left-handed Amoros to sprint to the left field foul line to put himself in position to make the catch. Sticking out his glove at the last moment, Amoros grabbed the ball in fair territory and quickly relayed it to shortstop Pee Wee Reese, who fired the ball to Hodges to double up Gil McDougald at first. Podres proceeded to blank the Yankees on eight hits, and Dodgers fans finally had a world championship to celebrate.[26]

What if Sandy Amoros had not caught Yogi Berra's fly ball in Game 7 of the 1955 World Series?

MAURY ALLEN: Brooklyn manager Walter Alston decided in the sixth inning to replace Junior Gilliam in left field with the left-handed Sandy Amoros, as Gilliam moved to second base, replacing Don Zimmer. Don Zimmer will joke to this day that if he hadn't been removed from the game, Brooklyn would have never won its one and only World Series. Berra went the other way, hitting a drive down the left field line, but the left-handed Amoros was able to extend the glove on his right hand to catch the ball near the foul line and the wall. Probably no other player on the Dodgers had the speed Amoros did to catch up to the ball and bring it down. It's very rare to have a left-hander playing in left field but it worked to the Dodgers' advantage in this case. Had Gilliam been in left, the ball probably would have gone all the way to the wall and been a double or a triple. The Yankees would have rallied, knocking Podres out of the game, and New York would have won the game and the series.

FORMER BROOKLYN PITCHER CARL ERSKINE: A catch like Sandy Amoros made usually happened to us against the Yankees. Gilliam was a fine defensive player but he was actually an infielder. He was kept in the game for his bat and his speed until we got the lead. It was then customary for Walter Alston to make some defensive changes. Putting Amoros in left, being a left-hander, made the catch much more possible. It was very close to the rail down the left field line. A right-hander, with his glove on his left hand, would have had to cross over with his glove to make the catch backhanded. I would say the fates were with us that day and credit our manager for putting Amoros in left field. He was a very quick fielder so he was able to race over to the left field line to grab the ball. The ball was tailing away from him toward the stands and it made the catch even tougher. Amoros was also able to relay the ball to Reese, who got it over to Hodges at first to double up McDougald. If Amoros does not make that catch, McDougald scores. The ball would not have bounced into the stands. It would have stayed in the ballpark, but Berra would have had at least a double and maybe a triple.

Winning the 1955 series was such a great achievement. The World Series had proven to be such a barrier for the Dodgers before 1955, with losses to the Yankees in 1947, 1949, 1952 and 1953. The Yankees never intimidated us, but in a short series, anything can happen. Ted Williams went to his grave a disappointed man, in one small respect, regarding his performance in the 1946 World Series. He only hit about .200 in that series and it really bothered him. That's typical, though, of what can happen in a short series. Anyone can have a big week or a bad week in the World Series.

ROB NEYER: If you watch film of the catch, it wasn't that difficult a play. Amoros had to run full out to get to the ball. Once he got to the ball, he had to reach out and caught the ball near his knees. It was a tough play, but it wasn't as difficult as some have suggested. Amoros had replaced Jim Gilliam in left, with Gilliam replacing Don Zimmer at second base. Gilliam and Amoros both played a lot of left field for the Dodgers in 1955 and 1956, and over those two seasons, Gilliam's statistics in left field were better. Presumably, they played behind the same group of pitchers, and it's my considered opinion that Gilliam would have made the same play that Amoros made. Alston made the move to get Gilliam to second base and Alston had made that move essentially all season. It wasn't like Alston made the move strictly for Game 7 of the World Series. If anything, I would compliment Alston for being consistent and not changing his strategy just because it was the World Series. He made the move he always made, and it worked out.

Go West

For nearly five decades, the 16 franchises in the major leagues had remained in the same cities they had occupied since 1903. However, a sharp decline in attendance in the 1950s prompted some owners to take their teams to where the fans were.[27] In 1953, the Boston Braves departed for Milwaukee. One year later the St. Louis Browns transferred to Baltimore, and the Philadelphia Athletics headed for Kansas City in 1955.

Geographically speaking, major league baseball became a national game in 1958. That's the year that the Dodgers and Giants, two franchises that had seen a steady drop in attendance, traveled westward to Los Angeles and San Francisco respectively.[28]

What if major league baseball had reached the West Coast before 1958? What if the Dodgers and Giants had remained in New York?

DEAN SULLIVAN: The only way the Dodgers and the Giants would have remained in New York would have been if Mayor Robert Wagner and Parks Commissioner Robert Moses had promised both clubs that they could build new stadiums locally. If this had happened, the teams would have continued to thrive on the field, and perhaps the shock of nearly losing the clubs would have persuaded their fans to flock to the ballparks. The Dodgers probably would have built a bigger, better version of Ebbets Field (which would have hurt pitchers like Sandy Koufax), while the Giants, wanting to avoid the eccentricities of the Polo Grounds, might have opted to custom-build a stadium to fit Willie Mays. The immediate impact of this would not be on West Coast expansion, which was inevitable, but on baseball expansion — the creation of new clubs.

New York responded to the loss of the Giants and the Dodgers by forming a commission led by lawyer William Shea. Shea's solution was to establish a new major league — the Continental League — with teams in New York, Toronto, Houston, Minneapolis and Denver, among other cities, some of which had already built stadiums. When baseball officials realized that Shea and Branch Rickey had the ability to carry out their threat, they eliminated the threat by promising to put new expansion teams in several Continental League cities. Without the loss of the New York clubs, this deal never would have been consummated.

Expansion and continued franchise transfers would have continued, but in a different form. Surely, teams would have been given to Los Angeles and San Francisco. Perhaps the Washington Senators, who moved to Minneapolis as part of the deal described above, might have transferred to California instead. In time they might have been joined by the Yankees, who after a sharp decline in the mid-1960s could not compete with their cross-town rivals' and might have been shifted by their new owners, the CBS network, to familiar territory in Los Angeles. Maybe in time the Yankees (renamed the Conquistadors) would have been purchased by Los Angeles Lakers owner (and prospective Toronto Continental League owner) Jack Kent Cooke, whose money and flamboyance might have helped them return to dominance rather quickly. Steinbrenner who?

Another new power might have been the Atlanta Braves. In the mid-1960s they lost out on USC pitcher Tom Seaver when they lost a coin flip with the New York Mets for his rights. With Seaver following knuckleballer Phil Niekro in the rotation, the Braves might have won the 1969 NLCS against the Chicago Cubs and challenged the Reds for dominance in the NL West for several years.

JIM VAIL: This question reminds me of the old magazine cover that purported to show a map of the United States from a New Yorker's viewpoint, with over 90 percent of the map taken up by the area from the eastern edges of Brooklyn and Queens to the west bank of the Hudson River, and the rest of America—from Hoboken to San Francisco—compressed into a tiny space at the back of the drawing. After all, the moves to the left coast by the Giants and Dodgers were not the first franchise relocations in major-league history.

The Milwaukee club that was a charter member of the American League in 1901 moved to St. Louis the following season (becoming the Browns), and the junior circuit's original Baltimore Orioles franchise moved to New York (where it became the Highlanders and then morphed into the Yankees) after finishing dead last in the AL for 1902. Much later, the Boston Braves moved to Milwaukee in 1953, the St. Louis Browns to Baltimore and third-generation Oriolehood in 1954 (given the birds' coloring, a move which it seems should have more rightfully made them the Baltimore Oranges instead) and the storied Philadelphia A's to Kansas City in 1955.

Granted, however, the Giants-Dodgers relocations were especially traumatic because (1) they deprived New York City — of all places— of two of its three teams, and (2) they came at a time when the Dodgers, after decades of relative mediocrity, were perennial challengers for the National League pennant, featuring one of the most stable and beloved lineups in baseball history. (It's no consolation to their New York fans, but the Giants were about to reap a bountiful harvest from their minor league system that included four future Hall of Famers— Orlando Cepeda, Willie McCovey, Juan Marichal and Gaylord Perry — and would keep them in pennant contention for most of the first decade after they moved to San Francisco.) Beyond that, there is no doubt that the shifts were sociologically and economically significant, because they directly connected major-league baseball with the Hollywood public relations machine. More important, they changed the landscape of the game into one that, for the first time ever, was truly transcontinental rather than stopping a couple hundred miles west of St. Louis.

All the same, it's my opinion that the landscape of big league baseball today would not be much different city-wise than it currently is, even if the Jints and Bums had stayed put. In the perfection of hindsight, it's obvious that the changing demographics of the American population, plus the economics of professional sports in general and of baseball in particular, were about to impose dramatic expansion in some form or another on the national pastime.

To begin with, when the two clubs moved west after the 1957 season, the Pacific Coast League had been making noises about "going major" for the better part of a decade. In truth, the PCL had made such threats far longer than that, but they lacked economic credibility before the growing migration of Americans to the West Coast that followed World War II. At the time, the PCL was an eight-team league just like the two majors, and for much of the 1950s it had featured two teams apiece in the Los Angeles and San Francisco areas. At the end of the 1957 season, its franchises included the Hollywood Stars, Los Angeles Angels, Portland Beavers, Sacramento Solons, San Diego Padres, San Francisco Seals, Seattle Rainiers and Vancouver Mounties (who had been the Oakland Oaks prior to 1956). So the left-coast league was truly "international" a decade before the majors first ventured into Canada in 1969.

Given all that, and without doubt, the Giants' and Dodgers' relocations were — beyond the obvious economic advantages implied by moving into already large and growing, virgin markets— in part a preemptive strike designed to prevent the PCL's threatened declaration of "majordom." The moves forced the PCL to abandon its two largest population centers, Los Angeles and San Francisco, moving the three franchises in those locales to Phoenix, Salt Lake City and Spokane, leaving it with a much less impressive roster of cities for the time and forever ending its hopes to go major. However, the fact that the preemption succeeded did not ease the pressure for further expansion.

Roughly coincidental with the Giants-Dodgers moves, and probably far more significant than the PCL threats, former Cardinals-Dodgers-Pirates general manager Branch Rickey began to organize an entirely new circuit, the Continental League. At the time, Rickey was teamed with Edwin Johnson, a former governor and U. S. Senator from Colorado, and William Shea, a New York attorney with heavy-duty political clout. All three men were quite cognizant of the fact that the Giants-Dodgers relocations had left a vacuum of sorts in the Big Apple and that there were several American cities of substantial population hungry for, but without, a major league team. So by the end of 1959 Rickey and his partners announced that their new league would include teams in Atlanta, Buffalo, Dallas, Denver, Houston, Minneapolis, Toronto and, of course, New York — thereby replacing the Jints and Bums, plus beating MLB as a whole to the Canadian market.

To prevent the Continental League from getting started, MLB made yet another preemptive strike in 1961–62. The AL expanded first, actually a year ahead of the agreed-upon schedule, with Calvin Griffith's old Washington

Senators moving to Minneapolis to become the Twins, a new team with the same name replacing the Senators in the nation's capital, and creation of the major-level Los Angeles Angels (largely because the AL did not want to grant the senior circuit a monopoly in the nation's then-third-largest urban area). The NL followed suit the next season, adding the New York Mets (a tit-for-tat denying the AL and Yankees a continuing monopoly in the Big Apple) and Houston Colt .45s.

The presence of major league franchises in three of the Continental League's eight cities—especially the new senior circuit franchise in New York—effectively scuttled the new league's formation. Through franchise relocation (the Braves to Atlanta in 1966 and new Senators to Dallas in 1972) MLB also moved into two of the other proposed CL locales within a decade. Another expansion in 1969 added four more teams, in Montreal, San Diego, Seattle and Kansas City (replacing the A's, who moved to Oakland in 1968), giving MLB the same number of clubs that would have existed as majors had either the PCL or CL gone that route and no expansions had occurred.

One can only speculate as to whether the Pacific Coast League or the Continental circuit would or could have survived as majors. On the minus side, the reserve clause was still in effect, so players who were contracted to major league franchises—including their minor leaguers—would not (barring legal challenge) have been available to either circuit. Also mucking things up for the PCL would have been the fact that its teams had contractual agreements to serve as farm clubs for major league franchises, and it's likely that MLB would have filed suit against any attempt to break those agreements, tying up a newly "major" PCL in court costs that might have doomed it from the start.

The Continental League would not have faced that latter problem, but in the first few years of its operation still would have been confronted by considerable difficulty fielding teams that, were likely to have been perceived as "major league" quality. Among the existing high minors, only the Mexican League was independent enough of the majors back then that the CL might have siphoned off some of its talent without serious legal repercussions. At the time, few if any in baseball believed that the talent in the Japanese leagues was equal or even moderately comparable to the American majors, and it was not until 1964 that pitcher Masanori Murakami became the first Japanese-league player to reach the Show—and he stayed only briefly when he did.

So to be relatively credible, the best either circuit could have done at the time would be to sign as many major league castoffs as possible (mainly old, fading guys the big-league clubs deemed no longer useful), to scout the still largely untapped Caribbean as thoroughly as possible (with the exception of a couple of clubs, MLB was still relatively negligent in that area), and to compete aggressively for unsigned high school and collegiate talent — predictably driving up the price of every ballplayer in the process. All in all, and at best, such a recipe assured that it would be several seasons before either circuit could claim to be "major league" quality with anything like a straight face.

However, the situation would not have been hopeless for either league. Recall that nearly coincident with all of this the fledgling American Football League faced virtually the same obstacles, vis-à-vis the older NFL, when it began play in 1961 (without any realistic option to sign Japanese or Caribbean players). Yet it achieved sufficient parity with the older league to justify a "Super Bowl" by January 1967, and to force a merger with the older league within a decade. Just a half-decade or so behind the new football circuit, the American Basketball Association also began operation, reaching a point of relative parity sufficient to justify a merger with the older NBA within another decade (although most of the ABA clubs were dissolved in the process).

More than anything else, the AFL and ABA benefited from an aspect of the same demographic changes that fostered postwar expansion in baseball. After an unprecedented surge in the birth rate following World War II, by 1960 or a couple years later the horde of baby boomers began to graduate from high school as, without much doubt, the most sports-minded and sports-engaged generation in American history. For baseball, this meant that the collegiate system, especially, was about to become a hitherto untapped gold mine of already well-coached talent.

Beyond that was the option, hinted at above, to legally challenge the majors' reserve clause, which events a decade later proved was ripe for negation. Throughout the 1960s, the composition of the U. S. Supreme Court was still dominated by the "Earl Warren liberals," so there seems little reason to doubt that the clause could have been overturned by the right lawsuit several years before the separate actions of Curt Flood, plus Dave McNally and Andy Messersmith. If the Continental League had made such a challenge, it would have been very interesting to see (1) whether the existent Major League Players Association, which was nowhere near as strong by the early 1960s as it was a decade or so later, would have broken ranks with MLB and sided with the CL upstarts (no doubt as part of an effort to unionize its players), and (2) exactly what kind of free-agent process inevitably would emerge from the outcome. One suspects that, with a rival league competing for talent, whatever free agency ensued would have been far more liberal in form than the one "negotiated" in the mid–1970s; given the likely escalation of salaries that would have ensued, it also would have proved to be an impetus for rapid merger between the CL and the two older circuits as a cost-cutting measure.

So it seems as though either a "major" PCL or the Continental League (most likely the latter, but certainly not both) could have succeeded — even thrived eventually — if it managed to survive for about five seasons, increasing its overall talent level each year. If that had happened, then the baseball landscape of the mid to late 1960s, sans expansion, would have theoretically looked like this:

National League	American League	Continental
Chicago	Baltimore	Atlanta
Cincinnati	Boston	Buffalo
Los Angeles	Chicago	Dallas
Milwaukee	Cleveland	Denver
Philadelphia	Detroit	Houston
Pittsburgh	Kansas City	Minneapolis
San Francisco	New York	New York
St. Louis	Washington	Toronto

The first and most obvious problem with this alignment would have surfaced when, inevitably, the Continental League was admitted to postseason play against the two older majors. If merger preserved the CL's separate identity, then unless the World Series was to be reduced to some kind of round-robin affair it would seem that a "wild-card" postseason qualifier would have been an inevitable outgrowth of any three-league setup, thereby adding that phrase (or something like it) to baseball's lexicon three decades earlier than it actually was. A similar complication would have occurred regarding all-star play. Of course, it's possible that, like the NBA-ABA merger of the mid–1970s, the Continental League franchises would have been dispersed among the two pre-existing majors, obviating the need for radical alteration of the postseason format (but creating 12-team circuits that, no doubt, would have fostered divisional alignments as occurred in 1969).

But whatever might have ensued with regard to postseason and all-star play, and assuming that the Kansas City A's would have moved to Oakland when they actually did, the three-circuit alignment above represents only marginal variation from the 24-club reality that existed by 1969. Among the CL cities, only Buffalo, Toronto and Denver were not part of the MLB landscape by that year (although the latter two of those acquired big league teams in 1977 and 1993, respectively). Among the expansion cities of 1961–62 and 1969, only Montreal, San Diego and Seattle (to any one of which the Braves might have moved in the mid 1960s) are not represented.

So if, hypothetically, the Braves moved to Montreal instead of Atlanta, then under the three-circuit format above — and barring other franchise relocations possibly triggered by the CL's formation and survival — the list of current major league cities not yet represented by 1969 would have included Anaheim, Oakland, San Diego, Seattle, Miami, Phoenix and Tampa; and Buffalo and Montreal (assuming the Braves, like the Expos, failed there) would have been the only cities with a club back then that are not a part of the current MLB landscape. Given that the majors have expanded on three other occasions since 1969 — in 1977, 1993 and 1998 — there's little reason to doubt that at least six of those eight cities would have joined later on, at similar intervals, perhaps with each of the three circuits adding one club apiece at each new tier of expansion. Such an outcome would have produced the same number of MLB franchises existent today (30), albeit aligned in a three-league set up instead of just two. It's my own guess, obviously based on hindsight, that Oakland and Tampa would have been the most likely cities ignored by such a growth pattern.

However, by breaking the hearts of more than half of New York's fans in 1957–58, Walter O'Malley and Horace Stoneham effectively prevented this alternative scenario from ever taking place. As a result, there has not been and probably never will be a major league team called the Buffalo Bisons.

Herb Score

A rocket off the bat of Yankees infielder Gil McDougald knocked Herb Score's career off its tracks in 1957. One of the best pitching prospects in baseball, Score had won 16 games for Cleveland as a rookie in 1955 and improved to 20–9 in 1956.[29]

Score's path to stardom was radically altered, however, on May 7, 1957, when McDougald's liner struck the Indians' left-hander near his right eye. Although Score returned to the Indians after a layoff, he eventually injured his arm and lost his effectiveness. Score would add just 17 victories to his career total after 1957, and would be out of the majors after 1962.[30]

What if Herb Score had avoided Gil McDougald's line drive in 1957?

JERRY ESKENAZI: Score was the real McCoy. He was simply spectacular before his injury. A young pitcher will often rack up some great numbers during their first few years and then fade. Score was beyond that. I know Bob Feller felt Score was going to be one of the all-time greats. You don't win 20 games as a rookie thanks only to dumb luck. Some people say it's always easier to deal with a young pitcher the second time around, perhaps in the year after his rookie season. I think teams might have seen Score year after year and it wouldn't have done them any good. Some think Score might have wound up as one of the top ten pitchers of all time.

DEAN SULLIVAN: Prior to nearly losing his sight to a Gil McDougald line drive (which did not end Score's career — a sore arm years later did), legends such as Tris Speaker described Herb Score as a sure-fire Hall of Famer. Even with a mediocre team like the Indians, Score would have enjoyed several more 20-win and 200-plus strikeout seasons by the end of the decade. Score's statistics would have improved even more during the deadball era of the 1960s, making him a strong candidate to amass over 3,000 strikeouts and

For two seasons, Herb Score ranked among the best pitchers in baseball. (Courtesy Cleveland Indians.)

200 victories in his career. By avoiding serious injury, Score would surely have made the Hall of Fame.

BILL MCNEIL: Herb Score first came to the public's attention in 1954 when he led the American Association in victories (22), winning percentage (.815), innings pitched (251), strikeouts (330), and earned-run average (2.62) as a member of the Indianapolis Indians. The next year he captured American League Rookie-Of-the–Year honors with the Cleveland Indians and, disdaining the sophomore jinx, he won 20 games in 1956.

Gil McDougald's line drive struck Score in the eye, putting him out of commission for the rest of the season. He tried to come back the next year, but could do no better than a 2–3 record with a 3.95 ERA. After three more disappointing seasons, when he was a combined 15–23, he retired from the game.

According to Score, however, the eye injury had nothing to do with his pitching demise. The following spring, he tore the tendon in his elbow pitching against the Washington Senators and in those days the only cure for that type of injury was rest. He returned to the mound four weeks after his injury and pitched the rest of the season with a sore arm, but he had lost the zip on his fastball. The answer to the question, what if Score hadn't been hit by McDougald's liner, is that it would not have affected his career. His arm was dead, and there was no Tommy John surgery available at that time to reconstruct his elbow. If he suffered that injury today, he might have gone on to a very successful career, maybe even a Hall of Fame career.

However, Herb Score wasn't the only pitcher in the 1950s to have a promising career ended with an arm injury. Karl Spooner was a Brooklyn Dodger farmhand whose brilliant pitching career was almost too brief to be noticed. The 6' tall, 185-pound southpaw came into his own in 1954 when he went 21–9 for the Fort Worth Cats of the AA Texas League, while leading the league in victories, strikeouts (262 in 238 innings) and bases on balls (162). He was called up to Brooklyn during the last two weeks of the season but was not expected to see any action because the Dodgers were battling the New York Giants for the National League pennant. When the Dodgers were eliminated from the race, however, the 23-year-old phenom was given the starting assignment against the Giants on the last Wednesday of the season. The nervous rookie walked the first three men he faced in the game. Then, after a brief meeting with catcher Roy Campanella, he fanned the next three batters including Willie Mays and Monte Irvin, and went on to baffle the New Yorkers with a three-hit 3–0 victory, liberally sprinkled with 15 strikeouts. Four days later, he corralled the Pittsburgh Pirates 1–0 on a four-hitter with an even dozen strikeouts. In so doing, he set a new National League two-game strikeout record, breaking the mark of 25 set by Dazzy Vance in 1922.

As the 1955 spring training camp opened, the Dodger faithful were counting on 'King Karl' to pitch their Bums to the pennant with at least 25 wins. But fate ruled otherwise. Spooner developed a sore arm in camp and was of little use during the season, pitching just 99 innings, all of them in pain, and finishing with an 8–6 record. He did have the distinction of pitching and winning the pennant clincher, however, as he handcuffed the Milwaukee Braves 10–2 on September 8. It was the earliest pennant clinching in National League history. Spooner then started Game 6 of the World Series against the New York Yankees, but was driven from the mound after just one-third of an inning, yielding five runs.

Karl Spooner never pitched another major league game. The zip never returned to his overpowering fastball, and he faded from the baseball scene forever, finished at the age of 24. His potential is unknown and unpredictable. His career might have been short and ordinary. On the other hand, he might have developed into one of the greatest pitchers of all time. We will never know.

The Bullpen View

For nearly four decades, it was business as usual in the majors. All of that changed in the years following World War II. The war itself wiped out careers and deprived several players of a possible spot in the Hall of Fame. Ted Williams and Bob Feller were among the stars whose lifetime numbers were diminished by military service. Steve Bullock and Bill Deane predicted that Ted Williams would have slugged nearly 700 home runs, and would have ranked as the game's all-time RBI leader, had the Boston outfielder not served in World War II and Korea. Bill McNeil concluded that Bob Feller would have accumulated over 300 wins and more than 3,800 strikeouts, if World War II had not intervened. Panel members listed several others who might have made it to Cooperstown if not for the war, including Dom DiMaggio, Cecil Travis, Joe Gordon and Buddy Lewis.

Several experts also predicted big numbers from stars of the Negro Leagues, if integration had taken place in the majors before 1947. John Holway speculated that Josh Gibson and Mule Suttles would have shattered Babe Ruth's single season home run record. While any speculation along those lines is certainly debatable, there's no disputing Gary Gillette's assertion that baseball would have been the richer if the majors had opened its doors to blacks years earlier.

Two of the more talented teams during the '40s and the '50s, the Red Sox and the Dodgers, developed a nasty habit of crushing the hopes of their fans. Take, for instance, Cleveland's victory over Boston in the 1948 AL playoff game, when Red Sox manager Joe McCarthy chose Denny Galehouse as his surprise starter. Bobby Doerr stated that the Red Sox might have beaten the Indians if left-hander Mel Parnell had received the starting assignment. On the other hand, Rob Neyer voiced his opinion that it was going to be difficult for any Red Sox hurler to outpitch Cleveland's Gene Bearden that day. Boston's failure to overtake the Indians in '48 and the Yankees in '49 certainly frustrated the Red Sox faithful, but Brooklyn's heartbreaking losses in 1950 and 1951 had to be even more devastating for Dodgers fans. It's impossible to imagine a more emotionally draining defeat than the loss Brooklyn suffered when Bobby Thomson homered to catapult New York to victory in the 1951 NL playoff series. Brooklyn manager Charlie Dressen had his choice of relievers and his choice of hitters to face.

Dressen chose to use Ralph Branca against Bobby Thomson. David Shiner claimed it was a mistake to pitch Branca, and predicted a Brooklyn victory if Dressen had gone with Carl Erskine instead. Four years later, the Dodgers finally delivered a World Series crown to Brooklyn, thanks in no small part to manager Walter Alston's decision to insert Sandy Amoros into Game 7 as a defensive replacement in left field. Amoros snagged Yogi Berra's fly ball, and Maury Allen maintained that if Alston had not made that defensive move, Berra would have had an extra base hit, and the Yankees would have rallied to win yet another championship.

Brooklyn fans had little time to celebrate. Within just a few years, their team had packed up and departed for California, joining the Giants, Braves, Athletics and Browns on the list of franchises that found new homes in the '50s. Expansion would take hold in the following decade, as the NL added new teams in Houston, Montreal, New York and San Diego, and the AL expanded into Kansas City, Los Angeles, Minneapolis and Seattle.

5

Decade of Growth: 1960–1969

Historical Highlights

For more than half a century, the AL and the NL maintained eight franchises, but expansion in the 1960s completely altered the picture. By the end of the decade, each league numbered 12 teams and featured two divisions, forcing clubs to win a League Championship Series in order to get to the World Series.

The '60s featured several World Series classics, including Pittsburgh's stunning victory over New York in 1960, San Francisco's narrow loss to the Yankees in 1962, and Detroit's hard-fought triumph over St. Louis in 1968. Just getting to the postseason was no sure thing, as the Phillies discovered in 1964. One of the decade's stronger teams, the San Francisco Giants, displayed a tendency to fall short in pennant races. Witness 1965, when Los Angeles nipped San Francisco for the NL flag, thanks in part to the decision by Giants pitcher Juan Marichal to use his bat for something other than hitting a baseball.

From an individual standpoint, two Yankees staged an electrifying home run derby in 1961. Although both Roger Maris and Mickey Mantle threatened Babe Ruth's single-season home run record, Maris was the one who hit 61. Injuries also undermined several careers, as arm problems forced Dodgers left-hander Sandy Koufax to seek early retirement, and Boston's budding superstar Tony Conigliaro was nearly killed by a pitched ball in 1967.

Several big trades in the '60s launched dynasties in St. Louis and Baltimore. When St. Louis picked up Lou Brock from the Cubs in 1964, the Cardinals got a speedy outfielder who helped them win three NL pennants in five seasons. Baltimore swiped veteran outfielder Frank Robinson from Cincinnati after the 1965 season and the Orioles proceeded to win four of the next six AL titles.

The Bad Hop

Pittsburgh proved in 1960 that the margin of victory is irrelevant. Despite the fact that the Yankees outscored the Pirates 55–27 in the World Series, Pittsburgh had the last laugh, winning a wild seventh game 10–9 on Bill Mazeroski's solo homer, a shot that turned Forbes Field into a madhouse.

Pittsburgh's victory celebration might never have erupted, had it not been for a bad bounce that gave the Pirates new life in the bottom of the eighth inning. With New York on top 7–4, Bill Virdon's potential double play grounder took a strange hop, striking Yankees' shortstop Tony Kubek in the throat. Reliever Jim Coates then failed to cover first base on Roberto Clemente's ground ball, as the Pirates pulled to within a run. Reserve catcher Hal Smith completed Pittsburgh's comeback with a hair-raising three-run home run that put the Pirates in front 9–7. When New York rallied for two runs in the top of the ninth, the stage was set for Mazeroski's series-ending heroics.

What if Tony Kubek had successfully fielded Bill Virdon's bad hop grounder in Game 7 of the 1960 World Series?

MIKE ROBBINS: Had a bad hop not changed a grounder off the bat of Bill Virdon from a probable double play to a single, the Yankees would have won the 1960 World Series. The Yankees were up 7–4 before that eventful bottom of the eighth, and with two out and no one on, it seems unlikely that the Pirates would have scored at all, much less the five runs they eventually pushed across.

Adding one more World Series victory to the Yankees' impressive resume wouldn't have changed their legacy very much, though perhaps the Yankees wouldn't have "retired" Casey Stengel after the season in favor of Ralph Houk, which might have slightly re-written both Yankee and Met history. However, had Kubek made the play, it likely would have dramatically altered Bill Mazeroski's place in history. Mazeroski was, without question, a wonderful defensive second baseman. However, being a wonderful defensive second baseman has never been a great way to ensure lasting fame. Without his dramatic Series-winning home run in the ninth inning of that game seven, the career .260 hitter would enjoy nowhere near the name recognition he does today.

FORMER PIRATES PITCHER BOB FRIEND: The 1960 World Series has been described as a wacky series due to the large scores in the Yankee victories and the close scores in our wins. The fact is we had a veteran ballclub and had beaten out some good teams to win the National league pennant, like Milwaukee and St. Louis. There was a lot of balance in the National League and it was very tough to repeat as a champion in the 1960s.

We knew how to play the game and I think the Yankees respected us. I think the Yankees felt they should have won, but we made the bigger plays in the final game. The Yankees had a great team, with good pitching, solid defense, and a tremendous offense with guys like Mantle and Maris.

We might have been a team of destiny. We had many games during the season where we made the plays in the late innings to win the game. There were several strange plays in the seventh game, like the grounder to Tony Kubek. Even if Kubek had handled the ground ball cleanly, I still feel the Pirates would have found a way to come back and win the game. The bottom line is that it was our series and we were going to win no matter what.

FORMER PITTSBURGH SHORTSTOP DICK GROAT: It's true, if Kubek fields the ground ball, perhaps the series turns out differently. Then again, what if Jim Coates had covered first base like he's supposed to on Clemente's ground ball? That's a basic play that pitchers work on all spring. The eighth inning would have been over before Hal Smith hit his big home run. Smith's home run is the forgotten home run in World Series history. I was on base at the time and that place was just a madhouse when Hal hit it. We really thought we had it won right there, but the Yankees, being a very fine offensive team, scored two runs to tie it up in the top of the ninth inning.

The best team won the World Series that year. Branch Rickey really deserves the credit for rebuilding the Pirates organization. He drafted Roberto Clemente and Elroy Face and signed Mazeroski and Bob Skinner. He made the trade for Bill Virdon and brought in Gino Cimoli. Rickey really put together that 1960 Pirates championship team. Branch Rickey also taught us when we were just kids in baseball that everyone wins the high scoring games at one time or another. Great teams find a way to win the close games, and we won every game we had a chance to win in the 1960 World Series.

61

Yankees outfielders Mickey Mantle and Roger Maris captivated the baseball world in 1961 with their pursuit of Babe Ruth's single-season mark of 60 home runs. Although many New Yorkers were undoubtedly pulling for Mantle, the record went to Maris, who hit his 61st homer on the final day of the 162-game regular season. Hobbled by a hip injury, Mantle dropped out of the race and finished with 54 home runs, playing in eight fewer games than Maris, with 76 fewer at bats.[1]

What if Mickey Mantle had remained healthy throughout the 1961 season?

DAVID VINCENT: Mantle was in the hospital for a while late in the season. Heading into September, Mantle trailed Maris, but Mantle wasn't that far behind and certainly had a shot at hitting 60 homers. For a good part of the 1961 season, Mantle led Maris in the home run race. In fact, Mantle was ahead of Maris as late as the middle of August. The injuries started to wear Mantle down and he did not hit a homer for the final 10 or 11 games of the season.

It was a fun race, and Mantle was the big star in New York, so I think a lot of fans were rooting for Mantle. At the rate that Mantle was hitting homers, he certainly would have surpassed Ruth's record of 60, if he hadn't missed games due to injuries. We might have seen two guys surpass the home run record, just as we did with McGwire and Sosa in 1998.

DAVID SHINER: Every time during the season that Mantle came to close to Maris in the home run race, Maris was able to pull ahead. It seemed to me in 1961 that Mantle was the great and talented star, the one who should be breaking Ruth's record, rather than Maris who wasn't well known, photogenic, or good copy.

Mantle did more things offensively than Maris in 1961. He drew more walks and he would bunt when needed. In the movie "61," they have Maris dragging a bunt to win a game, but it was really Mantle who did that. Maris just got more at bats from his plate appearances. Without the injuries, Mantle might have come closer, up to maybe 57 or 58 homers, but he still wasn't going to surpass Babe Ruth.

The Kansas City Pipeline

Roger Maris came to the Yankees from Kansas City after the 1959 season via a pipeline that often saw the best and brightest of the Athletics heading for the Big Apple. Between 1955 and 1960, the Yankees and Athletics swung 16 deals involving 58 players. While New York got future stars like Maris, third baseman Clete Boyer and pitcher Ralph Terry, Kansas City received over-the-hill veterans and second rate players in return.[2]

What if the Athletics had not supplied the Yankees with so many valuable players in the '50s and the '60s?

GARY GILLETTE: If Roger Maris hadn't been dealt to New York, he might have still been able to put together the power numbers he had with the Yankees. Kansas City could have easily traded Maris to the Angels who played at a true bandbox, Wrigley Field, in 1961. Maris' great season with New York in 1961 wasn't a fluke. People forget what a great season Maris had in 1960. He was the American League MVP and therefore was the league MVP two seasons in a row. Not too many people have done that. He wasn't a Hall of Famer but he certainly was a terrific player at the peak of his game. You put a left-handed pull hitter in Yankee Stadium in 1961, with the short right field line and a three-foot wall, and you had all the ingredients for a record-breaking season.

The New York-Kansas City pipeline was absolutely unconscionable, and it shows you how corrupt the American League was when the Yankees and Athletics could make these trades. The A's essentially served as the Yankees' quadruple-A farm team. It shouldn't have been allowed. The commissioner, Ford Frick, was a puppet. If these trades are disallowed, the Yankees probably still win the American League in many of the years they did, but it's possible the Cleveland Indians might have been able to break through and win one or two more pennants. The Indians won the pennant in 1948 and 1954 and finished a close second to New York on a number of occasions. Disallowing the trades wouldn't have prevented the Yanks from being a dominant team, but it might have allowed other teams, like the Tigers, Red Sox, White Sox or Indians to win a pennant or two and spark even more interest in baseball in those cities.

JIM VAIL: If the Maris trade had not occurred when it did, I believe the following can be said with relative confidence: (1) Mickey Mantle would have been the 1960 American League MVP; (2) Babe Ruth would have held the single-season home run record for 71 years (through September, 1998) rather than the 34 that he actually owned it; (3) the Yankees would have won at least four of those five straight pennants anyway; and (4) Maris might have lived a longer and happier life. He died of lung cancer in 1985 at age 51, apparently having never quite gotten over the ton of grief he incurred for beating Mantle in the chase for Ruth's home run record.

However, there is one caveat to the alternate outcomes above. It's my own belief that — absent the December, 1959, transaction — Maris would have been traded by the A's to New York anyway, no later than the winter of 1960–61.

At the time of the deal Maris ranked with Detroit's Al Kaline (age 24) and Cleveland's Rocky Colavito (26) as the top young, power-hitting outfielders in the junior circuit (Washington's Bob Allison might also be included, but he was coming off his rookie season with no assurance he would repeat his 1959 numbers). Among the three, Kaline and Colavito were both better established as stars. The former had won the AL batting crown and led the circuit in hits at age 20 in 1955, and was already a five-time all-star. The latter, like Maris, had made his first all-star squad in 1959 while leading the league with 42 homers, but also had swatted 21, 25 and then 41 big flies in the previous three seasons, driving in more than 100 runs each in 1958–59. Maris had three big-league seasons under his belt, but had not yet performed at quite the same level as Kaline and Colavito. Beyond that, Cleveland had swapped Maris to Kansas City at midseason 1958, in part because he and Colavito were both natural right fielders (with arms comparable to, but probably not as, good as Roberto Clemente's) and the club apparently lacked the imagination or desire to convert one of them — both were fast enough afoot at the time — into a center fielder (although both would play that position sporadically later in their careers).

The Yankees were brooding that winter over failing to win the pennant for the first time since 1954, and for only the second occasion in the previous decade. New York had finished third in 1959, 15 games behind Chicago, with a very un-Yankee-like record of just four games above .500. Hank Bauer, the Bronx Bombers' right fielder throughout most of the 1950s, had turned 37 during the 1959 campaign, with a commensurate decline in his batting numbers, and his advancing age was widely perceived as one of the Yanks' major (albeit relatively few) liabilities heading into 1960.

Predictably, New York management wanted a younger man, with some power, to replace Bauer. Yankee first baseman Bill Skowron was just 28 and already a perennial all star, so it's not likely they considered trading him instead. Also, several of the AL's slugging flychasers of the time — Roy Sievers, Jim Lemon, Minnie Minoso and Jackie Jensen, for example — were 31 or older and past their prime. Among the more youthful trio mentioned above, Kaline would have commanded a higher price than New York was likely willing to pay, and — given the intensity of the Yankee-Detroit rivalry of the era — Tigers fans might have lynched their general manager had he traded Kaline to the Yanks. The same may have been true of Colavito with Cleveland, although Indians GM Frank 'Trader' Lane was crazy enough that he shipped Rocco to Detroit for Harvey Kuenn during spring training of 1960 in an ill-advised swap of batting and home run champions. So Colavito may have been available to New York that winter, but one suspects that Lane would have demanded nothing less than Mickey Mantle in return — a deal that was not about to happen.

So New York shipped Bauer, 1956 World Series hero Don Larsen, 26-year-old outfielder-first baseman Norm Siebern and (the not yet, but truly less than) Marvelous Marv Throneberry to KC for Maris, DeMaestri and Hadley. Among those seven, only Maris and Siebern had significant impact on subsequent history. With the exception of Maris and Siebern, all of the others involved played part-time roles for both clubs in 1960, and were gone from either team by the end of 1961.

With regard to the 1960 MVP, along with his league-leading RBI total, Maris also topped the junior circuit with a .581 slugging percentage that season. His other key MVP stats included 39 home runs and 290 total bases (both second-best to Mantle's numbers), plus a .283 batting average that proved to be the highest of Roger's career (no one paid any attention to on-base percentage back then, so it had no impact on MVP voting). Teammate Mantle was runner-up for the award, just three points behind Maris (225 to 222), with season stats that included a league-best 40 homers and 294 total bases, plus 94 RBI and batting and slugging marks of .275 and .558. Placing third, and the only other man above 200 points in the voting, was second-place Baltimore's Brooks Robinson, with 14 homers, 88 RBI, 262 total bases, plus .294 and .440.

Without Maris, Kansas City finished last in 1960, seven games behind seventh-place Boston and 13 games out of sixth. Maris was approaching star status by the start of that season, and it is likely — had he stayed with Kansas City — that his numbers would have surpassed those of the previous year. But the A's offense was dismal in 1960: their team batting average declined from .263 in 1959 (which tied Cleveland for the league leadership) to just .249, third-lowest in the AL; their runs-scored total dropped from 681 to 615; and their on-base percentage of .316 was the worst in the circuit. So, with likely few men on base ahead of him, Maris would have been hard-pressed to equal the 112 RBI he posted for New York that year. In turn, whatever his individual stats may have been, they were not likely to get the A's any higher than a seventh-place finish.

Although Maris' 1960 numbers with the Yanks clearly benefited Mantle (and vice versa), given New York's economic advantages it's also virtually certain that — absent Maris — the Yanks (who won the 1960 pennant by eight games over Baltimore) would have acquired someone else of average or above-so offensive output over the winter of 1959–60 to supplant Bauer in right field. Given that, Mantle's numbers would have been something similar to—probably a little less than—what he actually produced, but still far more likely to earn MVP recognition with a first-place club than whatever Maris might have done with a last- or seventh-place team. Beyond that, if Mantle's numbers had not approached what he really achieved, and/or Baltimore had actually won the pennant as result, then Robinson also would have been more likely to be the MVP than Maris.

With regard to 1961, whether Maris played for the A's or Yankees that season, he would have enjoyed the benefits of diluted expansion pitching and his home run total would have increased commensurately. But given KC's wimpy lineup of 1961, his prospects of hitting anything close to 61 dingers with the A's were slim and none. The team hit just 90 homers that year, dead last in the majors, and the only club in either circuit to swat less than 100. Also, the Kansas City ballpark was not conducive to high home run totals, as only three players (Gus Zernial in 1955, Bob Cerv in 1958 and Rocky Colavito in 1964) hit as many as 30 dingers in any of the years the A's played in KC. So had he stayed with the A's in 1961, Maris would have lacked both the lineup protection and the park configuration that abetted his assault on Babe Ruth's record.

It's also doubtful that Mantle could have challenged the home run mark had the Yankees acquired one of the AL's other premier young outfielders to replace Bauer in 1960. Kaline, Colavito and Allison were all righthanded batters. Given the expanse of Yankee Stadium's left-field Death Valley, no righty—not even Harmon Killebrew—could have produced a Maris-like home-run total in 1961 or any other year. So it's difficult to conjure Mantle achieving the symbiosis that he did with Maris with any of the other potential replacements; and it seems probable that, even with a full season of diluted pitching, the best Mantle might have done without Maris in 1961 was to approach the 54 dingers he actually hit.

As a result of all that, and with no serious challenge posted at any time in between, Ruth's 60 homers of 1927 would have remained the all-time seasonal mark until Mark McGwire and Sammy Sosa made their big splash in 1998. In turn, Maris might never have suffered the hostile press he encountered during his chase of Ruth's record; he may have kept his hair instead; and because it's well documented that he much preferred playing in Kansas City (nearer to his Fargo, North Dakota, home), he might have lived a longer, happier life as just one more very good—but not quite Hall of Fame caliber—outfielder from his era.

Given all that, the Yanks would have won at least four consecutive pennants (1960–63) anyway. The New York franchise was rich enough at the time that, if not Maris or Colavito, they still would have acquired someone of average or better replacement value to supplant Bauer as the right fielder in 1960, a season when they won the pennant by a comfortable eight-game margin. If that player proved to be nothing but a stopgap, they would have improved upon him by 1961, when they enjoyed another eight-game victory margin. They won by five games in 1962 and by ten and a half the following season. When you add to that the fact that the second-place teams changed identities every year (Baltimore in 1960, followed by Detroit, Minnesota and Chicago in subsequent seasons), it's evident that no other AL franchise was consistent enough to challenge New York on a perennial basis during that period. So without Maris, the only pennant during their five-year reign (1960–64) that is in some doubt is 1964, when New York edged Chicago and Baltimore by margins of one and two games, respectively — and that outcome is just too close to call with anything but pretentious authority.

As indicated above, however, it's my own suspicion that — even if the 1959 trade involving Maris and Siebern as principals had not materialized — KC would have dealt Roger to New York anyway, no later than the winter of 1960–61. My justification for that suspicion is the special relationship that existed between the A's and Yankee ownership during the period in question.

In November, 1954, Arnold Johnson, a Chicago-based vending machine and real estate tycoon, bought the Philadelphia A's from 90-year-old Connie Mack for $604,000 and promptly moved the team to Kansas City for the 1955 season, marking KC's first return to the majors since its Federal League franchise of 1914–15. After Johnson died of a heart attack in March of 1960, his heirs — headed by his widow — ran the club for a season before selling it to Charles O. Finley in December of that year for $1.975 million. At the time of Johnson's purchase, one of his real estate holdings included (at least partial) ownership of Yankee Stadium, so he already had a close working relationship with New York owners Dan Topping and Del Webb.

To evidence the degree and depth of that friendly relationship I made a list, using the trade register of the old Macmillan *Baseball Encyclopedia*, of all the transactions (trades, sales and waiver deals) made by Kansas City during the Johnson-family ownership. There were 52 of them in all, too many to list here, involving every team in the majors except the Cubs and Giants, and none of them involved more than the A's and one other club. The deals are broken down numerically below, according to the team involved and whether the swaps were a multi-player or one-for-one trade, a straight player sale, return of a player traded earlier (perhaps damaged goods) or a waiver transaction.

Kansas City Transactions During Johnson Era (1955–60)

Deal Type	Bal	Bos	Chi	Cle	Det	NY	Was	B/LA	Cin	Mil	Phl	Pit	StL	Tot
Trade (Multi)	1	0	0	0	2	9	0	1	0	0	0	1	0	14
Trade (1-up)	4	1	1	2	0	3	0	0	1	1	0	2	0	15
Sale	0	0	0	3	3	4	2	0	0	1	0	1	0	14
Return	0	0	0	0	0	1	0	0	0	0	0	0	0	1
Waiver	0	0	0	0	1	1	0	1	1	1	1	1	1	8
Totals	5	1	1	5	6	18	2	2	2	3	1	5	1	52

Among the deals listed above, 18 out of the 52 (35 percent) were transactions with the Yankees. In comparison, the six trades with Detroit, second-highest team figure on the list, represent just 11.5 percent of the total. What's more, 12 of Kansas City's 29 trades during the Johnson era (41 percent) were with New York, including nine of its 14 multi-player deals (64 percent). Seven of KC's swaps during the period saw five or more players change uniforms, with the A's receiving a total of 31 players in exchange for 27 (Maris was a figure in two of them). Four of those seven "cattle-car" deals (57 percent) involved the Yankees, with KC acquiring 17 players in exchange for 15. Overall, among the 18 transactions between the A's and Yanks during that era, KC obtained 36 players from New York, while the Bronx Bombers got 26 from their "farm" club. So there is little doubt from the data above that New York was, by far, the A's favored trading partner during the Johnson era.

It's often been claimed that financial distress was the major reason for KC's trade behavior, and that the Yankees—being the wealthiest team in the majors—were the most logical source of quick cash. In that light, any good player the A's had was likely to be trade bait for New York, and the list of best men Kansas City shipped to the Yanks during 1955–60 seems on the surface to support that view. The group included: Clete Boyer, Art Ditmar and Bobby Shantz (sent to the Yanks in February, 1957); Ryne Duren (traded to NY in June of that year); Duke Maas (June, 1958); Ralph Terry and Hector Lopez (May, 1959); Maris (December, 1959); and Bob Cerv (May, 1960). Boyer, Lopez and Maris all became lineup regulars for the Yanks during their early 1960s dynasty, while Ditmar, Shantz, Duren, Maas and Terry all played key pitching roles (albeit in some cases briefly) sometime during the period 1958–64. Cerv joined Johnny Blanchard to give the Yanks baseball's premier righty-lefty pinch-hitting combo for several seasons. In turn, and predictably, the list of players KC received from the Yankees during this era included numerous "has beens" (Ewell Blackwell, Eddie Robinson, Johnny Sain, Irv Noren, Enos Slaughter and Murry Dickson, for example), quite a few "never was" (e.g., Bob Martyn and Marv Freeman), and only a handful of players with any kind of future at the time they were dealt (notably Siebern, Jerry Lumpe and Woodie Held).

As a result of all this, during the six seasons of the Johnson-family ownership (and in retrospect since), the A's were often criticized — with considerable justification — for behaving like a major-league farm club of the Yankees. Beyond that, there is no doubt that Arnold Johnson's heirs were anxious to get out of baseball after his death in March, 1960, and it's likely given the sporadic attendance in KC — that the club was strapped for cash that last season, especially compared to 1955. Also, pitcher Bud Daley, who (with Maris) was KC's other all-star in 1959 and its only representative in 1960, was swapped to New York in June, 1961 (by Charles Finley, no less) — so the habit of shipping the A's players to the Yankees survived the Johnson-family era, at least briefly. With all that in mind, it seems probable that — barring the prior acquisition of someone like Colavito — Maris, as KC's primary talent, would have been traded to New York shortly after the 1960 campaign at the latest, perhaps even at mid-season.

So it's my view that Maris would have become integral to the Yankee dynasty of the early 1960s anyway. But how that might have affected the 1961 home-run derby is hard to predict. Given Maris' well-known discomfort in New York, it seems he would have necessarily spent all of 1961 adjusting to his new surroundings, and seems unlikely he could have challenged Ruth's record in his first season in the Big Apple. Because no one approached hitting 60 homers again for 37 more seasons, it also seems doubtful that Maris might have done so in 1962 or later. But then again, no one knows for certain.

Finally, it does seem safe to say that, although their cozy relationship with Kansas City during the Johnson-family era helped the Yankees maintain their American League dominance, New York would have enjoyed similar, probably equal success during 1955–60 without it. With the exceptions of 1948 and 1954, they owned the junior circuit during the years 1947–58, most of those seasons coming before Johnson acquired the A's. They had the richest, best-attended team in baseball throughout the two decades that followed World War II. Their front office was clearly astute, and their farm system was still among the best in baseball as late as the early 1960s — developing in-house players like Bobby Richardson and Elston Howard in the late 1950s, plus Tom Tresh, Jim Bouton, Mel Stottlemyre, Al Downing and Joe Pepitone slightly later. They didn't need Arnold Johnson's friendship to win pennants every year, but it didn't hurt them any either.

So Close

One of the most memorable seasons in San Francisco Giants history ended on October 16, 1962, when the Yankees blanked the Giants 1–0 in Game 7 of the World Series. Although New York right-hander Ralph Terry tossed a complete game shutout, San Francisco certainly had chances to win the championship in the team's final at bat.

With two outs and the speedy Matty Alou on first, Willie Mays lined a double to right. Yankees right fielder Roger Maris raced over, cut the ball off before it went to the wall, and fired a relay to second baseman Bobby Richardson, whose throw home convinced the Giants to hold Alou at third.[3]

Left-handed slugger Willie McCovey now headed toward the plate and Yankees manager Ralph Houk suddenly had some tough choices to make. Would Houk pitch around McCovey and go after the on-deck hitter, right-hander Orlando Cepeda, who would hit an anemic .158 in the series? Would Houk stick with his starting pitcher or bring in a reliever? Houk kept Terry in the game and elected to challenge McCovey.

Yankees fans held their breath as McCovey ripped a vicious liner toward right field, but the ball went directly into Bobby Richardson's glove. San Francisco had missed a championship by just a few feet and New York had survived to win yet another crown.

What if the Giants had sent Matty Alou to the plate on Mays' double in the ninth inning of Game 7? What if the Yankees had walked McCovey in the ninth and pitched instead to Cepeda?

MAURY ALLEN: In hindsight, the Giants might have sent Alou, a fast runner, from third to try to score on Mays' double to tie the score. It would have taken perfect throws by the Yankees to nail Alou at the plate, but Maris was an excellent outfielder, and he had made a fine play to cut the ball off. I think if Alou had been sent home that he would have been out at the plate. With McCovey and Cepeda due up next, I think the Giants thought they would take their chances and hold Alou at third base. No manager wants to lose the seventh game of the World Series by having your man thrown out at the plate to end the game.

Ralph Terry, the Yankees pitcher, had gone all the way and New York manager Ralph Houk had to decide which hitter he wanted to face. He could walk McCovey and let Terry face Orlando Cepeda, but Houk decided to let the right-handed Terry face the left-handed McCovey. The platoon situation wasn't as crucial in 1962 as it is viewed today. In those days, managers often stayed with the starting pitcher and Terry was pitching a great game up to that point. Terry also had a good curve ball and Houk thought

Terry could handle McCovey, who was a fast ball hitter. A base hit with men on second and third would have won the game for the Giants, but McCovey lined a pitch right at Bobby Richardson for the final out.

FORMER SAN FRANCISCO PITCHER BOBBY BOLIN: Matty Alou would have been dead at the plate if he had tried to try to score. Roger Maris made a great play getting to the ball, cutting it off, and then throwing to the cut off man, second baseman Bobby Richardson. There was no way Matty could have scored. You could second-guess the decision to hold him at third if the throw was way up the line, but the Yankees made the defensive plays to keep him at third base.

Some of the moves the Yankees made in the ninth inning surprised me. I was totally surprised they pitched to Willie McCovey. With Alou on third and Mays on second, I expected the Yankees to walk McCovey because his run didn't mean anything. I've heard all types of things as to why the Yankees didn't want to walk McCovey to pitch to Cepeda, including that they might throw balls in the dirt to try to get Cepeda out and one might get away for a wild pitch. The Yankees liked to throw a lot of curve balls in the dirt to Cepeda. It was a close call. When McCovey hit the ball, I jumped up in the air, thinking it was a hit. By the time my rear end hit the bench, we had lost the World Series. Richardson only had to move a few feet to catch McCovey's line drive.

I was also a little surprised that the Yankees left Ralph Terry, a right-hander, in the game to pitch to McCovey, a left-hander. Back then, managers didn't really think that much about going with a left-handed pitcher to face a left-handed batter. In those days, you stuck with your starting pitcher a lot longer.

THOM HENNINGER: There is a common thread in eyewitness accounts of the Willie Mays double in the ninth inning of Game 7. Most of the players, coaches and sportswriters at the game believed that Matty Alou would have been out at home in a two-out attempt to tie the deciding game of the 1962 World Series. Alou was held at third, as Roger Maris cut off Mays' double and fired a crisp throw to second baseman Bobby Richardson, who rifled an impressive relay home to protect New York's 1–0 lead over San Francisco.

The two throws to the plate were on the money, and that was required to keep Alou from scoring. Yet there wouldn't be any discussion about Alou's chances of coming home on Mays' double if Maris hadn't executed his on-the-run grab of the hard-hit ball, keeping it from rolling to the wall at Candlestick Park. The Yankees' right fielder, running toward the right-field line, quickly set himself for a shoulder-high throw to relay man Richardson. Without Maris' move to cut off the ball, Alou goes home, perhaps Mays is at third and Willie McCovey comes to the plate with the score knotted at 1–1.

While having a World Series conclude with a play at the plate makes for good drama, the Giants made the right move. Unless Alou was going to flatten Yankees catcher Elston Howard, the correct decision was letting clean-up man McCovey and possibly number five hitter Orlando Cepeda take their swings with Giants on second and third and two outs in the ninth.

After all, McCovey had homered off Yankees starter Ralph Terry in the Giants' 2–0 victory in Game 2. Two innings earlier, the Giants' slugger had tripled for one of the four hits Terry allowed in his Series-clinching 1–0 shutout. McCovey's success against the 26-year-old right-hander probably had many fans thinking that Terry's day was over. If the Yankees were going to walk the left-handed hitter McCovey to load the bases, they would have to face Cepeda, a dangerous threat from the right side.

New York manager Ralph Houk went to the mound with options. Veteran lefty Bud Daley and right-handed starter Bill Stafford were warming up in the Yankees' bullpen. Daley, a key cog in the pen all season long, worked a scoreless final frame in Terry's 2–0 loss in Game 2. Stafford had gone the distance in New York's 3–2 victory in Game 3. If Terry was departing, Daley might have gotten the call against the left-hander McCovey. The other match-up might have been Stafford against Cepeda after an intentional pass to McCovey. Cepeda had gone hitless in four trips against Stafford in Game 3.

While these alternative scenarios look promising on paper, it's possible McCovey would have hit a ball far less hard off Daley, which may have lazily dropped between the infield and outfield for the Series-clinching hit. It's hard to argue against the eventual winner of the Terry-McCovey showdown.

It surprised many at Candlestick Park when Houk returned to the dugout alone. In that era it was much more common to find a starting pitcher still working the ninth inning, and a manager often stuck with his starter even if he encountered trouble getting the last three outs. Seeing Terry stay in the game may be less surprising when you consider that the starter went the distance in all four New York wins in the 1962 World Series. Whitey Ford worked a 6–2 win in Game 1. Stafford claimed a 3–2 decision in Game 3, surviving an Ed Bailey two-run homer in the ninth without Houk going to the pen. Then Terry went the distance in a pivotal Game 5, securing a 5–3 victory that put the Yankees up three games to two.

Game 7 came down to the last out with Terry still on the mound. It had been the right-hander's best big league season. Only in 1962 did he win 20 games, going 23–12 with a solid 3.19 ERA in an American League-leading

298.2 innings. He also topped the AL in wins after breaking out with a 16–3 record in 1961. Over those two summers, Terry's control had improved markedly, and that was critical to his big 1962 campaign. Although he gave up a major league-high 40 home runs, he had allowed just 257 hits and only 57 walks in his 298.2 innings, generating a .268 opponent on-base percentage that ranked second in the league behind the .267 mark of Detroit's Hank Aguirre.

On this night, Terry had been perfect through six, and he had been at the top of his game. There are plenty of baseball observers, however, who say letting Terry face McCovey was one of the worst baseball decisions ever in such a key situation. It's an understandable position, in light of McCovey's homer off Terry in his Game 2 loss. Plus, the Giants' slugger had ripped a two-out triple against the right-hander in his last at-bat in the seventh inning.

To say the least, it was a bold decision to have Terry pitch to McCovey, and it was made by the pitcher himself. "I was tempted to put McCovey on in the ninth," a pale and drawn Houk told reporters soon after the final out, "but Terry said he'd prefer to pitch to him and that was all right with me." That says a lot about Houk's tendencies with his starters in games that are being decided on the final pitches of the day. As for Terry's decision-making, sometimes it's better to be lucky than good. He had been good all season, but he was lucky that second baseman Bobby Richardson barely had to move to snare McCovey's bullet to nail down the 1–0 victory.

Interestingly, Terry's logic was to keep a bag open and pitch to McCovey. "If I walk the bases loaded," Terry explained after the dust had settled on the biggest game of his career, "I've got to pitch too carefully to Cepeda. Now suppose I get behind him on the count. I take two chances then. I might walk the tying run home, or I might groove one too good and there would go the ball game."

It was a gutsy call to face McCovey. The ace of the 1962 Yankees came away with his second World Series victory over the final three contests, capping off his dream season with the performance of a lifetime.

The Dodger Meltdown

Although San Francisco had missed a world championship by the narrowest of margins, the Giants almost didn't make it to the 1962 World Series. To earn a date with the Yankees, San Francisco first had to overcome Los Angeles in a three-game NL playoff series.

The Dodgers seemed to have the NL pennant race well in hand, but went 1–6 down the stretch to give the Giants new life. Los Angeles' offense completely disappeared during the final weekend series against St. Louis; the Cardinals blanked the Dodgers twice and swept the three-game series, allowing San Francisco to forge a tie at 101–61. Just like in 1951, a three-game playoff would decide the NL title.

After San Francisco shut out Los Angeles in the first playoff game 8–0, the Dodgers rebounded to win a wild second game shootout 8–7. The entire season came down to the third playoff game on October 3, 1962, at Dodger Stadium. With the Dodgers ahead 4–2 in the top of the ninth inning, Los Angeles manager Walter Alston relied on his bullpen to close out the Giants, namely pitchers Ed Roebuck and Stan Williams. Alston's relievers crashed and burned, issuing four walks in the inning, as San Francisco rallied for a 6–4 victory.

What if Los Angeles manager Walter Alston had handled his bullpen differently in Game 3 of the 1962 NL playoff series?

THOM HENNINGER: The Los Angeles pitching staff was showing the wear of a long season, with starters working some short outings in late September, and a tired Dodgers bullpen losing three games and posting a 5.06 ERA during the club's final seven contests.

The Los Angeles pen mostly was a three-headed monster, featuring right-handed veterans Larry Sherry and Ed Roebuck alongside second-year southpaw Ron Perranoski. Both Roebuck and Perranoski worked more than 100 innings in relief, posting the best ERAs in the pen, but they were running out of gas. During the Dodgers' 1–6 skid into the playoffs, they took the three losses, and each of them allowed runs in three of their last four appearances, combining to cough up ten earned runs over 12 innings.

For the final playoff that would decide the National League champion, San Francisco manager Al Dark sent right-handed ace Juan Marichal to the hill on three days' rest, something the veteran did frequently in 1962, while Los Angeles skipper Walt Alston decided to go with left-hander Johnny Podres, who would be starting on two days' rest for the first time in his career. The 30-year-old veteran had gone just 15–13 with a so-so 3.81 ERA in a career-high 40 starts in 1962, but he had allowed only a single run in each of his three previous outings, claiming the Dodgers' final two victories of the 162-game schedule. Still, Alston may have been predisposed to keep Podres' 40th time out brief if he got into trouble. The entire season was on the line.

A quick hook for Podres meant a heavier workload for a Los Angeles bullpen that had been called on for significant innings in the first two playoff games. Sandy Koufax departed the Giants' 8–0 romp in the opener at Candlestick Park after allowing the first two batters to reach in the second frame, when San Francisco took a 3–0 lead. Five relievers followed Koufax to the mound. In the second game, Don Drysdale didn't finish the sixth, and the Dodgers fell behind 5–0 and went to the bullpen four times before pulling even in the series.

Right-hander Ed Roebuck came in and shut the door on the Giants for four scoreless, one-hit innings when he replaced Koufax in the first game, and he was the first man in when Drysdale was done. When Alston headed out to the mound to pull Podres in the sixth inning of the finale, the 31-year-old Roebuck entered his sixth game in seven days.

Podres was the victim of three Dodger errors in the third inning, when the Giants jumped out to a 2–0 lead. The score was 2–1 in the sixth, when the Giants greeted the southpaw with successive singles by Orlando Cepeda, Ed Bailey and Jim Davenport to load the bases with no one out. Podres had allowed nine hits and a walk without fanning anyone, and it wasn't hard to foresee the Dodgers' season slipping away if the left-hander couldn't turn it around against the next few batters.

Alston gave the ball to Roebuck, who induced a force out at home from Giants shortstop and number eight hitter Jose Pagan, then got Marichal to ground into an inning-ending double play. The move looked like the key to the game when Tommy Davis stroked a two-run homer in the bottom half of the sixth, and the Dodgers took a 4–2 lead into the final frame. If the Giants had taken a larger lead against Podres or another reliever, perhaps the Dodgers wouldn't be three outs from a World Series berth opposite the defending champion Yankees.

Remarkably, when Giants skipper Al Dark sent Matty Alou to the plate as a pinch hitter to open the ninth, Roebuck still was in the game. He had held the Giants scoreless for three innings on this day, and for a total of 7.2 frames in the three-game playoff. He had pretty much shut down San Francisco's hitters for three straight days.

Alou greeted Roebuck with a single to open the ninth, collecting just the fifth Giants hit off the veteran reliever during the playoff. After San Francisco leadoff man Harvey Kuenn hit a grounder that forced Alou at second base, Roebuck's control deserted him. He walked both pinch hitter Willie McCovey and Felipe Alou to load the bases with one out. Number four hitter Willie Mays stepped in and drilled a hard grounder that caromed off Roebuck, but stayed in the infield. A run came home to cut the Dodgers' lead to 4–3, and the bases remained loaded.

Alston pulled Roebuck at this point, perhaps too late, setting up the Dodgers' skipper to be second-guessed. Who he called on to replace Roebuck was a key decision as well, and it's likely that Alston wasn't especially confident in most of his options on the final day of the 1962 regular season.

Perranoski might have been running on empty, as the 26-year-old lefty had allowed runs in five of his last six outings, including a pair in the first two games against San Francisco. Sherry was touched for three hits and two runs in one-third of an inning in the opener against the Giants, and he had walked the bases loaded in the ninth inning of his previous appearance against St. Louis on September 29. Neither was on top of his game. The other options were rookie right-handers Phil Ortega, Jack Smith and Pete Richert, as well as veteran starter Stan Williams.

With Cepeda batting right-handed in the number five spot for the Giants, Alston called on Williams, the right-handed veteran who ranked third in the National League with 98 walks allowed in 1962. Cepeda lifted a fly ball to right field for the second out, which scored the tying run and allowed Felipe Alou to advance to third base. Mays stayed on first, but moved up to second when a Williams pitch to Bailey rolled a few feet from the plate. With runners on second and third with two out, Alston ordered a free pass for Bailey, once again loading the bases. The Giants went ahead 5–4 when Williams issued a walk to Davenport. Perhaps Williams should have pitched to Bailey.

With the Dodgers now behind, Perranoski entered looking for the last out. He induced the grounder the Dodgers were looking for, but Larry Burright, a defensive replacement at second, fumbled the ball behind the bag and Pagan reached, Mays scored and the Giants led 6–4. With a two-run cushion, the Giants turned to Billy Pierce, who had blanked the Dodgers on three hits in the opener. The 35-year-old lefty worked a 1–2–3 ninth inning to complete the Dodgers' slide.

With the always dangerous Cepeda stepping into the batter's box, should Alston have gone with Perranoski or Sherry, who were stalwarts of the bullpen all season long, over Williams? That's certainly the safe approach; it minimizes the second-guessing when a manager can say he went with what got him to this point. That approach can make decision-making very black and white as well, but with the struggles of the pitching staff over the previous week, Alston knew he didn't have an easy decision.

While Perranoski and Sherry had been giving up runs more frequently, Williams had turned in a pair of scoreless relief appearances during the last week of the season. He had worked the last 1.2 innings of the Dodgers' come-back win a day earlier, picking up the "W," so bringing in a starter with 12 games out of the pen during the season seems reasonable. The mistake may have been walking Bailey intentionally to load the bases with two outs. By calling on Williams, having a base open to put someone proved more important than having a play at any base with Davenport at the plate.

The Collapse of the Phillies

Phillies fans will remember 1964 for quite some time. St. Louis outlasted Philadelphia, Cincinnati, San Francisco and Milwaukee for the NL flag, in a race that the Phillies seemingly had locked up just weeks earlier.

Led by infielder Richie Allen and starting pitchers Jim Bunning and Chris Short, the Phillies owned a five and a half game lead with 11 games to play, but ten straight losses wrecked Philadelphia's title hopes.[4] St. Louis clinched the championship on the final day of the regular season with an 11–5 victory over the Mets.

Several factors led to Philadelphia's late season collapse, including an injury to veteran Frank Thomas. Acquired from the Mets in early August, Thomas briefly carried the Phillies with a hot bat, until he suffered a broken thumb in a game against the Dodgers. Phillies manager Gene Mauch also received criticism for overusing Bunning and Short.[5] Between them, the two pitchers started 70 games during the 1964 season, often on just two days' rest down the stretch.[6]

What if Philadelphia manager Gene Mauch had used his starting pitchers differently during the final month of the 1964 season?

FORMER PHILLIES OUTFIELDER FRANK THOMAS: My injury hurt the club. When I arrived in Philadelphia, they were a half-game in front in first place and I took them to a six and a half game lead within a month. I was red hot and was hitting the ball pretty good, hitting a lot of home runs in the late innings to win ballgames. I broke my thumb. I think if I hadn't suffered that injury, the Phillies would have won the pennant. When you're red hot as a home run hitter, you can carry a club for a week or two. My replacement, Vic Power, didn't pan out.

Gene Mauch, the Phillies manager, pitched Jim Bunning and Chris Short with three days, rest for much of the final few months. When he gave them an extra day of rest at the end of the season, they both won games in the final two games of the season. Mauch has been criticized for using Bunning and Short without giving them enough rest between starts. When I went back for the 25th anniversary, Mauch said the main reason the Phillies lost the pennant to St. Louis was my injury.

I think going to the Phillies was perhaps my best shot at getting to the World Series. I had the pennant handed to me when I went to Philadelphia and it was taken away with my injury. It's one of those unfortunate things that happen in the game of baseball. I felt bad about it because I never got a chance to play in a World Series. I think if Philadelphia had faced the New York Yankees in the 1964 World Series, we had the pitching to win. We had good hitting and we were a good defensive club.

ROB NEYER: Mauch was criticized for basically going with his two best starting pitchers down the stretch, Jim Bunning and Chris Short. He would give them one day of rest and use them constantly for the last week of the season. Mauch tried something radical and it didn't work. I never like to criticize managers for doing something different because if it had worked, Mauch would be viewed as a genius, and it almost did work. But it didn't work, and it's fair to suggest that if Mauch had tried to use a few of his other starting pitchers down the stretch, perhaps his third-best starter, the Phils probably would have tied for the NL pennant or won it outright.

FRAN ZIMNIUCH: I don't believe the Phillies choked. They just ran out of gas. It was almost a dream for Phillies fans for 150 games and then it went down the drain the last few weeks. One key was the expanded schedule of 162 games, as opposed to 154 games as it had been before the Mets and Colt .45s joined the National League in 1962. Had the league expanded without extending the schedule, the Phillies would have won the NL in 1964.

The Phillies had some key injuries and their manager, Gene Mauch, lost confidence in some of his starting pitchers. Jim Bunning and Chris Short won 19 and 17 games respectively. Mauch had a young right-hander by the name of Ray Culp who was in Mauch's doghouse that year. Culp won 14 games in 1963 and 14 games in 1965, but won only eight games in 1964. He was young, healthy and a good pitcher but he rather disappeared. Art Mahaffey won 12 games for the Phillies but disappeared down the stretch. Left-handed pitcher Dennis Bennett had his best season in the majors with 12 wins. He had some arm problems and Mauch ignored him. Another intriguing option Mauch had was 19-year-old Rick Wise, who won 188 games in his career. He won five games in 1964 but Mauch relied instead on Bunning and Short.

Mauch also made some questionable moves with respect to his bullpen. He had Jack Baldschun with 21 saves and a good screwball, and Ed Roebuck with 12 saves and a good sinkerball. You saw those two relievers coming into games earlier and earlier as the Phillies' September swoon continued, and Mauch was forced to use relievers like Bobby Shantz and Bobby Locke late in games.

The Phillies made a late season trade and picked up Frank Thomas. Thomas really energized the team but broke his thumb while diving back into second base on a pick off attempt. The Phillies picked up Vic Power, but he just wasn't the answer and barely hit over .200 for the remainder of the season. The combination of fatigue, possible misuse of the pitchers by Mauch, and the hole at first base doomed the Phillies.

Lou Brock

As Philadelphia stumbled and collapsed during the final few weeks of the 1964 regular season, St. Louis surged to the NL title bolstered by outfielder Lou Brock, a midseason acquisition from Chicago. The Cardinals sent veteran pitcher Ernie Broglio to the Cubs in a trade that seemed to favor Chicago. Broglio had won 60 games the previous four seasons; Brock had never hit higher than .263 or stolen more than 24 bases.

Brock and Broglio would see their careers head in drastically different directions. While Broglio would win just seven games for the Cubs, Brock would go on to steal 938 bases for his career, and would fuel St. Louis' drive to a world championship by hitting .348 in 103 games in 1964.[^]

What if the Cubs don't trade Lou Brock to the St. Louis Cardinals?

DAVID SHINER: The Cubs had a fair number of young prospects coming up in the early to mid 1960s. Leo Durocher, who would eventually come on board as the Cubs manager, was good at deciding which of the young kids could play, and I think he would have decided that Brock was one of them. With Billy Williams in left, Brock would have had to play centerfield. Playing in center would have stretched Brock's defensive skills. With Wrigley Field as Brock's home field, the Cubs were not likely to use Brock as a base stealer. The Cubs were not looking at Brock as a leadoff type of hitter, but more as a George Altman type of hitter, a second-rate slugger with good speed. Brock didn't draw a lot of walks, but he was capable of hitting .300, and he could turn singles into doubles with stolen bases. St. Louis tended to play small ball in the 1960s and 1970s, and that suited Brock perfectly. Stan Musial said getting Brock was the key to St. Louis winning the NL pennant in 1964, and I agree.

FORMER CARDINALS SHORTSTOP DICK GROAT: Lou had a fantastic year and really ignited the Cardinals to win the National League in 1964. He was just an outstanding player in every possible way. Brock was phenomenal when he came over to St. Louis, and I am not sure we could have won the National League pennant without him. He was a better player in St. Louis than he had ever been with the Cubs.

To me, the ironic part of the trade was that St. Louis general manager Bing Devine, who made the deal for Brock, was fired at mid-season. We went on to win the World Series and Devine was elected General Manager of the Year in Major League Baseball, although he was no longer with the team. Bing Devine was one of the finest people I have ever known in baseball, a first-class gentleman in every possible way.

Marichal's Bat

One of the more talented franchises during the '60s also happened to be the perennial bridesmaid of the National League. Led by Willie Mays, Willie McCovey and Juan Marichal, the snake-bit San Francisco Giants won only one NL title, despite piling up 823 regular season victories between 1961 and 1969.

Perhaps San Francisco's best shot at a second league pennant during the decade came in 1965. On August 22, with the Giants and the Dodgers vying

for the league lead, an incident involving San Francisco ace Juan Marichal and Los Angeles catcher John Roseboro weakened San Francisco's pennant hopes. Marichal took exception to one of Roseboro's return throws to pitcher Sandy Koufax, possibly thinking that Roseboro's toss had ventured too close to Marichal's head. The Giants pitcher responded by taking his bat and smashing Roseboro over the head, picking up a fine and a nine-day suspension for his troubles. Marichal went 3–4 in his final seven decisions of the season, after winning 19 of 28 before the Roseboro incident.[8]

The 1965 pennant race went right down to the final weekend, with the Dodgers taking three out of four from Milwaukee to

John Roseboro locked horns with San Francisco's Juan Marichal in the heat of the 1965 NL pennant race. (Courtesy Los Angeles Dodgers, Inc.)

nip the Giants by two games in the standings. It would be the first of five straight seasons that San Francisco would finish as league runner-up.[9]

What if San Francisco had Juan Marichal available throughout the 1965 NL pennant race?

BRUCE MARKUSEN: Marichal missed at least two starts during his suspension. He started 37 games in 1965, and that was a time when many staff aces would make 40–42 starts a season. So if Marichal had received those two or three extra starts, as opposed to your fifth best starter pitching, I'd say it's likely that the Giants would have won the NL pennant. At that point, we're talking about the Giants and Twins in the 1965 Series. As it was, the Dodgers edged the Twins in a seven game series, thanks mainly to the Dodgers' great pitching staff. Los Angeles' team ERA was 2.81 in 1965. The Giants had a pretty good pitching staff but not nearly as good as the Dodgers. The Giants had a team ERA of 3.20. Therefore, I think the Twins would have scored a few more runs off the Giants' pitchers. My feeling is the Twins, led by pitchers Jim Kaat and Mudcat Grant and with a pretty powerful lineup led by Tony Oliva and Harmon Killerbrew, might have been able to beat the Giants in the 1965 series.

THOM HENNINGER: Marichal was fined $1,750 and suspended for nine days. With the 19–9 right-hander working every fourth day, the time off shut him down for one start and delayed his subsequent outing by a day. San Francisco manager Herman Franks voiced his opinion that Marichal's suspension would kill the Giants' playoff chances, even though his Giants were just one game behind in the loss column when Marichal attacked Roseboro.

The Dodgers on the other hand were seething, believing that league president Warren Giles had gone too easy on Marichal. While they had taken two of the first three games in the series, their indignation certainly didn't spark a winning streak. A three-run homer by Willie Mays off Koufax, just minutes after the third-inning fracas at home plate, gave the Giants a 4–3 win in the series finale, and the Dodgers lost seven of ten games after Marichal's assault.

The Giants faced a doubleheader a few days after the incident, and with their ace out of action, they had to call on swingmen Ron Herbel and Bob Bolin to make starts. This put a significant strain on the bullpen, which was nothing more than the trio of Frank Linzy, Mashi Murakami and Bill Henry with Marichal sitting out. Facing the Pittsburgh Pirates, Bolin worked a 3–3 tie that was rained out in the tenth inning, Herbel absorbed an 8–0 beating, and the Giants went just 4–5 during Marichal's suspension.

Marichal returned for a Labor Day doubleheader on September 2, with his club trailing the Dodgers by the same three and a half game margin as when he was ejected on August 22. In his second go-round for his 20th victory, he lost a 4–3 decision to Chris Short and the Phillies. Two days later, however, the Giants ignited a 14-game winning streak with a 7–3 win behind Herbel. Marichal won three straight starts during the streak, allowing just three earned runs in three complete games. After the Giants' 14th consecutive victory on September 16, they were 87–69 with a four and a half game edge over the Dodgers.

On the same day San Francisco claimed the final win of its red-hot run, with just 16 days left in the season, the Dodgers kicked off a 13-game winning streak of their own. They had gone 10–12 immediately following the attack on Roseboro, but closed the season with a 15–1 flourish. In those final 16 games, the Los Angeles pitching staff stepped up and tossed eight shutouts.

Meanwhile, on September 17, Marichal and the Giants were soundly beaten 9–1 by Milwaukee and a future Hall of Famer, 26-year-old Phil Niekro, making his first major league start. The loss marked the end of San Francisco's 13-game tear, and the beginning of an 8–8 finish that left the Giants two games behind the Dodgers when the season came to a close.

After Marichal's suspension, that understaffed Giants bullpen took just one loss through the end of the season, and the club's fate was determined in the final two weeks of the season, not on August 22. While Marichal lost three straight starts during that mediocre 8–8 wrap-up, and was roughed up twice in the final two weeks of the season, that may have had more to do with approaching 300 innings for the season than anything else.

Perhaps having Marichal's first start after the suspension delayed a day from his normal turn could have been a factor. If the suspension had been for one fewer day and Marichal had moved up a game through the end of the season, he would have been available to make another start on the final day of the campaign. As the season played out, the Dodgers clinched the NL flag on the final Saturday, rendering Sunday's season finale meaningless.

With the Dodgers closing with a 15–1 surge, it's easier to attribute the final outcome of the 1965 race to the stellar performance of the Los Angeles pitchers than Marichal's attack or any failures of the San Francisco staff. The Dodgers allowed just 17 runs over their final 16 contests. The string of eight shutouts during that span began on September 16. Claude Osteen turned in eight scoreless innings against the Cubs at Wrigley Field that afternoon, and Koufax worked a 1–2–3 ninth to save a 2–0 win, exactly one week after throwing a perfect game against Chicago at Dodger Stadium.

Koufax threw three shutouts of his own in the final two weeks. A pair by the lefty combined with two by Don Drysdale produced four shutouts in six days to close out September.

On Saturday, October 2, on just two days' rest, Koufax four-hit the Milwaukee Braves for a 3–1 pennant clinching win. He fanned 13 for a second straight start to close out the year, thereby setting a modern-day record for strikeouts in a season with 382 and dashing the 1965 pennant hopes of the San Francisco Giants.

An Old 30

"An old 30" is a phrase that Cincinnati fans would like to forget. After the completion of the 1965 season, Reds General Manager Bill DeWitt somehow concluded that power-hitting outfielder Frank Robinson was on the downward spiral of his career. Cincinnati traded Robinson to Baltimore for outfielder Dick Simpson and pitchers Milt Pappas and Jack Baldschun.[10]

It wasn't like Robinson had given any indication that he was over the hill. Robinson had hit 33 homers in 1965, to go with a .296 batting average; in ten seasons with the Reds, the veteran outfielder had launched 324 home runs and had surpassed the .300 mark five times.

In perhaps the worst deal Cincinnati has ever made, the Reds shipped a future Hall of Famer to Baltimore; the Reds, a pennant contender in 1964 and 1965, floundered badly in 1966, finishing 18 games behind the Dodgers. Meanwhile, Baltimore soared to its first World Series title in 1966, led by Robinson's 49 homers and .316 batting average. Robinson would go on to lead the Birds to three additional AL pennants through 1971 and a World Series victory over the chagrined Reds in 1970.

What if the Reds had not traded Frank Robinson to Baltimore?

FORMER BALTIMORE THIRD BASEMAN BROOKS ROBINSON: It would be hard to envision the Orioles winning all of those championships in the late '60s without Frank Robinson. We had a good club before Frank arrived, but we never could get over the hump. We had chances to win the American League in 1960 and again in 1964. The trade for Frank Robinson, which was the most significant trade in Orioles' history, made the difference. To me, when you talk about some of the greatest players in baseball at that time, you have to talk about Frank Robinson. People like to mention Mantle, Mays and Aaron, but you have to include Frank Robinson in that group. It seems like Frank is always a notch below those guys. He was a tough guy who had a great instinct for the game.

If we had not picked up Frank in that trade with Cincinnati, it is hard to say whether we would have been able to win the World Series in 1966.

Frank Robinson proved to the Reds that he still had a few good years left. (Courtesy the Cincinnati Reds.)

We had a good club before Frank got here, and we had good young players, like Paul Blair and Davey Johnson. We also had a very good pitching staff. With pitchers like Jim Palmer, Wally Bunker, Dave McNally and then Mike Cuellar in 1969, we could afford to trade Milt Pappas. We needed Frank's hitting and his leadership.

GABRIEL SCHECHTER: This trade hurt the Reds more than it helped the Orioles. That is, the Orioles still would have been strong contenders in the AL because of their strong pitching staff. They still had Brooks Robinson and Boog Powell, strong defense, and a solid lineup without Frank Robinson, so I think they would have won two pennants from 1966–1971 instead of four. The Reds, of course, still would have had pitching woes in the late 1960s, but by keeping Robinson, they would have been able to trade some-one else to shore up the pitching. With Robinson in the outfield, Pete Rose could have stayed at second base, making Tommy Helms expendable. Or if Rose stayed in the outfield, they could have done better in dealing Alex Johnson or one of their other outfielders. Even without Robinson, they led the NL in runs scored in 1968–69, and with him their lineup would have been fearsome, launching the Big Red Machine a few years earlier. Picture Robinson, Pinson, and Rose in the outfield, Bench catching, Perez and May on the corners, and it's more of a 1990s lineup than one from the 1960s. I think the Reds definitely would have won one or two pennants in the late '60s with Frank Robinson.

REDS BROADCASTER MARTY BRENNAMAN: We have no way of knowing how productive Frank Robinson might have been for Cincinnati in the early 1970s. He could have made a major difference for the Reds in the late '60s and in 1970 when Sparky Anderson took over as manager. It's hard to say whether having Frank Robinson would have resulted in a World Series title for the Reds in '70. Anyone who says Frank would not have made a difference is crazy. He was an impact player. The trade that sent him to Baltimore was the worst trade the Reds have ever made. Robinson went to the Orioles and became the Most Valuable Player of the American League.

The Reds management argued that Frank Robinson was too old and that he was heading into his lesser years, which obviously was not the case. Although the trade occurred before I arrived in Cincinnati, I can say that Frank Robinson certainly would have strengthened the Reds in the years following the trade.

Resurrecting Sandy

For a five-year period in the '60s, Sandy Koufax was the top pitcher in baseball and arguably the best southpaw since Lefty Grove. Between 1962 and 1966, Koufax won 111 games, picked up three Cy Young Awards, and grabbed five straight ERA titles. It all ended in November of 1966 when the 30-year-old Koufax, plagued by an arthritic-pitching elbow, decided to retire rather than risk a serious long-term injury.[11]

Dodgers team physician Dr. Robert Kerlan had diagnosed Koufax's condition, which arthroscopic surgery could have addressed, had it been available in 1966. In fact, less than a decade after Koufax's retirement, Kerlan's partner and successor, Dr. Frank Jobe, performed the first elbow reconstruction on Tommy John, adding 12 years to John's career.[12]

What might have happened if Kerlan had been able to carry out such a procedure on Sandy Koufax? In the following fictional account, Jeff Katz magically extends Koufax's career into the 1970s, much to the regret of National League hitters.

What if modern day medicine had been available to Sandy Koufax in 1966?

JEFF KATZ: How improbable it all seemed now, the last season ending like the first. Back in '55 he was too fresh, too unproven and too untested to pitch in the Series at all. Well, that was as far as Alston was concerned. Now

What if Sandy Koufax could have taken advantage of modern medical techniques? (Courtesy Los Angeles Dodgers, Inc.)

his old foil and present manager, Tommy Lasorda, gave him this gift. In his final year, at 41 years old, Sandy Koufax was pitching the bottom of the ninth inning of Game Seven of the 1977 World Series, at Yankee Stadium against his old foes.

Could this have ever been foreseen? Back in 1966, when Robert Kerlan, Koufax's trusted doctor and silent partner in his battle against an ever-worsening arthritic left arm, suggested surgery so "far out" (as they said) as to sound like science fiction, Sandy felt his career was over.

He had gone all out in 1966 on the assumption that this was it. He pitched 323 innings, completing 27 games, equaling his personal best of the year before. Everything hurt. The medications were killing him. Butazolidin was eating his insides, and the Empirin with codeine made him spacey. The Capsolin was burning his flesh, but nothing hurt as much as the pitching itself.

But Kerlan had had an idea. If Sandy's arm could be rebuilt with other parts from his own body, perhaps he could pitch again. The doctor thought that he could replace what seemed to be a stretched ligament in Koufax's left arm with, maybe, a tendon from his forearm. Sandy wanted to know only one thing: could he come back and be himself? He was not going to embarrass himself and get knocked around. He had watched his good friends and teammates fade fast and it was tough. Carl Erskine had ERAs of over five and over seven in his last years. Joe Black, his guardian in that tough first spring of his rookie year, burnt out so fast it was hard to remember how great he was in his magical rookie season, winning 15 games in 1952. It was not going to happen to Sandy. He wouldn't allow it, and he was not going to let people bear witness to his failure.

Kerlan was outwardly confident that it could work, that it would work, and Sandy trusted him. When he was wheeled in for surgery on November 18, 1966, he knew it was a risk worth taking. Kerlan was at his bedside when he awoke and, although he assured Sandy it was a successful operation, it seemed hard to gauge what would be considered successful for something that had never been done before.

It wasn't until four months later that Sandy picked up a ball in his huge hand. It wasn't at Dodgertown. Florida would not see him that spring. In fact, he was in Hawaii, having already rented a house on Oahu for April, originally to be far from baseball when spring training arrived. He knew the pain of being away from the game he loved would hurt him as much as his arm had done, he hoped, only in the past.

The ball felt wonderful in his hand and, although his arm was stiff from inactivity, it didn't seem to hurt that badly. All of that 1967 season, as he watched his friends reel from his absence and finish 28.5 games out of first place, almost exactly equal to his 27 wins of the year before, he worked harder than ever. He gradually threw harder, although not from a mound, and longer distances. He lifted weights, violating a baseball taboo. His program worked to strengthen his rebuilt arm, but, again, the front office was none too pleased when they heard about it, fearing he would get too bulky and limit his mobility.

While passing a local high school, he hailed the team's catcher and suggested that the boy could help him out, meeting him every day for an hour on a diamond far from the school grounds. The boy was sworn to secrecy. He couldn't believe that he was going to catch a Sandy Koufax fastball and couldn't tell a soul.

Getting back on the mound was scarier than any game he had ever pitched in, scarier than his first World Series appearance before 48,000 crazed White Sox fans in 1959. It felt funny, physically, being back on the hill. It had been the longest time he had ever gone without pitching. The mound was fine, although not Dodger Stadium high. He felt ready, and with his perfect mechanics intact, let it rip. Sandy knew what his catcher did not. It was not a Sandy Koufax fastball, but it was close. Maybe it was in the mid–80s but that was not enough to get back. He needed to see better results.

All winter he worked in the gym. More weight training, more running, and more pitching. Alston called asking if he'd be back for 1968 and Sandy said he didn't think so, not just yet. He wasn't about to put his reputation on the line for Alston, who never understood him, or Bavasi and O'Malley, who used him just as they used all the other players. He would do it all for his teammates who needed him. However, it was obvious that they needed him at his best. The Koufax of 1966 would be what they deserved, he thought, not a shadow of that towering figure.

The "Year of the Pitcher" is what they called 1968. Gibson's record-setting ERA and McLain's 30 wins were just the highlights of a year that saw all pitchers, great and not so great, record unparalleled feats. Yet the best pitcher of them all fought on to regain his skill. It came back hard fought. The fastball got faster and started to explode, going up just as it used to. The curveball was later in returning and it was inconsistently regaining its straight North Pole to South Pole drop. He worked harder than ever, feeling so very close to getting it all back. He was only 32 years old that summer and his arm was only two. And when every fastball started to pop and every curve started to fall that winter, he knew he was ready to return.

When a simple statement was released saying, "Sandy Koufax will be starting the Dodgers first home game of the 1969 season against the San Diego Padres on Tuesday night, April 15," the baseball world was in disbelief. Stories had leaked out about a revolutionary surgery and the possibility of return, but they seemed far-fetched. Sandy had been out of sight for over two full years and with that came a certain mythologizing. Yet, it was true and it was the most anxiously awaited sports event in anyone's memory.

Koufax was nervous but ready. When he strolled to the Dodger bullpen, he was floored by the noise. He had never heard it so loud in Chavez Ravine. The Dodger crowd, known for arriving late and leaving early, was not going to miss this. The stands were filled by 5:30, and the atmosphere was electric. Electric was an understatement. It was like the discovery of electricity. It had never been seen, a player as perfect as Koufax was, disappearing from the scene for two years and then reappearing. It sounded like a magic trick, and it was.

As he neared the mound, Sandy realized how different it felt. First was the tone of the crowd. Second, as he climbed to the mound, he felt how much it had changed. After the pitching dominance of 1968, the Major Leagues had lowered the mound and, while it was still higher at Dodger Stadium, it was much lower than the last time Sandy had been on it. And the San Diego Padres? They hadn't even existed in 1966.

The time to throw the first pitch had arrived, and when home plate umpire Ed Vargo shouted, "Play Ball," all the waiting, all the anxiety and all the change melted away. He didn't even know who these Padres were, and he didn't care. When Jose Arcia led off, Sandy took a deep, deep breath. Then, with his left foot slightly angled on the rubber, he started his windup and let fly a rising fastball. Arcia had never seen anything like it. Jeff Torborg, who caught Sandy's perfect game, was incredulous. "He hasn't lost anything," he thought, and told Vargo, "This is gonna be fun."

It was great fun and Sandy felt in total control. When his ex-teammate and fellow Brooklyn boy Al Ferrara came up third and promptly struck out on three straight fastballs, he turned and said, "Jeff, I was awfully glad he retired before I had to face him. Why's he coming back now?" Fastballs and curves, just like he had never left, and the Dodger offense, exhilarated by his return, scored 14 runs. His first game in two years, and he had pitched a shutout! It couldn't be this easy, Sandy reflected quietly, as the pandemonium of the crowd and his teammates surrounded him. When Vin Scully, who had watched him since day one and had seen up close the suffering of 1965 and 1966, interviewed him after the game, he was touched to see his friend shed a tear. He almost shed a tear of his own when Sandy said, without bravura, that his arm felt better than it ever had. Koufax had no pain and when he instinctively went back to the clubhouse to soak his arm in the whirlpool filled with ice, he came to a surprising realization that he didn't need to. His arm felt fine.

The rest of 1969 was a success for Sandy Koufax and a disappointment for the Dodgers. While not as dominating as when he left in 1966, Koufax won 19 games and had an ERA of 2.29, just behind Jerry Koosman of the upstart Mets for sixth best in the National League. He also struck out 251 hitters, good enough for third in the league and tops on the team. The Dodgers did win 90 games that year, 14 more than the year before and finished tied for second (with the Giants, of course!) in the inaugural season of the NL West. The nicest part of it all was just being back, laughing in the clubhouse with his friends and enjoying the game without the agony.

Everyone expected great things for Los Angeles in 1970, their ace being, as in the old days, Sandy Koufax. Sandy felt a bit more alone that year as Don Drysdale was forced to retire after it was discovered that his rotator cuff was torn. There would be no miracles for Don as there had been for Sandy. Just as the Dodgers felt less than whole when they had Don and no Sandy, so they were incomplete with Sandy and no Don. These two proved that the twain could indeed meet, and while they were as different as the coasts they were born on, they were close friends and missed each other on the club.

Sandy was one of the top pitchers that year, finishing with 22 wins, 275 Ks and an ERA of 2.99. He finished second to Bob Gibson for the Cy Young Award, although his numbers were better in every category. He was not the most dominant pitcher in a league that had old stars like Gibson and newer ones like Tom Seaver and Fergie Jenkins. However, he was content to be back close to the top and to be seen as one of the best again, proving that 1969 was no fluke. The Dodgers again finished second in 1970, winning 92 games. It was a slight improvement, but they couldn't compete with the new Big Red Machine of Cincinnati.

That was the way it would continue for the next three years: Sandy achieved personal success while the team was just shy of a division title. He won 20 games in 1971 and in 1972 he won 25 games, his most since 1966, but lost the Cy Young Award to a younger lefty, Steve Carlton, who won 27. He slumped to winning only 17 in 1973, but in 1974, at 38 years old, he won 20 games as the Dodgers went to the World Series for the first time in eight years. While they lost in five games to the explosive Oakland A's, Sandy won the only game he started.

Entering the 1975 season, Sandy needed only 12 wins for 300. He was no longer the number one starter. Despite his numbers the year before, he and the team felt he should cut back on his workload. He was now 39 and realistically, he could only pitch a few more years. He felt fine physically but even Warren Spahn stopped being dominant at 42. Sandy was fine with it. Baseball was still fun for him and having had two years taken from him already, he was not ready to leave. A lesser role was no big deal and he still won 15 games, including number 300.

The next year was more of the same. Being a third starter was fine; it afforded him the rest that his now 40-year-old body needed. He won 15 games again, and the Dodgers finished behind the Reds. After the season, Walter Alston resigned after 23 years on the bench. He was the only manager Sandy had ever known and while they were never close, it was a relationship of long standing and Koufax was a little sorry to see him go.

Sandy announced early in 1977 that this would be his last year. He had nine more years than he had dreamed of during those last days of 1966 and was glad to be going on his own terms. Lasorda took the opportunity to thank Sandy and hoped he wouldn't mind being a spot starter and long reliever. The slight was accepted graciously because Sandy knew he would have fun in his last go-round, regardless of the new skipper.

The 1977 season saw the Dodgers win 98 games to finish first in the West. Koufax appeared in 40 games, starting 20, winning 12. In the National League Championship Series, they beat the Phillies in four games. Sandy pitched the last three innings of Game Three and got the win. Then, it was on to the World Series against the Yankees.

This was the first meeting between these two archenemies since the Koufax-dominated 1963 Series. It was a much different experience for the now graying veteran. Instead of being the ace, he was now sometimes the fourth starter. As such, he did get a start in Game Four, a 4–2 loss in Los Angeles. It was bittersweet, being at the scene of so many glorious moments and not being able to guarantee the team a victory, although he pitched very well.

It was a great series. Reggie Jackson had already hit five home runs through six games, hitting three in Game Six to tie the series. This set the stage for what looked to be a tension-filled Game Seven at Yankee Stadium, the first one held at the big ballpark since the Yanks defeated the then Milwaukee Braves in 1957.

Tension-filled it wasn't. The Dodgers jumped out to a big lead early on, with two home runs in the first — a two-run shot by Reggie Smith and then another two-run dinger by Dusty Baker off of starter Ron Guidry. Tommy John, the present ace of the staff and 20 game winner, started for the second time in the series. Unlike his first start, a 5–3 loss at Chavez Ravine, John was in complete control. The Yankees hit ground ball after ground ball, the Dodger infield making all the plays on this cool, 51-degree New York night.

By the eighth inning, the Dodgers were leading 7–0, and it was clearly over. From the bullpen, Sandy watched New York's finest, billy clubs swinging at their sides, surround the perimeter of the field. Then the bullpen telephone rang, and Koufax heard Coach Monty Basgall say, "Sandy, Tommy wants you in the ninth." Koufax got up slowly, surprised and appreciative that Lasorda was letting him go out on top, as the man on the mound for the final out.

He felt good, really good, warming up. The fast ball was still hard and rising, maybe mid–90s, he thought. While the curve didn't drop as perpendicularly as before, it was still a very good major league curve.

The Stadium crowd stood on their feet as he walked to the mound.

Over 56,000 people, his people, New Yorkers, screamed at the top of their lungs for a man who had beaten them so soundly, so long ago. While he was no longer that pitcher, the noise in the stands gave him that old feeling. He was not going to get hit, not now. When Lasorda handed him the ball and joked, "Okay, let's see why they kept you and cut me," Sandy smiled.

Graig Nettles, in his anxiousness to get something started, hit the first pitch to Bill Russell at short. An easy grounder for out number one. Left fielder Lou Piniella was up next, always a cagey hitter. Sandy threw two fastballs, good ones that Piniella could only foul back. When Sandy caught him with a curveball on the third pitch, Piniella was fooled badly. He had thought that Bert Blyleven had the best curve he had ever seen, but this pitch was like a waterfall, straight down for a called strike three.

The potential last hitter, shortstop Bucky Dent, walked deliberately to the plate. After two quick fastballs, at which Dent flailed helplessly, Sandy paused and looked around. He soaked it all in, thinking of where he had been. He started with such failed promise, with no one in the Dodger organization on his side and willing to give him a chance. Then he had what many considered the greatest five-year stretch of any pitcher in the history of the game. Thinking now that it all could have ended so abruptly in 1967 made him shudder. For two long years after Dr. Kerlan's miracle surgery, Sandy had worked so hard to get back to where he had been and, while he never was the same as that five-year wonder, he had been one of the best pitchers for almost another decade. He felt a surge of pride at all he had done and a joy that he had the opportunity to do it.

He got set and started his motion. As he rocked back on his left leg, he reached back, back through space and back through time, and with cap flying off, unleashed a 100 mile per hour fastball, which exploded into the strike zone. It was over now, exactly as it should have been.

Tony C

One of the rising stars in baseball in 1967 was Boston outfielder Tony Conigliaro, who had blasted 84 homers in his first three seasons. At the age of 22, Conigliaro's future looked bright. Unfortunately, Tony C had also developed a penchant for injuries from pitched balls, missing five weeks in 1964, and nearly four weeks in 1965.[13]

Conigliaro's darkest day came on August 18, 1967, when California pitcher Jack Hamilton beaned Tony C on the left cheekbone nearly killing the Red Sox slugger, who would never again have proper vision out of his damaged left eye.[14] Conigliaro returned to action in 1969, and although he hit 56 home runs over the next two seasons, his vision grew steadily worse.

Traded to California, Conigliaro hit just .222 in 74 games for the Angels in 1971 and retired in July. A comeback attempt with Boston failed in 1975.

The dark clouds followed Conigliaro even after his retirement: he suffered a massive heart attack in 1982 and died of kidney failure in 1990 at the age of 45.[15] Hall of Fame pitcher Jim Palmer was quoted as saying that with Conigliaro's swing and with his home games coming at Boston's Fenway Park, Tony C could have wound up owning several home run records.[16]

What if Tony Conigliaro had avoided his near fatal beaning in 1967?

BILL MCNEIL: Tony Conigliaro's ill-fated career is one of the most tragic stories in major league baseball history, second only to the beaning death of Ray Chapman. The 6' 3", 185-pound right-handed slugger tore up the Class A New York–Penn League as an 18 year old in 1963, hammering a league-leading 42 doubles and 24 homers in just 83 games, while stinging the ball at a .363 clip. The next year he was a member of the Boston Red Sox, where he batted .290 with 24 homers before breaking his arm in August. In 1965, he led the American League in home runs with 32 and followed that with a 28-home-run year in 1966.

He had hit 20 homers in 95 games in 1967 when tragedy struck. On August 18, 1967, a Jack Hamilton fastball crashed into his face, shattering his cheekbone and damaging his eyesight. He never fully recovered from that accident.

Looking back at Conigliaro's potential, it is a good guess that if he had stayed healthy, he might have challenged Ruth and Aaron for the career home run record. At the age of 22 years and seven months, he had already hit 104 home runs. By comparison, Ken Griffey, Jr. had hit 66 homers by the same age, Hank Aaron had hit 66, Barry Bonds had hit 16, and Babe Ruth, who was a pitcher at the time, had put just nine balls over the fence.

BILL DEANE: Conigliaro apparently liked to crowd the plate and had a lot of injuries from being hit by pitched balls, including a broken arm in his rookie season of 1964 and another injury in 1965. He missed about a month of action both times due to being hit by a pitch, so it seemed as if he was an accident waiting to happen. He was well on his way to a Hall of Fame type career, but his injury history was such that you couldn't be sure he could keep that up. I don't know that we can say with any kind of confidence that he was heading for the Hall of Fame because of his injury history.

ALAN SCHWARZ: There was actually some talk initially about Conigliaro being a guy who could threaten Babe Ruth's home run record. Had Jack

Would Tony Conigliaro have wound up in the 500 home run club if he had remained healthy? (Courtesy Boston Red Sox.)

Hamilton not hit Conigliaro in 1967, Conigliaro would have been in a position to take advantage of the jump in offense in the majors in 1969, becoming perhaps a high–30s, low–40s homer guy year after year. He also might have benefited from the American League's designated hitter rule as he grew older in the late 1970s. It's possible that Conigliaro could have played as many years as Carl Yazstremski did. Outside of his batting average, it's certainly fair to think that Tony Conigliaro might have had career stats comparable to Yaz, with probably more power, maybe 500 homers. Everyone who saw Conigliaro play in his early years thought he was a 500 home run hitter waiting to happen.

The '68 Series

St. Louis looked unbeatable in 1968. With a pitching staff anchored by ace right-hander Bob Gibson, and a team ERA of 2.49, the Cardinals had every reason to be confident heading into their World Series clash with the Tigers. Detroit manager Mayo Smith knew he had to find a way to get more offensive production; that meant getting outfielders Al Kaline and Jim Northrup into the lineup whenever possible.

Shortstop was unquestionably the weak link of Detroit's offense: Ray Oyler, Tommy Matchick and Dick Tracewski combined to hit just .165 in 654 at-bats during the regular season.[17] Smith's radical solution was to shift Gold Glove center fielder Mickey Stanley to short. The gamble succeeded. Stanley committed just two errors in seven games, and Kaline and Northrup combined to drive in 16 runs.[18]

Despite Smith's unorthodox maneuver, St. Louis won three of the first four games, and appeared to be primed to take the series when the Cardinals jumped out to a 3–0 lead in Game Five. A defensive play by Detroit left fielder Willie Horton turned the game around. With the speedy Lou Brock on second, Orlando Cepeda singled to left. Horton fielded the ball cleanly and fired a strike to catcher Bill Freehan, who tagged out an upright Brock, who had tried to score standing up rather than sliding. Detroit rallied to win 5–3.

Detroit pasted St. Louis 13–1 in Game Six, setting the stage for the decisive seventh game in St. Louis, pitting Detroit's unheralded southpaw Mickey Lolich against the indomitable Gibson. Both pitchers tossed shutout ball for six innings before Detroit finally pushed across three runs in the seventh, thanks to Jim Northrup's two-run triple over the head of center fielder Curt Flood, who misjudged the ball and then slipped. Lolich had all the support he needed; Detroit's 4–1 victory gave Tigers fans their first World Series title since 1945.

What if Tigers manager Mayo Smith had not shifted Mickey Stanley to shortstop for the 1968 World Series?

BILL DEANE: It's another one of those World Series events that I think is way overrated. I've often wondered if that move made the Tigers such a better team, why didn't they make the move all season? As for the 1968 World

Series, Detroit might simply have benched Stanley with the same results. He batted an Oyler-like .214 and fielded just .939.

DAVID SHINER: Mayo Smith's decision to play Mickey Stanley at shortstop was the key. Smith wasn't a great manager or a great innovator, but his decision to move Stanley to shortstop was a stroke of genius. The big question heading into the series was how the Tigers were going to get the bats of Kaline, Horton, Stanley and Northrup in the lineup for each Series game. All of the outfielders were healthy and there was no DH rule at the time. Smith's decision to position Stanley at shortstop was a great move in hindsight. It takes a lot of guts to make that kind of move and risk being second-guessed by the fans and the media in the postseason. Smith wouldn't have been second-guessed for playing Oyler or Matchick at shortstop because Smith could have said that's what was done all season long. If Stanley had committed five errors in the series, Smith turns out to be a goat. He didn't.

BRUCE MARKUSEN: Moving Stanley to shortstop was important, not for his offense but for his defense. He only hit .214 in the seven game series. The Tigers regular shortstop during the season, Ray Oyler, hit about .170. The big difference was in the Tigers outfield. If Detroit's manager, Mayo Smith, had kept Stanley in center field, the Tigers probably would have platooned Jim Northrup, a lefty, and Al Kaline, a right-hander, in right field. By moving Stanley to shortstop, Kaline and Northrup could play every game for Detroit. As it turned out, Kaline was one of the offensive heroes for Detroit in the seven game series. Kaline hit .379 with two homers and eight runs batted in. Northrup contributed offensively as well with eight runs batted in. Smith's decision to take a chance and play his regular center fielder at shortstop, allowing Kaline and Northrup to play full time in the outfield, was a daring move. You probably wouldn't see too many managers these days making that kind of a move. There's so much media second-guessing and criticism these days. Without that move and the added offense, I think St. Louis wins the series. It was a close series with several low scoring games and the Tigers really needed the extra offense to win.

GARY GILLETTE: The move by Mayo Smith was brilliant. It was not the kind of move you would expect from him. Smith was certainly not a great tactician, but his bold and unexpected idea worked for the Tigers. I think the Tigers could have still have won the series with Stanley in the outfield and Ray Oyler at shortstop. Oyler only hit .135 during the season. The Tigers usually let Oyler get two at bats, then they would pinch hit for him if they were behind and would move Dick Tracewski or Tommy Matchick into the shortstop position. Tracewski was a good defensive player, but not much of a hitter, while Matchick was a better hitter with a little power. If the Tigers had played Stanley in center field, they could have used Matchick or Tracewski as backups at short and they still could have won the series.

FORMER DETROIT OUTFIELDER JIM NORTHRUP: The move of Stanley to shortstop was the logical move. Mickey Stanley would not have been in the outfield. The Cardinals had an all right-handed pitching staff so I was going to play in center, Willie Horton would play in left and Al Kaline would be in right. That would have left Mickey on the bench. There was no reason Stanley couldn't go to shortstop. He was a gifted athlete and we all had faith in him. Mickey played very well at shortstop in the series. A lot of managers wouldn't have had the guts to make that move but it made sense to all of the players on the team. We weren't worried for one second about Mickey's ability to do the job at shortstop.

What if Lou Brock had slid into home plate in Game Five, rather than trying to score standing up?

BILL DEANE: I think sliding into home plate is overrated. There are two purposes for sliding; one is to stop quickly, at second or third base, when you don't want to overrun the bag. The other is to create a smaller target for the fielder attempting to tag you. Sliding slows you down if anything, and in this instance, Freehan tagged Brock near the knees. If Brock were sliding, Freehan still would have had enough of a target to tag Brock. I don't really think that was a key play. It looks bad when you go in standing up, but I really don't think sliding into home increases your chances of scoring in most cases.

BRUCE MARKUSEN: If St. Louis wins Game Five, they win the Series. To this day, Brock says he would have been out at the plate, whether he slid or went in standing up. I do think he would have had a better chance at being safe if he had slid, simply because Bill Freehan caught the ball chest high. If Brock had slid, Freehan would have had to sweep down with the tag to get Brock. With Brock coming in standing up, Freehan didn't have to sweep down to make a tag, and that gave him plenty of time to tag Brock. It really was a huge play. It not only cut off a run but also potentially stopped a big inning for the Cardinals. The Cards had the momentum up until that point, in the Series and in Game Five. The Series really turned around on that one particular play. If Brock isn't thrown out, I think the Cards win the game and the Series is over in just five games.

FORMER DETROIT OUTFIELDER JIM NORTHRUP: Game Five was the turning point. Lou Brock was very fast but he had no idea that Willie Horton was going to throw that ball to home plate. Brock figured that with his speed he might make it home without a play so he chose not to slide. If he slides, I'm sure Brock would have been safe. If he's safe, it would have changed the whole complexion of the game and we would have been in trouble. You never know in the game of baseball how things will turn out. It was a critical mistake by Brock but that happens. We made the right plays. Willie Horton made a great throw and Bill Freehan made a great decoy and tag.

What if Curt Flood had caught up to Jim Northrup's long fly ball in Game Seven?

BILL DEANE: Flood broke in a few steps initially, but I'm not sure he would have caught the ball, even if he hadn't broken in on the ball first. Bob Gibson certainly didn't blame Curt Flood. St. Louis wasn't scoring runs off Mickey Lolich either. St. Louis didn't score until after there were two outs in the bottom of the ninth inning when Mike Shannon hit a home run. You can't win if you don't score any runs. I think it's unfair to blame the loss on Curt Flood.

FORMER TIGERS OUTFIELDER JIM NORTHRUP: I don't think Flood would have caught the ball, even if he hadn't misjudged it or slipped. I've seen the film many times and Flood was clearly 15 to 20 feet away from the ball. He did slip a little. It was wet in the outfield. One of the problems you had in Busch Stadium was that it was a low stadium and didn't have a very high facade. It was a bright sunny day with practically an all white-shirt-sleeve crowd in the stands. In their first few steps, outfielders almost had to guess where a line drive was hit, until the ball got above the stadium. At that point, you could see the ball. Flood broke initially where he thought the ball might be and slipped a little, but the ball short-hopped the center field fence and he wasn't going to catch it.

 If he had caught it, it would have been a whole different ballgame. It really had been a pitchers' duel in Game Seven between Bob Gibson and Mickey Lolich. Gibson was the best pitcher in 1968 in the National League and we had two of the best pitchers in the American League in Denny McLain and Lolich. Gibson in Game One was just amazing. For one game, Gibson's performance was the most dominating that I have ever seen. I still can't believe we ever got a hit off him. He had the best stuff I ever saw in my major league career. His fastball was hopping and he had a wicked breaking ball. However, we had confidence heading into Game Seven with Mickey Lolich. We blew St. Louis out in Game Six and we knew then that we were going to win the final game.

Four Divisions

From 1901 through 1960, both the National League and the American League operated as eight-team leagues. However, the '60s turned out to be a decade of growth, as the AL added two teams in 1961 and the NL followed suit a year later. More expansion came in 1969 with the addition of Montreal and San Diego in the NL, and Kansas City and Seattle in the AL. Each league now split into two divisions. The result was a new postseason playoff format where division winners had to clear the extra hurdle of a League Championship Series. The days when fans could count on World Series participants owning the best record in their league were long gone.

What if baseball had not gone to four divisions in 1969?

BILL JAMES: The split into divisions had been tried in other sports, and it was something that baseball finally caved into. I don't think there had been too much pressure for the majors to split in to divisions before the 1960s.

The man who was responsible for bringing the four-division format about was the AL president, Joe Cronin. When baseball expanded from ten to 12 teams in 1968, many owners wanted to maintain the format of one league champion advancing to the World Series. Cronin kept saying that you couldn't sell a 12th place team. Cronin was able to persuade AL owners to split into two divisions of six teams each.

I wasn't in favor of the decision at the time, but then again I was a teenager, what did I know? The danger of expanding the playoffs is that you create fewer meaningful games rather than more. If you expand the playoffs to the point where teams can coast in to the postseason, then the regular season becomes meaningless. It's not necessarily a bad thing to have upsets in the playoffs. Without upsets the major league playoffs would be boring. The NBA suffers from that problem, where there isn't enough chance — enough randomness — in the system. You basically know who's going to win most of the playoff match-ups before the series actually start. You need a degree of randomness to keep things interesting.

BRUCE MARKUSEN: Going to four divisions in 1969 really changed the playoff picture. For instance, teams that wouldn't have made the playoffs instead found themselves in the World Series, such as the 1973 Mets. Those Mets were 82–79. If it were just one league, as it was before 1969, the Reds would have beaten the Mets by 17 games. The Mets would have been behind the Giants, Dodgers and barely ahead of the Astros. The Mets would have been fourth in the NL rather than making a trip to the World Series.

The 1988 Dodgers were another team that benefited from the decision to go to two divisions. The Dodgers upset the Mets in the NLCS and upset the A's in the World Series. It was not a vintage ballclub. Of all the champions I have seen in baseball over the years, the 1988 Dodgers may have been the weakest champions in terms of player personnel. The Dodgers had Franklin Stubbs, Jeff Hamilton and John Shelby in their everyday lineup. Los Angeles did not have great players, with the exception of Kirk Gibson and Orel Hershisher. The Dodgers featured an excellent manager in Tommy Lasorda and got clutch hitting when they needed it. Los Angeles wouldn't have made the postseason with the two-division format because in 1988 the Mets owned the best record in the NL. Recently teams like Florida and Anaheim have claimed World Series titles without owning the best record in their league.

It was a huge change for baseball to go initially with a two-division and eventually a three-division approach. It allows weaker teams to win the World Series. Some may criticize that, but I think it makes for a much more exciting postseason, to have several playoff rounds, as opposed to the old way where you had league champ versus league champ. The decision to go to four divisions in 1969 was one of the best decisions baseball ever made and created some special postseason memories.

JIM VAIL: Even if they hadn't been created when the majors expanded to 12 teams in 1969, divisional alignments within each league were probably an inevitable by-product of expansion. At the very least, it seems that when the American League added Toronto and the second Seattle franchise in 1977, the circuit's moguls would not have wanted a 14-team race for just one "pennant," especially given the added revenue that an extra tier of playoffs provides.

But for me, the historical facts involved in this question inevitably produce a lament. There is simply no way I can analyze it without focusing on what has been lost.

For six decades (1901–60), when there were eight teams in each league and a 154-game regular-season schedule, each club played a balanced slate of 22 contests (11 home, 11 away) against each of its seven league opponents, for 77 home and road games apiece. Given the economic inequities inherent in major-league baseball in all eras, no type of schedule could have possibly guaranteed competitive balance, and the dominant success of the Yankees during much of that period was a testament to that fact.

But the balanced-schedule format did produce fair and perfect competitive equity. At the end of each season, because every team had played each league opponent an equal number of times at each venue (discounting rainouts), there was no possible dispute over which team was the best in either circuit for the year and deserved to advance to the World Series. Even if two clubs tied for first and a pennant playoff was required, at the end of that playoff the equity of their head-to-head competition was still preserved and the winner was clearly the best team in the league for that season, if only by a game.

With the first tier of major-league expansion (1961–62), both ten-team leagues preserved that competitive equity by adopting 162-game regular-season slates, which had clubs play each of their nine league opponents 18 times apiece during the season (nine home, nine away). So scheduling fairness was retained through 1968.

That commitment to scheduling balance was integral to baseball's charm during the first seven decades of the National and American Leagues' coexistence. The ability of the game's long season to legitimately identify the best team in each circuit stood in stark contrast to the shorter regular seasons played by pro basketball and hockey, as both of them often left some reasonable doubt about the best clubs' identities, thereby legitimizing — beyond the economic motives involved — those sports' long-standing preferences for multi-tiered playoff formats.

But when both leagues went to 12-team formats in 1969, MLB faced a dilemma which presented two options. In option one, retention of perfect competitive equity required either a retrenchment to the 154-game schedule (with each club playing its 11 league opponents 14 times each, seven home, seven away) or adoption of a 176-game slate (with each team playing a 16 total, eight home-eight away; format). The longer schedule was untenable because, more often than not, it would have required opening the season in bad weather at several venues and enhanced the possibility of playing the World Series on a white-covered field with snow plows tearing it up between innings. The shorter one, presumably, was rejected because owners didn't want to give up revenue from the additional four home dates provided by a 162-game slate.

Option two, the one that was chosen, was to split each league into six-team divisions and add a potentially lucrative League Championship Series (LCS) to the postseason format. The divisional alignment was adopted largely on the seemingly logical public argument that 11th- and 12th-place teams would be an extremely hard sell, attendance-wise. But a 55–107 record or thereabouts will usually make you the 12th-worst team in any league, whether or not you officially finished "sixth." So whatever was said in public, I would never underestimate the likelihood that greed imposed by retention of the 162-game slate and the prospect of an added tier of playoffs was the real decisive factor for most owners.

The result was a semi-balanced schedule in which clubs in the new, six-team divisions played each of their five divisional rivals 18 times apiece (nine home, nine away), and the six teams in the other division 12 times each (six home, six away). At the same time, the existence of two divisions in each circuit often exacerbated the natural disparities in competitive balance, because there was simply no way to guarantee that the average quality of all teams in both league divisions was equal. In turn, perfect competitive equity was forfeited, and has remained so ever since.

With regard to competitive equity, things have only gotten worse since 1969. The AL's unilateral, two-team expansion in 1977 required distinctly different schedule formats for both leagues. Theoretically, that disparity was rectified when the NL also went to 14 teams in 1993, but any semblance of the concept of competitive equity was tossed out the window when the majors realigned each circuit into three divisions of unequal size in 1994, then adopted inter-league play and shifted the Milwaukee Brewers to the senior circuit to accommodate it in the late 1990s.

Over time, all of that produced a situation where, in recent years, many teams played clubs from other divisions on a three-home, six-away basis (or vice versa); most divisional schedules included a one-game (ten-home, nine-away) advantage; inter-league match-ups occasionally involved games played at just one team's venue, and — worst of all — some clubs even enjoyed a three-game home advantage against various divisional rivals. Given the inevitability of inequity in talent from one team and division to the next, the net result is a situation where regular-season records are no longer truly indicative of superior talent or achievement. In turn, one team might post a won-lost record ten games better than any other club in its league, but one or two teams in another, much stronger division might totally dominate the first team during the regular season and post winning records against the other two divisions, and yet fail to qualify for the post-season (even with the wild-card) because they finished third or fourth in a division where the teams all played roughly .500 baseball in head-to-head competition using a schedule that emphasized divisional rivalry. In terms of competitive equity, the current situation — imposed by the combination of unequal alignments and inter-league play — is a complete farce.

To bring in yet more revenue, MLB has given us the wild-card playoff format, and cleverly sold it as a means to keep more teams in postseason contention, and therefore enhance attendance, later in the season. Given that sales pitch, a solid majority of fans have gobbled it up.

But even beyond the scheduling inequities involved, the net effects of the three-division alignment required to justify the wild-card format are multi-fold, several of them aesthetically negative. First, there is no such thing as a "pennant race" anymore, and hasn't been since 1969. Second, even divisional championships are now rendered meaningless. Third, more good teams than at any time before now spend the last week or two of the regular season, after clinching their division, treading water and — in many cases — losing their competitive edge in the process just before the playoffs begin. Fourth, it often over-rewards teams that enter the playoffs on a hot streak built during the wild-card race. Fifth, the artificial third division in each circuit actually assures that two more teams from each league get into the playoffs that wouldn't have been there before 1995, rather than just one, thereby diminishing the overall quality of the participants as a group. Finally and inevitably, the relative quality of World Series winners, as measured by regular-season success, has declined from a .639 average winning percentage for the period 1903–1968 to just .596 in the period 1995–2004.

All of this may be healthy for baseball during the build-up to the playoffs, for the added postseason excitement it creates and the number of upsets produced. But the fact is that the schedule required to maintain this system makes a mockery of the whole purpose of baseball's long season, is competitively unfair to every team in both leagues, and severely muddles the identities of which teams should really be in the playoffs and which teams shouldn't.

The Amazing Mets

Who can explain 1969? Heading into the season, the New York Mets had never won more than 73 games in the team's brief seven-year history. In 1969, the Mets won 100 games, outfought Chicago for a divisional title, beat Atlanta in the NLCS, and then upset the powerful Baltimore Orioles in the World Series.

For much of the season, Chicago looked to be the team to beat in the NL East. With hitters like Ernie Banks, Billy Williams and Ron Santo, and a pitching staff anchored by Ferguson Jenkins, Ken Holtzman and Bill Hands, Chicago's lead approached ten games in late August. The Cubs soon hit the skids, however, as manager Leo Durocher played his starters without letup. At the same time, the Mets sizzled: New York won 38 of 49 down the stretch to win the division by eight games over Chicago.[19] Cubs fans were left to wonder what might have happened if Durocher had given his top players an occasional rest during the summer of '69. Seven of the Chicago starters played in 130 games or more, five played in at least 150 games, and Jenkins, Hands and Holtzman combined for 122 starts.[20]

New York's magic continued into October. The Mets swept Atlanta in the first ever NLCS and then shocked the baseball world by knocking off the Orioles in the World Series. After Baltimore beat Mets ace Tom Seaver in the opener, New York took the next four behind outstanding pitching, timely hitting, and spectacular catches by outfielders Tommie Agee and Ron Swoboda. The Orioles scored four times off Seaver in the opener; Baltimore would manage just five more runs in the final four games.

What if Chicago manager Leo Durocher had used his starters differently in the 1969 NL East pennant race?

BRUCE MARKUSEN: There's no question the Cubs were, man for man, a more talented team than the Mets in 1969. Leo Durocher has been criticized for not resting his regulars more during the season, but in all fairness to Leo, he really didn't have much of a bench. Durocher didn't have the opportunity to platoon in several positions as the Mets did. The Mets could platoon Donn Clendonon and Ed Kranepool at first base and Art Shamsky and Ron Swoboda in right field. Platooning gave the Mets the lefty-righty advantage and gave the Mets a chance to rest players. The Cubs essentially had a regular eight-man lineup, and if Leo substituted for any of his starters, it would have been a big falloff in the talent level. Durocher had bench players like Willie Smith, Paul Popovich and Al Spangler. The Cubs were simply not a deep ballclub.

The Cubs lineup wasn't necessarily an old team. Banks was 38, Hickman was 32, and Billy Williams was 31. The rest of the regulars were all in their mid to late 20s. It was a veteran team, but it wasn't really an old club. Durocher played it the right way in wanting his regular starters on the field as much as possible. I can't blame Durocher, especially in light of the fact that he had fewer bench options compared to Gil Hodges, the Mets manager. The Cubs also lost to the Mets by eight games in the NL East race. When you lose by eight games, I have a hard time pinning it on the manager. Give credit to the Mets. The Cubs may have had superior talent, as far as the regular position players might be concerned. However, the Mets had the superior starting pitching staff, more platoon options, and the Mets won when they had to down the stretch.

What if the Mets had not made several big plays in the '69 World Series, including great catches in the outfield by Tommie Agee and Ron Swoboda?

BRUCE MARKUSEN: The Mets lost the opener to Baltimore in the 1969 World Series and many people were probably thinking at that point that the Orioles were going to take the Series in four to five games. New York rebounded to win the next four games, thanks largely to great pitching and some phenomenal defensive plays by Tommy Agree and Ron Swoboda. Swoboda's diving catch in right field in Game Four was arguably the greatest catch by an outfielder in baseball history.

There were a number of turning points and every one of them seemed to favor the Mets. It shows you that in a short series, when you have the kind of pitching that New York did, the Mets were capable of beating anybody. The Mets needed every break and needed to play nearly perfect baseball to beat a team like the Orioles in five games. Even beating Baltimore in a seven game series would have been stunning enough.

FORMER BALTIMORE THIRD BASEMAN BROOKS ROBINSON: The 1969 loss to the Mets really wasn't the biggest disappointment of my career. My biggest disappointment was losing to Oakland in the ALCS in 1973 and 1974. When you play so hard all year to win your division, it's tough to get beat in the LCS. The playoffs started in 1969. We won three years in a row and won all nine playoff games. Then in 1973 and 1974, we got beat by Oakland, and those losses were probably the most difficult losses for me to take.

The loss to the Mets in 1969 was certainly a shock. We won 109 games that season, probably the best team I was on in my career. The Mets were no fluke. They won 100 games that year and beat Hank Aaron's Braves in the National League Championship Series. When you can start a Tom Seaver and a Jerry Koosman, and than add a Gary Gentry as a third starting pitcher, you're going to win a lot of games.

We beat Seaver in the opener and then lost four straight. The Mets made plenty of great plays. I tell Ron Swoboda every time I see him that no one would have ever heard of him if I hadn't hit that line drive to right field. Swoboda made a great catch and Tommie Agee made several great catches. Those defensive plays were made when we had men on base.

When we lost the third and fourth games of the Series in New York, we were just hoping to win Game Five and get back to Baltimore to see what we could do. Looking back, I think we may have panicked a bit. We got to a point where everybody was trying to do things they couldn't do. Some of our hitters were trying to hit homers rather than trying to get on base. We were trying to turn the Series around in a hurry. The bottom line is that the Mets simply outplayed us and deserved to be the World Champions.

The Bullpen View

The fate of several World Series matchups in the '60s could have easily turned on a single play. In 1960, the Yankees were closing in on another championship when Bill Virdon's ground ball took a nasty bounce and struck New York shortstop Tony Kubek in the throat, allowing Pittsburgh to rally. Mike Robbins predicted another title for the Yankees, if not for that strange hop, although Bob Friend claimed that the Pirates would have found a way to win. Eight years later, St. Louis was a single victory away from repeating as World Series champions when Detroit outfielder Willie Horton gunned down Cardinals outfielder Lou Brock at the plate. Brock failed to slide, and Bruce Markusen maintained that Brock might have scored if he had hit the dirt, and the Cardinals would have won the series if Brock had scored that run.

A couple of trades turned St. Louis and Baltimore into dominant franchises. The Cardinals pilfered Lou Brock from the Cubs, and David Shiner pointed out that St. Louis was the perfect location for a speedster like Brock, whose career might have gone in a completely different direction in Chicago. Meanwhile, Cincinnati's trade of Frank Robinson to Baltimore ranks as the worst transaction in Reds history, according to Cincy broadcaster Marty Brennaman. Gabriel Schechter also suggested that the Big Red Machine might have arrived a few years ahead of schedule if Robinson had stayed in Cincinnati. Instead, he directed Baltimore to four AL pennants in six seasons, and Brooks Robinson questioned whether the Orioles could have achieved that kind of success without Frank Robinson.

The career of Boston's Tony Conigliaro went south after a near fatal beaning in 1967, and Bill McNeil stated that Tony C might have challenged for the all-time home run record if he had remained healthy. Alan Schwarz asserted that Conigliaro would have benefited from both a jump in offense in 1969 and the designated hitter rule in 1973, perhaps concluding his career with more than 500 homers.

Thanks to expansion in the '60s, Major League Baseball was larger than ever. In the pivotal decade of the '70s, a new AL rule would create controversy and an arbitrator's decision would finally free the players from the power of the hated reserve clause.

6

A Whole New Ballgame: 1970–1979

Historical Highlights

Few decades can boast as many landmark changes as the 1970s. The most significant development came in 1975, when an arbitrator's ruling invalidated the long-standing reserve clause, opening the floodgates for free agency.[1] While several teams took advantage of the new goldmine of talent, others did not. The Oakland Athletics, winners of the AL West from 1971 through 1975, faded from contention, as owner Charlie Finley rid himself of players that he could no longer afford.

The addition of the designated hitter rule in the AL in 1973 meant that offensive stars, who were liabilities in the field, suddenly had enhanced job prospects. In 1974, baseball had a new all-time home run king, as Hank Aaron surpassed Babe Ruth with his 715th career homer.

In one of the decade's biggest trades, Cincinnati's Big Red Machine acquired second baseman Joe Morgan from Houston. A good Reds team suddenly became a dominant team and Cincinnati won World Series titles in 1975 and 1976, with the victory over Boston in 1975 possibly ranking as the most exciting championship series of them all.

Retooling the Machine

In conquering the National League in 1970, Cincinnati relied on its power game to flatten opponents. However, the following season was a

different story, as the Big Red Machine sputtered, winning 23 fewer regular season games. Reds general manager Bob Howsam astutely judged that
Cincinnati needed more speed to contend in 1972. In a bold move, Howsam
sent power hitting first baseman Lee May, second baseman Tommy Helms,
and utilityman Jimmy Stewart to Houston. In return, the Reds got second
baseman Joe Morgan, third baseman Denis Menke, pitcher Jack Billingham, and outfielders Cesar Geronimo and Ed Armbrister.

Morgan turned out to be the essential ingredient in a recipe that
resulted in the Reds dynasty of 1972–76. Morgan won back-to-back MVP
awards in 1975 and 1976 and earned his bronze plaque in the Hall of Fame
in 1990.[2]

What if Cincinnati had not picked up Joe Morgan from the Houston Astros?

REDS BROADCASTER MARTY BRENNAMAN: The Reds would not have accomplished all that they did in the 1970s without Joe Morgan. Morgan and the other
players Cincinnati got from Houston, including Jack Billingham and Cesar
Geronimo, were the final pieces to the puzzle. It was the foresight and the wis-
dom of Bob Howsam that allowed the Reds to make the trade. Howsam realized that the artificial turf of Riverfront Stadium called for speed in the lineup,
as well as good defense. The Reds picked up a Gold Glove second baseman;
an excellent center fielder in Geronimo, who was the best defensive center
fielder in the game; a solid starting pitcher in Billingham; and Ed Armbrister, who contributed coming off the bench. When you matched those players
with the cast that had already been assembled, including Pete Rose, Johnny
Bench and Tony Perez, the Reds were going to be tough to beat.

Without Joe Morgan, I don't believe the Reds would have won World
Series titles in 1975 and 1976. I know there were many people in Cincinnati who were opposed to the trade. Whenever Bob Howsam was ready to
make a trade, he would call all of his baseball people in to talk about the
pros and cons of the deal. People had the freedom to express their feelings
about the proposed trade. At the end of the meeting, Bob Howsam would
make the decision, with the understanding that everyone would be on board
with whatever the final decision was.

If the deal had not been made, I don't believe Joe Morgan would have
become the type of player he later became. By coming to Cincinnati, Joe
got out of the Astrodome, which was a very tough place for power hitters.
Once Joe came to Cincinnati, he was a power hitter. He hit 25 to 30 homers
almost every year. That probably would not have occurred if Joe had kept
on playing his home games at the Astrodome.

The acquisition of Joe Morgan solidified the Big Red Machine. (Courtesy Cincinnati Reds.)

There was a perception that Joe was a malcontent when he was with the Astros, but I think that stemmed from Joe having major disagreements with Harry Walker, Joe's manager in Houston in the 1960s. I don't think Joe was a malcontent. He never showed that in Cincinnati. Joe would also be the first to tell you that had the trade not come about, Joe's chances at

making the Hall of Fame would have been diminished. By playing in Cincinnati with guys like Bench, Rose and Perez, Joe had a chance to become the
best player he could possibly be. If the Frank Robinson trade ranks as the
worst deal in the history of the Reds, then the Joe Morgan deal would have
to rank as one of the best trades in franchise history, if not the best.

ALAN SCHWARZ: Without Joe Morgan, the Reds would not have developed
into the dynasty they did in the 1970s. Morgan was the Reds' best player
and the best player in the NL in 1975–76, the seasons the Reds won the
World Series and forged their legend as one of the great teams of all time.
Clearly, the Morgan deal made the Reds complete.

People forget how much talent the Houston Astros had in the '70s. In
addition to Morgan, Houston also had Jimmy Wynn, Cesar Cedeno, Bob
Watson, and good pitchers like Larry Dierker, Don Wilson and J.R. Richard.
It appears as if the Astros were a team that underperformed horribly in the
'70s. You have to think that if Morgan stays with the club, the Astros are
going to be a strong team in 1974 and 1975. They might have been one of
the dominant teams in the National League West if they could have kept
the club together, in the wake of free agency. Perhaps the NL West wouldn't
have always come down to the Reds and Dodgers between 1973 and 1978.
Perhaps we might have seen the Astros in the mix.

Morgan himself was an All-Star in 1970 and led the NL in triples in
1971. He was 28 when he was traded to the Reds. Morgan certainly blos-
somed with the Reds, and he benefited from playing with teammates like
Rose, Bench and Perez. Morgan got on base and scored tons of runs thanks
to the Reds power hitters. If he doesn't get traded, it's hard to say what
Morgan's offensive numbers might have been had he continued to play in
a pitcher's park like the Astrodome. It was a terrible park for hitters and
several Houston hitters suffered as a result, like Jose Cruz.

GABRIEL SCHECHTER: The Reds were a sub-.500 team in 1971 with May and
Helms. They had problems in the outfield, as newly acquired George Foster hadn't matured. Without the trade, they would have continued to struggle for two or three years until Foster and Griffey became fully productive,
instead of turning into immediate winners. However, it wasn't just Morgan. Cesar Geronimo was a big piece of the puzzle, a terrific defensive center fielder on a team whose pitchers usually needed defensive help. They
also got Jack Billingham in the trade, and he was their most consistent starting pitcher over five seasons. Take away Geronimo or Billingham, and Morgan probably doesn't lead the Reds to four pennants in five years by himself.

BRUCE MARKUSEN: It was as pivotal a trade as was made in the 1970s. It
reconfigured the Reds and made them stronger up the middle. It gave them

more speed, better defense and really didn't take away that much power from the Reds lineup. In 1972, the Reds ended up beating the Houston Astros by ten and a half games. If the Reds don't trade for Morgan, I think the Reds still win their division in 1972, but I don't think they would have beaten the Pirates in the NL playoffs. Without Morgan, the Reds don't win back-to-back World Series titles in 1975 and 1976. You can argue that Morgan would be on your all-time team at second base. I would say after Johnny Bench, Joe Morgan was the Reds' most valuable player.

Designated Hitting

Love it or hate it, no rule change in baseball history draws more comments than the designated hitter rule. After it was adopted exclusively for the American League in 1973, offensive production received an immediate jolt, as AL scoring rose by 23 percent in the first season of the DH, the biggest increase since 1911.[3]

Several veterans served as designated hitters during the rule's debut season, including Orlando Cepeda with Boston and Tony Oliva with Minnesota. Hal McRae spent most of his years in the majors serving as Kansas City's designated hitter, and Hank Aaron concluded his superlative career as Milwaukee's DH in 1975 and 1976.

What if the AL had not approved the designated hitter rule?
What if the DH was employed even earlier in the 20th century?

GABRIEL SCHECHTER: It's hard to say with certainty that this or that modern AL hitter would not have seen "the light of day" without the DH. Prominent DHs like Harold Baines and Edgar Martinez played in the field for years before switching to DH. If the DH had never been invented, their managers would have had the age-old dilemma of balancing someone's offensive contributions with their defensive liabilities. I think Baines and Martinez would still have had long and productive careers, had they been forced to play the entire game of baseball the way it is supposed to be played. George Brett and Paul Molitor could have continued playing first base for years to reach their batting milestones.

The more interesting question is what would have happened if the majors had adopted the suggestion Connie Mack made before 1920, advocating a DH. For one thing, Babe Ruth might have turned out to be an earlier Lefty Grove, instead of the original Bambino. Many strong hitters who were relegated to the minors because of fielding deficiencies would have thrived, such as Buzz Arlett and Ox Eckhardt. Many other records and careers would have been affected. Rogers Hornsby would have zoomed past

3,000 hits instead of falling just short because leg injuries kept him from playing the field. Ralph Kiner and Hank Greenberg would probably have added years to their careers instead of retiring early because of back problems. Maybe the most dramatic effect would have been on the career of Mickey Mantle. Mantle had so many leg injuries that it wore him down just having to run back and forth from center field to the bench nine times a game. If he had had nothing to do but hit, his energy would have been channeled more efficiently, and it would have added at least another 50–100 home runs to his career. Paul Molitor became a DH at a young age, not because he couldn't play the field, but because his managers were afraid he would continue to be injured and lose playing time. As a DH, he was rarely hurt and lasted a long time. I think that if the DH had existed in 1950, as soon as Ted Williams hurt his elbow in the All-Star Game, his manager would have forbidden him to play in the field again. He would have been happy as a DH, since all he really wanted to do was hit anyway.

MIKE ROBBINS: When it comes to hitters of the past who would have made excellent designated hitters, four names come immediately to mind: Buzz Arlett, Ike Boone, Smead Jolley, and Moose Clabaugh. All four were great hitters in the highest levels of the minors in the 1920s and 1930s, but all saw their major league careers derailed by their inability to play defense. Arlett hit .341 with 432 homers in the high minors between 1918 and 1937; Ike Boone .370 with 217 homers; Smead Jolley .366 with 334; Clabaugh .339 with 346. There's every reason to believe that their hitting would have made them stars—if only their fielding hadn't severely limited their time in the majors. The DH rule could have done that.

Chasing the Babe

Perhaps the most notable career record fell in 1974, when Hank Aaron supplanted Babe Ruth as the all-time home run king; two years later, Aaron concluded his career with 755 homers. Even so, it's interesting to speculate whether another slugger might have smashed his way to the record, under a different set of circumstances. Both Ted Williams and Willie Mays lost seasons to military service; others, like Mickey Mantle, had to contend with nagging injuries and poor health throughout their careers.

Let's not forget the heavy hitters of the Negro League, like Josh Gibson, who pounded nearly 800 home runs in his career, including 75 in a single season.[4] There are also international stars like Sadaharu Oh, who blasted 868 homers in a 22-year career in Japan.[5]

Could another player possess the all-time home run record,
perhaps Ted Williams, Willie Mays, Mickey Mantle,
Sadaharu Oh, or one of the Negro League stars?

DEAN SULLIVAN: If we eliminate racism and nativism, then sluggers like
Sadaharu Oh and Josh Gibson might have challenged the record. Given the
power record, however, of Japanese hitters after moving to the majors (not
impressive), and Gibson's status as a catcher (which would wear out his
body before he could play long enough to challenge the record), we can
probably eliminate them from consideration. If Ruth had switched to full-
time hitting earlier, obviously the home run record would have been higher,
but in the deadball era, even Ruth wouldn't have hit that many more home
runs. His pitching talent was such that some questioned the move to the
outfield as it was, so it's not realistic to consider that he would have been
moved much earlier than he was.

If Mays, Mantle and Ted Williams, among others, had not lost time to
war and injury, the race would have been closer, but not by much. Mays
was still quite young in 1952–53 and might not have hit many more than
40–50 homers during that time. If he had played during those two seasons
however, it might have taken off time at the end of his career, since he
would have more wear and tear to consider. The same is true of Williams,
who might have added about 200 home runs, if not for war and injury, but
whose career would have ended several years earlier as a result.

Even if any of these scenarios had played out, Aaron simply could have
continued playing for several more years as Milwaukee's DH, in order to
break the record.

JIM ALBRIGHT: When it comes to the career home run mark, you need to
start with the man who popularized four baggers, Babe Ruth. The first question is whether he would have hit more homers if he had become an everyday player earlier. There are two issues that cloud the picture on this point:
Ruth was allowed to develop his then-unique style of hitting precisely
because he was a pitcher; and the shift to home run hitting was a result of
the serendipitous convergence of several events, including Ruth's arrival,
Ray Chapman's fatal beaning, and the Black Sox scandal. If Ruth had become
a regular much sooner, there's a strong possibility baseball would have taken
steps to clamp down on homers. Another question is how many homers
the Babe would have gotten had he used a little less (ahem) idiosyncratic
training methods—like eating right, working out a little more, stuff like
that. I think there's little doubt his career numbers would have been even
better had he done so. But then he wouldn't have been the overgrown kid
that was the Babe. Besides, quantifying how many more homers he would

have gotten is wild speculation with little basis in fact. The lack of factual basis for quantifying such injury-based what-ifs is a sufficient reason to reject them in my mind. Having taken that position, I'll leave out any discussion of how Mickey Mantle and/or Willie McCovey would have done had they stayed healthy. Another problem of these conditioning/injury what-ifs is the players' conditioning and injuries have a tremendous influence on the shape and duration of players' careers.

The questions I find more interesting are those which focus on factors which are not only beyond the control of the player, but which are also not the result of the player's personality, choices or playing style. Examples of the kinds of issues I am talking about are the exclusions of Negro Leaguers and Japanese ballplayers and time spent in military service. I'll stay away from moving people around in time as well.

There are five Negro Leaguers who I'd like to comment on, but I am confident enough to come to a conclusion on only three of them. Josh Gibson was a great, great hitter and slugger — but he was also a catcher. No major league catcher has more than 60% of Ruth's total. I am sure Gibson would be much closer to Ruth than that, but it is hard to see him closing the entire gap when you think of the beating catchers take. Turkey Stearnes and Mule Suttles are possibilities, though I'd like to know how much their home parks favored them. If they didn't get too much help, I'd look at them closely. Two players who may have had the talent but couldn't surpass 714, if born on the real-time date they were born, are Oscar Charleston and Cristobal Torriente. They started too early, and the early start would have doomed their chances of surpassing 714 in the major leagues, in my opinion.

I am confident the only Japanese player likely to get even 500 homers in a full MLB career is Sadaharu Oh. I've projected him between 525 and 555 homers in a neutral major league park. He was a dead pull hitter, so if he played in a park with a short right field porch like Yankee Stadium, he would have had even more than my projection. However, it's hard to project him to add at least 20 percent more homers due to his park. Oh would have to have over 60 percent of his career homers at home to get close to 714 homers. Outside of Mel Ott, I can't think of a top-notch slugger (450 or more homers) with that kind of home field edge. I am confident Oh was a great player, but it is very unlikely he would have hit over 700 homers in the major leagues.

Ted Williams lost three full seasons to World War II, and lost all but 40 or so games in two seasons due to his service in Korea. In cases like this, the method I like to use for projections is to base each missing season (or part of it) on one-third the season before the gap, one-third after the gap, and one-third an average season not affected by military service. Ted Williams had 30 homers in an average year not affected by military service. His two seasons surrounding his WW II service yield another 74 homers. Since we're doing three seasons in this case, the projection is 104 lost homers to WW II. For his Korean service, his before and after years total 59 homers. Add in the 30 average year homer figure, divide by three and then multiply by 1.7 to restrict the projection to the games he missed, and you get 50 more homers. Thus I project Ted to have 675 homers at the time he hung up his spikes. The question becomes whether or not Ted would have played another two or three years to beat Ruth's mark. I can see the argument that he would have made it, but only barely. I can't accept that he would have enough homers to keep Aaron from passing him sometime in 1974 as Aaron finished that year with 733.

Willie Mays lost what I'll call 1.8 seasons to military service during the 1950s. Interestingly, when we apply the projection methods used above for Ted Williams, the projection adds precisely 55 homers to Willie's total. Of course, this puts Willie at 715, one ahead of Ruth. Willie's final year was well below full-time, and if he had been chasing Ruth, I think he would have gotten enough opportunities to make it to 715. Again, though, I can't see him finishing with more than the 733 Aaron had at the end of 1974. Al Downing might well have lost the "distinction" of being the guy to give up the record-breaking blast, but somebody who faced Aaron in 1974 would have.

In sum, it is certainly possible Willie Mays would have surpassed Ruth before Aaron, though possibly after Ted Williams. However, in either case, I believe Aaron would have held the mark before the end of the 1974 season and would still hold it today.

BILL McNEIL: Babe Ruth pitched five full seasons for the Boston Red Sox between 1915 and 1919. During that time, he played 386 games, exactly half the number of games he could have played as an outfielder. He hit 49 home runs over that period, which means he could have hit an additional 49 homers as a position player. That would have increased the Babe's total to 763 homers, eight more than Aaron's total. Obviously, that's too close a call to say that Ruth would have beaten Aaron, but it would have been interesting.

Sadaharu Oh hit 868 home runs as a member of the Yomiuri Giants between 1959 and 1980. However, as I noted in my book, *The King Of Swat*, it was much easier to hit home runs in Japan than it would have been in the major leagues. I developed a formula, based on actual statistics involving hundreds of thousands of at-bats of players who played in both leagues, to predict how a Japanese league player would perform in the major leagues. That formula, which was developed in 2000, has since been verified by the exploits of Ichiro Suzuki, Hideki Matsui and others. According to my formula, Sadaharu Oh would have batted .283 if he had played in the major leagues and would have hit 506 home runs, and average of 23 homers for every 550 at-bats.

Josh Gibson, as I noted in another segment of this book, would have batted .312 in the major leagues with 61 home runs for every 550 at-bats using my conversion formulas. If he had played the same number of years he played in the Negro Leagues, which was 17, he could have hit as many as 854 home runs in his career. However, catchers usually don't get as many at-bats as other position players due to the high risks associated with their trade. If he had the same number of at-bats per season as the game's greatest catchers did, about 400 at-bats a season, he would have hit 748 home runs during his career. Once again, it would be a tossup between him and Aaron.

Ted Williams finished his career with 521 home runs, while missing almost five years to military service. If he had played those five years, he could conceivably have hit another 171 home runs, giving him a career total of 692. It is doubtful he could have challenged Babe Ruth, let alone Hank Aaron.

Willie Mays lost almost two years to military service, but it was near the beginning of his career, and the 21-year-old slugger had not yet fully developed physically. He might have added another 36 to 60 home runs to his total, giving him somewhere between 696 home runs and 721 home runs for his career. He could have passed the mighty Bambino, but wouldn't have come close to Aaron.

Another celebrated slugger who should be mentioned is Mickey Charles Mantle. The charismatic Oklahoman hit more home runs by the age of 30 than any other hitter. His 404 home runs easily outdistanced both Babe Ruth (309) and Hank Aaron (366). Unfortunately for Mantle and his fans, he battled demons throughout his career. Many of the male members of his family died young, including his father, Mutt, so Mantle took a fatalistic view of life and decided to live it up while he had the time. As a result, he spent the bulk of his off-field time partying and slowly destroying his body. He was physically spent by the time he was 30 and although he played six more years, he was just a shadow of his former self. Over his last four years, playing in 518 games, he hit just 82 home runs. Mickey Mantle might have been the greatest slugger in baseball history if he had taken care of himself, but the demons won out.

There are many what-if's in baseball history, but the only important thing is, what-is. And in that arena, Hank Aaron is still the king.

JIM VAIL: In order to have a legitimate shot at breaking Babe Ruth's career home run record, a player would need to combine relatively injury-free longevity with a demonstrated ability to hit home runs at something approaching the Bambino's pace. Ruth played 22 seasons (1914–35), averaging one homer every 11.76 at-bats and 32.5 dingers per season.

The Babe also enjoyed four seasons when he hit 50 or more big flies, along with another seven years with a total in the 40s, and it would seem that the ability to post several high-total seasons like that would also help considerably. But Hank Aaron, who had only one season in his career above 45 home runs, and a total of seven others with 40–45, proved you didn't have to swat 50 or more several times to surpass the record.

At the start of the 1974 season, Aaron trailed Ruth by just one homer, and promptly tied him on opening day. The table below includes every man who had at least 400 career home runs through the 1973 season, plus the two other men with smaller totals who nonetheless had at least four years of 40 taters or more. The data columns include statistics through 1973 only, and give each player's career span (Career), his number of major league seasons (Yrs), his career home run total (HR), the number of 40-homer-or-better years he'd enjoyed (40+), his career at-bats total (AB), plus his number of dingers averaged per season (HR/Yr) and his rate of at-bats-per-home run (Rate, with the lower the number the better). Players who were active in 1974 or later are italicized.

Player	Career	Yrs	HR	40+	AB	HR/Yr	Rate
Babe Ruth	1914–35	22	714	11	8399	32.5	11.8
Hank Aaron	1954–73	20	713	8	11288	35.7	15.8
Willie Mays	1951–73	22	660	6	10881	30.0	16.5
Frank Robinson	1956–73	18	552	1	9344	30.7	16.9
Harmon Killebrew	1954–73	20	546	8	7502	27.3	13.7
Mickey Mantle	1951–68	18	536	4	8102	29.8	15.1
Jimmie Foxx	1925–45	20	534	5	8134	26.7	15.2
Ted Williams	1939–60	19	521	1	7706	27.4	14.8
Ernie Banks	1953–71	19	512	5	9421	26.9	18.4
Eddie Mathews	1952–68	17	512	4	8537	30.1	16.7
Mel Ott	1926–47	22	511	1	9456	23.2	18.5
Lou Gehrig	1923–39	17	493	5	8001	29.0	16.2
Stan Musial	1941–63	22	475	0	10972	21.6	23.1
Willie McCovey	1959–73	15	413	2	5919	27.5	14.3
Duke Snider	1947–64	18	407	5	7161	22.6	17.6
Ralph Kiner	1946–55	10	369	5	5205	36.9	14.1
Hank Greenberg	1930–47	13	331	4	5193	25.5	15.7

Given their relative proximity to Ruth's career home run total and their frequency of seasons with 40 homers or more, it's fair to claim that the 15 men listed with Ruth and Aaron above, all but three of whose careers fell entirely between 1923 and 1973, had the best chance of anyone during that era of breaking Babe's mark before Hank did. In turn, I believe it's specious to argue that someone like Tony Conigliaro—who had 56 homers at the age of 20 and 104 in his first four big-league campaigns before his career was ruined by an eye injury—had a legitimate shot, because there are simply too many "what ifs?" involved. Besides, Tony C was only 28 when the 1974 season began, so—absent the injury, and even if all the "what ifs?" fell in his favor—he clearly would and could not have topped Babe's mark before Aaron did it.

Several of the players above can be dismissed from consideration fairly easily. Willie McCovey, Frank Robinson and Ernie Banks would have had to average an unprecedented 47.7, 39.7 and 37.6 home runs per season, respectively, for their entire careers to have passed Ruth before the start of 1974, and none of them missed significant portions of enough seasons due to injury, military or Negro League service to warrant any speculation about what might have been. Neither Stan Musial nor Duke Snider ever put a string of more than five seasons together in which their per-at-bat or per-season home run rates were truly Ruthian, and their career rates were otherwise simply too low. Eddie Mathews was actually well ahead of Babe's career pace at ages 25 (222 homers to 103 for the Bambino) and 30 (399 to 309), but—like the others just mentioned—he enjoyed a fairly healthy career and missed no seasons, so there is no real basis for speculation about his prospects either.

Beyond Aaron, that leaves nine other players from the list—Mays, Killebrew, Mantle, Foxx, Williams, Ott, Gehrig, Kiner and Greenberg—who arguably had a shot at the record. In each of their cases there is also some room, due to missing or injury-shortened seasons, for speculating about "what if?"

Starting at the bottom of the list, Hank Greenberg had one at-bat at age 19 for the Tigers in 1930, then never appeared in another major-league game until 1933. He also lost all of 1942–44 to World War II military service, and missed substantial portions of the 1936 and 1941 seasons, plus about half of 1945 for other causes. So, arguably, his career was shortened by about seven and a half seasons all told. Five of those years (1936, 1941 and 1942–44) also came during what is normally considered a player's prime (ages 25 through 33). During the rest of that prime, 1937–40, Greenberg hit 172 home runs (43.0 per season). Even if you argue—too liberally, no doubt—that Hank could have averaged 43 dingers for each of the seven and a half seasons he missed, that comes out to an additional 323 home runs, or a career total of 654, still 60 shy of the Babe.

Ralph Kiner's biggest problem is the brevity of his career, which lasted just ten seasons. He spent 1941–42 in the minors, leading the Eastern League in homers in 1942. He graduated to the International League for 1943, but spent most of that season and all of 1944–45 in the military. He retired at the end of the 1955 season, at just 32 years of age, due to chronic sciatica. So, it's fair to argue that military duty (two years) and physical woes (any-where from three to eight years) cut about seven seasons from his career. If you credit Kiner with his career, per-season home run average for each of seven additional years (again, a very liberal estimate given his high home run rates), that adds 258 dingers to his actual career total of 369, leaving him with 627, 87 short of Ruth.

Lou Gehrig joined the Yankees at age 20 in 1923. He had only 38 at-bats in his first two seasons, and then retired early during 1939 (age 35) due to the illness that took his life in 1941. In between, he was as injury-free as his 'Iron Horse' nickname implied, and there's little reason to doubt that without the disease named for him, he could have played until he was 40. If you give him an extra five seasons at the end of his career, assume he was a full time player for 1923–24 (which is definitely stretching credibility) and credit him with his career, per-season home-run average, then he jumps from 493 dingers to about 696, just 18 behind the Babe.

Mel Ott came to the majors in 1926 at age 17, and had only 223 at-bats during his first two seasons. He retired in 1947 at age 38, having hit just one homer in only 72 part-time at-bats during 1946–47. Given his youth, I think it's specious to credit him with any more production at the start of his career than he actually had. But, even if you do that, claim that he could have played until he was 40, and apply his per-season HR average (23.2) to the four partial and two extra seasons involved, then subtract the dingers he actually hit for 1926–27 and 1946–47 combined, it only adds another 137 big flies to his career total of 511, giving him 648, or 66 less than Ruth.

Then there is Ted Williams, the poster boy for almost every "what if?" batting scenario conjured by man. The Splinter joined the Red Sox in 1939 at age 20, and was an immediate full-timer. He missed all of 1943–45 plus virtually all of 1952–53 to military service in World War II and Korea, and almost half of the 1950 season due to a broken elbow incurred during that year's All-Star game. Williams also suffered a broken collarbone that cost him about one-third of the 1954 campaign, and was retired briefly for part of 1955. His seasonal at-bat and home run totals declined beginning in 1954, but he was still effectively Boston's regular left fielder through his true retire-ment at the end of 1960, at age 42. Given all that, he may merit credit for an extra six seasons, at most. In the four years on either side of his World War II service (1941–42 and 1946–47), Williams averaged 35 homers per year. For the comparable years on either side of 1952–53, his per-season average was 28.8. If, being as liberal but fair as possible, you apply those averages separately as full-season values for 1943–45 on one hand, and to 1950 plus 1952–53 on the other, and then subtract the number of dingers he actually hit in the partial years involved, the grand total comes to about 149, giving him a career total of 670, 44 behind Ruth.

Like Mel Ott, Jimmie Foxx came to the majors at a very young age (joining the Philadelphia A's at 17 in 1925) and spent his first two seasons as a bench warmer (41 at-bats in all), followed by a 130-AB campaign in 1927. So as with Ott, it's specious to credit any more production to those young seasons. After that, Foxx was a full-timer during 1928–41, a 14-year period in which he swatted 516 of his 534 career homers, for an average of 36.9 per season. Foxx's problem was booze, which began to take its toll in 1942, a season in which he hit only eight home runs for the Red Sox and Cubs combined, prompting a temporary retirement, at age 35, for all of 1943 and most of the next season. A brief swan song ensued for 1944–45, in which he had 7 dingers in 244 at-bats. If (again very liberally) you give Foxx his career, per-season average of 26.7 big flies for each of the partial seasons at the front and back of his career, plus the two years he was "retired," those six extra seasons (minus the ten home runs he actually hit) adds 150 to his career total, giving him 674, or 40 shy of the Babe.

Beyond Ted Williams, Mickey Mantle is the other player who seems to encourage the most speculation regarding the "what ifs?" in his career. They, of course, involve playing his entire career on bad legs (after a high school ankle injury and twisting a kneecap after running into an outfield drain pipe during the 1951 World Series), and an alcohol problem similar to Jimmie Foxx. Despite that, Mantle had just two seasons (his rookie year of 1951 and 1963) when he played in fewer than 100 games and only four others (1953, 1962 and 1965–66) when he appeared in less than 140 contests. In all, he had 2,045 at-bats in those six abbreviated seasons (an average of 341 per year), compared to 6,057 AB (and 505 per season) in his 12 "full-time" campaigns. At an average difference of 164 at-bats per shortened season, there is no reason to credit him with more than two extra years for the partial seasons missed — a total which is certainly not abnormal for injuries in any 18-year career. If you credit Mickey with his 29.8 per-season career home run average for two extra seasons, that adds 60 homers to his career total of 536, leaving him at 596, or 118 behind Ruth.

Harmon Killebrew came to the majors at age 18, and spent his first five seasons (1954–58) as a bench-warming bonus baby for the original

Washington Senators, getting only 254 at-bats that produced 11 home runs. In 1959, his first season as a regular, he led the American League with 42 dingers as a third baseman, and except for an injury-shortened season in 1968 never hit less than 25 over the next 14 years. He then was a part-timer for his final three campaigns (1973–75). Killebrew spent his career as a man without an obvious position, playing four of his full-time seasons at third base, seven at first and three in the outfield. When he joined the Senators in 1954, Washington had a very good third sacker, Eddie Yost, who remained the club's regular at the position through 1958. But Washington finished last in three of Harmon's five bench-sitter campaigns, plus sixth and seventh in the other two; and the club employed no fewer than three regular first basemen (Mickey Vernon in the twilight of a solid career, Norm Zauchin and Pete Runnels) and 12 outfielders (the best of whom were Roy Sievers and Jim Lemon) who appeared in as many as 85 games in any season during that five-year span. Given the club's ineptitude, its revolving-door outfield and first base situations, and the fact that Killebrew was obviously more than ready to be a regular by 1959, it's astounding that the Senators never found a place for him as a lineup regular before that season, and by 1957 at the latest. As a result, in estimating Harmon's "what if?" prospects of catching Ruth, it may be fair to credit him with four full seasons (1955–58) at his career, per-season home run rate of 27.3. That would add another 109 dingers to his career total of 573, giving him 682 overall, just 34 shy of Ruth.

Finally, there is Willie Mays, the man who many in the mid–1960s thought had the very best chance of breaking Ruth's record. After a rookie season with 20 homers in 1951, Mays missed about three-fourths of 1952 and all of 1953 due to Korean War-era military service. Thereafter, he was a lineup fixture (never posting fewer than 403 at-bats) for the Giants in every season up to the moment he was traded to the Mets in early 1972, at age 41. So the only significant time Mays lost during his career was 1952–53. Mays had 92 homers in 1954–55. If you add them to his 20 for 1951, you get an average of 37.3 per season. If you credit him with that liberal rate for the 1.75 seasons he missed, it adds 65 big flies to his career mark of 660, for a total of 725, or 11 more than Ruth hit.

All of the above seems to indicate that only Willie Mays had a legitimate chance to break Ruth's career home-run record before Hank Aaron did it. Subjectively, it's my own opinion that, given perfect circumstances (and less booze in the former case), both Jimmie Foxx and Harmon Killebrew could and would have made a run at the record. The facts remain, however, that Mays retired at the end of 1973, and Aaron smacked 20 homers in 1974, for a career total of 733 by the end of that year. So if 'Say

Hey' had retired as the all-time leader with 725, or thereabouts, his reign as the long-ball king would have lasted for less than a season.

As for the Babe, he was used exclusively as a pitcher during his first four seasons (1914–17), swatting nine homers in 361 at-bats, for an overall rate of one for every 40.1 ABs. Then, in 1918, he played 59 games in the outfield, 20 as a hurler and 13 as a first baseman, winning his first home run title with 11 in 317 at-bats (a rate of 28.8).

The American League home run leaders for 1914–17 were (consecutively) Frank Baker with nine dingers in 570 at-bats (a rate of 63.3), Braggo Roth with seven in 384 AB (54.9), and then Wally Pipp twice, with 12 in 545 AB (45.4) and nine in 587 (65.2). Except for 1914, when Ruth hit no taters at all, Babe's seasonal at-bats per-homer rates (23.0 in 1915, 45.3 in 1916 and 61.5 in 1917) were better in each of those years than the league's actual home run leader, and it's conceivable he would have led the AL in big flies in each of those three seasons had he been used as a non- (or merely part-time) pitcher from the start of his career. But if you apply each of those seasonal rates for 1915–17 to a 431-at-bat year (his AB average for the first five seasons he played the outfield), Ruth would have had consecutive totals of 19, ten and seven homers during those seasons, leading the league in 1915 only, and adding 27 dingers to his career mark for a total of 741 (which Aaron surpassed about two-thirds of the way through 1975).

Sadaharu Oh hit 868 home runs in the Japanese majors in a 22-year career (1959–80) exactly contemporary with that of Willie McCovey. In the process, Oh hit 50 or more homers in three different seasons (with a high of 55 in 1964), and had ten other campaigns with 40 dingers or more. With no major league statistics to work from, any estimate of what Oh might have achieved in the United States is totally and unavoidably subjective. A recent (2005) publication about Oh by the Society for American Baseball Research included comments from ten American players of the era who saw him play during off-season exhibitions. Among them, estimates of Oh's likely home run prowess in America ranged from a low of 20–25 per season to as many as the low 40s. The publication also noted that 612 (or 70.5 percent) of Oh's home runs were to right field. In that context, it seems safe to say that Oh's relative success in America would have depended greatly upon the configuration of his home park(s), and that — blessed with a 22-year career in a venue like Yankee Stadium — he may well have challenged for a spot among the all-time top five or ten home run hitters, if not a ranking with Aaron, Ruth and Barry Bonds.

A Buyer's Market

December 23, 1975, turned out to be one of baseball's most significant dates. It was on that day that federal arbitrator Peter Seitz issued his ruling on the reserve clause, stating that under his interpretation, a player could become a free agent by playing out his option year without a new contract.[6] Owners and players eventually agreed to a compromise that would make players ineligible for free agency until they had played at least six seasons in the majors. Nonetheless, free agency would transform the game; on average, salaries tripled within five years of Seitz's ruling.[7]

Teams felt the impact as well. The Oakland A's, winners of three straight World Series titles between 1972 and 1974, were obliterated by free agency and finished dead last in the AL in 1977. While Oakland plummeted, the New York Yankees soared behind the addition of free agents like Catfish Hunter, Goose Gossage and Reggie Jackson. Yankees owner George Steinbrenner used his newfound talent to win back-to-back World Series crowns in 1977 and 1978.

What if free agency had not become an option for teams to use in the 1970s?

REDS BROADCASTER MARTY BRENNAMAN: Bob Howsam felt that free agency was going to ruin baseball. In my opinion, free agency became one of the greatest things that ever happened to baseball. Some people were concerned that the major market clubs in New York, Los Angeles and Chicago would dominate baseball, leaving the smaller market teams in Cincinnati and Kansas City in their wake, and that didn't happen. Free agency actually created parity in baseball rather than becoming the ruination of the game. Arbitration has become actually the biggest negative in baseball.

When free agency came in, the Reds let Pete Rose leave. Rose ultimately signed with Philadelphia. Joe Morgan became a free agent and signed with Houston in January of 1980. Tony Perez was traded to Montreal after the 1976 season. The Reds dynasty was systematically broken up. Had the Reds management had the foresight to recognize that free agency was not going to be the ruination of the game, and had kept the Big Red Machine together, the Reds had a good shot at winning at least one more World Series title.

The Reds also had a chance to pick up Vida Blue in a deal with Oakland, but Commissioner Bowie Kuhn vetoed the deal. I was never a big fan of Bowie Kuhn, but I could understand some of the reasons he vetoed the trade. Taken in the context of the way the game is played and operated today, the trade probably would have been approved. When you consider, however, that Charlie Finley was systematically trying the best he could to destroy the Oakland franchise before he ultimately sold the team, I think Kuhn's decision to veto the Vida Blue deal was the right decision. Had Kuhn allowed the trade to have been made, there's no telling how good the Reds might have been, because Vida Blue was on top of his game at that point in his career. It would have been something to see Blue join Tom Seaver in the Reds rotation, and it would have been rather scary for the other National League clubs.

BILL MCNEIL: Free agency was caused by the major league owners' practice of treating players like slaves over a period of 100 years, using the heinous reserve clause to keep a player tied to one team for his entire career unless he was traded. The Peter Seitz arbitration decision essentially abolished the reserve clause and led to a negotiated settlement between the owners and the players' union that permitted players to become free agents after playing in the major leagues for one team for six years. This unfortunate situation, which the owners brought on themselves because of their greed, opened a Pandora's box of problems for owners, players, teams, and even fans.

The two most serious problems created by free agency are the unhealthy player salaries and the loss of family that was part of every major league team between 1876 and 1975. The astronomical salaries have led to lackadaisical play, inflated egos, and any number of off-field problems that have impacted a player's career. As for the family issue, it shouldn't be dismissed lightly. In "the old days," in Ebbets Field for instance, the coziness of the ballpark put the players in close proximity to the fans and, with the same players representing the team year after year, many of the fans and players were on a first name basis. In fact, the players lived in residential areas near the park, and many of them rode the subway to the park. The same situation existed in places like Fenway Park, Wrigley Field, and Sportsman's Park, where fans could relate to their players on a personal level. Sadly, those days are gone forever.

BRUCE MARKUSEN: Free agency had a huge impact in the 1970s on several franchises including the Athletics and the Yankees. You start with Catfish Hunter, who became a free agent before we actually had a free agent system in place. Charley Finley had failed to pay a $50,000 insurance premium. It was a technicality, but he had violated Hunter's contract and an independent arbitrator ruled that Hunter was a free agent. This was after the 1974 season and the free agency picture we know today really did not appear until 1976. The A's won the AL West in 1975 for a fifth straight season but then got blown out in the ALCS by Boston. The A's missed Hunter in that playoff series. Oakland missed having a dominant right-hander to pitch at Fenway Park. If the A's had Hunter in 1975, it certainly would have been a more competitive series, and you can make a reasonable argument that Oakland would have won that series in four or five games.

After the 1976 season the A's continued to lose players to free agency, including most of the key players from the World Series winners in 1972, 1973 and 1974, players like Gene Tenace, Don Baylor, Sal Bando, Bert Campaneris and Joe Rudi. Charley Finley tried to make several trades and sales of players that did not go through. The baseball commissioner, Bowie Kuhn, disallowed the trades. Finley was trying to sell Rudi and Rollie Fingers to the Red Sox and Vida Blue to the Yankees.[8] A deal that would have moved Blue to the Reds was also nixed. The Reds only lost to the Dodgers by two and a half games in 1978 so you could argue that Blue might have put the Reds on top in the NL West race. Blue was a great lefty and was going to a new league, where batters hadn't seen him. You also wonder what impact Fingers might have had for Boston in the Red Sox bullpen in the late 1970s. Instead, the Red Sox had to make do with a relatively mediocre bullpen.

GARY GILLETTE: If free agency had been delayed, the Oakland A's might have been able to win another pennant and a few more AL West titles. It wasn't like the A's were going to win the AL West for eight or nine years in a row. Oakland lost several players that later wound up with the Yankees, including Hunter and Jackson. If Oakland had kept those players, maybe the A's would have been the team to go to the World Series in 1977–78 and beat the Dodgers. Of course, Charlie Finley might have broken up the team even without free agency. He had to pay these guys and Finley might not have been willing to give them hefty raises.

It would also have been interesting to watch George Steinbrenner try to put together a championship club without the ability to buy free agents. George Steinbrenner rose to fame essentially because he's a prima donna and has more money than God. You have to remember that the Yankees had a lot of success with free agency up until 1982. After 1981, you have a very long drought until the Yankees made the postseason again in 1995. Steinbrenner was still spending money in those years when the Yanks didn't make the playoffs, but free agency failed to produce results for the Yankees in those years.

Boston's Near Miss

Arguably the most exciting World Series of all time, Cincinnati's victory over Boston in 1975 included plenty of heroes and some controversy. One run separated the two teams in five of the seven games. In a series this

tight, both teams needed to be at full strength, but the Red Sox were without the services of outfielder Jim Rice, who had broken his arm in a late
season game with Detroit.[9]

After a split in the first two games in Boston, the series shifted to
Cincinnati for Game Three, a contentious extra inning affair. In the bottom of the tenth inning, Reds pinch hitter Ed Armbrister tried to sacrifice
Cesar Geronimo into scoring position and wound up colliding with catcher
Carlton Fisk, knocking Fisk off balance. The catcher's subsequent throw to
second base sailed into center field. Cincinnati suddenly had runners on
second and third, and despite Red Sox protests, home plate umpire Larry
Barnett refused to rule interference against Armbrister. Joe Morgan ended
the game with a line drive over the head of center fielder Fred Lynn.[10]

Boston rebounded to win two of the next three, setting the stage for
the decisive seventh game. The title was clearly within Boston's grasp when
Red Sox left-hander Bill Lee took a 3–0 lead into the top of the sixth inning.
With one out and Pete Rose on first, Lee induced Johnny Bench to hit what
appeared to be an inning-ending double play ball. Second baseman Denny
Doyle's relay to first, however, sailed over the head of Carl Yastrzemski,
giving Tony Perez a shot at Lee. Perez made the most of his opportunity,
blasting a hanging curveball for a two-run homer that sliced the Red Sox
lead to 3–2. The resurgent Reds added single runs in the seventh and the
ninth to rally for a 4–3 victory, giving Cincinnati its first World Series championship in 35 years.[11]

What if Boston's Jim Rice had played in the 1975 World Series?

BRUCE MARKUSEN: The absence of Jim Rice hurt the Red Sox. It was a
series where the DH was not allowed, so that factor took an extra bat away
from the Red Sox. Rice himself had a terrific regular season for Boston, and
even if he couldn't DH, he could still have been an effective pinch hitter
from the right side for Red Sox manager Darrell Johnson. It was a series
where one run decided several games. Having a guy like Jim Rice to pinch-
hit late in a game could have made the difference between winning and losing for the Red Sox.

FORMER BOSTON PITCHER BILL LEE: Bernie Carbo should have been starting and playing in left field. Every at bat he had in the 1975 Series was unbelievable. He was really in a zone and hitting the ball well. Darrell Johnson
kept switching guys around. He put Yastrzemski in left and Cooper at first
base, and Cooper just didn't have a great series offensively. The Reds had
George Foster in left and we were really hurt by not having Jim Rice in left.
We were playing with one hand tied behind our back. In a seven game series

like this one, with each game as close as it was, Jim Rice certainly would have had an effect in one of the ballgames, and could have made the difference against the Reds' left-handed pitching. Just think if Rice had been available to pinch hit for Yaz against Will McEnany in the bottom of the ninth inning in that seventh game. Our manager probably wouldn't have taken Yaz out of the game in that situation. He popped up to end the 1978 season in the playoff game with the Yankees and popped up to end the '75 season.

REDS BROADCASTER MARTY BRENNAMAN: The biggest story of the 1975 World Series was the absence of Jim Rice. You're talking about one of the greatest players in the game at that time. Rice was one of the greatest run producers, one of the greatest impact players, and he did not get to play at all because of the injury. If Jim Rice had been able to play, and had been on top of his game, the Series outcome might have been different. When you consider the fact that Boston pushed the Series to the seventh game and nearly won the Series without Rice, one can certainly make the argument that Boston would have won the Series with Rice in the lineup.

There's no question in my mind that the Reds were the better club when you compare the two teams. I don't think there's any doubt about that. The fact of the matter is that you put Jim Rice in the heart of that Boston lineup and he could have been the difference to allow Boston to win the series. Anyone who would say that Rice would not have made a difference is dreaming.

What if the umpires had ruled interference against Ed Armbrister on his bunt attempt in Game Three?

FORMER BOSTON PITCHER BILL LEE: Umpire Larry Barnett's call in Game Three on the bunt by Armbrister was a terrible call. From then on, Barnett was booed in Fenway Park. Armbrister interfered with Fisk, hit his elbow and caused him to throw the ball high and away to second base on the bunt. If there was ever interference in a game, it was right there. Intent is not a factor. A batter cannot make contact with an infielder while he's trying to make a play. When Fisk was trying to field the ball, he was an infielder. The rules are the rules.

BRUCE MARKUSEN: Ed Armbrister's bunt was a tough call for the umps. To this day, there's still some confusion as to what was the right call. You could interpret the rulebook one way and call it interference; then again, there was another rule where the interpretation might be that it was not interference. The home plate umpire decided there was no interference, the

Would Jim Rice have led Boston to the 1975 World Series title? (Courtesy Boston Red Sox.)

Reds eventually scored as a result of the bunt, and went on to win the game. We don't know if the Red Sox would have won the game if interference had been called. At best, the game would have remained tied and moved into the 11th inning. If the call had gone against the Reds, at least Boston would have still been alive with a chance to go on top in the top of the 11th.

What if Bill Lee had not hung a curveball to Tony Perez in the sixth inning of Game Seven?

FORMER BOSTON PITCHER BILL LEE: We were ahead 3–0 and the Reds had Rose on first with one out and Bench at the plate. I had the feeling that our coaches had moved Denny Doyle, our second baseman, away from second base because Bench had hit me earlier in the opposite direction. When you're leading by three runs in the late innings, you have to play aggressively on defense. Any ball hit on the ground needs to be turned into a double play. That means moving your second baseman and shortstop closer to second base. Bench hit a perfect double play ball but Doyle was late covering.

Bill Lee was tossing a shutout in Game Seven until he hung a curveball to Tony Perez. (Courtesy Boston Red Sox.)

Doyle leaped into the air, and while some say Rose intimidated Doyle by barreling into second, Rose was nowhere near making contact with Doyle. Doyle says Yaz stretched off first base for the ball too soon.

If we had turned the double play, then Perez would have led off the seventh inning. Most managers would have taken me out of the ballgame at that point, brought in a right-handed reliever to face Perez, and then brought in a lefty to pitch to the top of the order. The team's top closer would then be used in the ninth inning. That's the way things are done today. The Reds may still have come from behind and won. They were a good come-from-behind team as we saw in Game Two and Game Seven.

I wished I hadn't thrown the pitch I threw to Perez, but I was upset. I felt we should have turned the double play and I was visibly upset. That's when the pitching coach needed to come out to the mound and settle me down, to let me know that with first base open we could afford not to give Perez anything good to hit. The first pitch I threw to Perez was just kind of laid in there. I wish I had wasted one on the first pitch, maybe a sinker away and got him to pop it up to right field, but that didn't happen.

BRUCE MARKUSEN: Bill Lee was cruising. I think it was important for Boston's starting pitchers to go as deep into a game as possible. Boston had the starting pitching to match up with the Reds, but the Red Sox really didn't have a great bullpen and didn't have a dominant reliever. Boston had journeyman types in its bullpen, guys like Dick Drago, Roger Moret, Reggie Cleveland and Jim Burton. Boston didn't have the kind of depth we saw in the Reds bullpen. Boston really needed Lee not to make the mistake he made to Tony Perez, and needed Lee to probably finish off the game to beat Cincinnati in Game Seven. Lee's pitch to Perez was a pitch he might throw if he thought the hitter was looking for a fastball. You can argue, however, that late in the game, you don't throw a pitch that might actually be your third or fourth best option.

Reggie's Hip Shot

One of the most successful franchises in the '70s, the Los Angeles Dodgers, proved to be unable to win a Fall Classic during the decade, falling to Oakland in 1974 and losing to the Yankees in 1977 and 1978. The '78 defeat was especially frustrating, since the Dodgers won two of the first three games and led 3–0 in the bottom of the sixth inning of Game Four. New York's Reggie Jackson singled home a run, but Los Angeles appeared to be on the verge of escaping further damage when Lou Piniella hit a low line drive to shortstop Bill Russell. Russell dropped the ball, stepped on second, and fired a relay to first baseman Steve Garvey in an effort to get

Tony Perez: his two-run homer sparked Cincinnati to victory in the final game of the 1975 World Series. (Courtesy Cincinnati Reds.)

an inning-ending double play. An object blocked the path of the ball. On his way to second base, Jackson stopped dead in his tracks, extended his right hip into Russell's throw, and deflected the ball into right field. Despite desperate pleas from the Dodgers, the umpires refused to rule interference against Jackson, and the Yankees rallied to win both the game and the series.[12]

What if the umpires had ruled interference on Reggie Jackson in Game Four of the 1978 World Series?

FORMER DODGERS THIRD BASEMAN RON CEY: The 1978 World Series loss to the Yankees was the most disappointing moment of my career, as far as what could have been accomplished. If you look at the replays of Game Four, when the throw to first struck Reggie Jackson in the hip, you'll see that it should have been ruled interference. The play changed the game and the Series. If the umpires had gotten together to discuss the play, as they do today, I think they would have called interference. That's what a player wants. He wants the correct call made on the field. He doesn't want an umpire to make a bad call and decide the outcome. Umpires in 1978 were more concerned about trying to avoid stepping on toes. They believed that the umpire responsible for the call should make the call, without any of the other umpires stepping in. If interference had been called, I think we would have won the game and gone on to win the Series.

The decision not to call interference allowed New York's rally to continue and the Yankees went on to win the game in extra innings. So it was a long night and Game Five was going to be an afternoon game the following day. Even with our veteran club, it was going to be very difficult psychologically and emotionally to bounce back from that kind of defeat. Perhaps it might have helped us if the fifth game had been a night game, to give us a few more hours to deal with the defeat and prepare for Game Five. We came in flat and New York went on to win the game and the Series. If we had won Game Four and were up 3–1, I think it's quite possible we would have won the Series in five games. I think psychologically that the Yankees might have had trouble being ready to play the afternoon game, had they lost Game Four.

BILL McNEIL: Reggie Jackson's infamous hip-shot was obviously intentional, and should have been ruled so by the umpires, but they blew the call. If the umpires had correctly ruled Jackson out for interference, the Dodgers would have escaped the sixth inning with just a single run scoring, and their lead intact. The rest of the game would have gone exactly as it did, with Bob Welch entering the game in the eighth inning and preserving a 3–2 win.

That would have given the Dodgers a comfortable three games to one lead in the Series, and would have made them overwhelming favorites to capture the World Championship, with two home games remaining, if necessary. The Dodgers probably would have maintained their momentum and would have closed out the Series in Game Five. However, the Yankees would have thrown Catfish Hunter at them instead of Jim Beattie and, if he had won, they would have had Ron Guidry ready for Game Six, which would have been played in Dodger Stadium. Tommy Lasorda, the great motivator, would have had his cohorts up for the last two games. Beating Guidry would have been a monumental task, however, as "Louisiana Lightning" had just finished a career season, going 25–3 with the third highest single season winning percentage up to that time. If Hunter had won Game Five, it is likely the Series would have gone seven games, with Ed Figueroa, 20–9 on the season, facing Tommy John who would already have won two games in the Series. I believe, in that case, the Dodgers would have won the finale in a tight pitcher's duel.

As for the Reggie Jackson incident, that type of flagrant play would have very little chance of succeeding today because the umpires now have conferences after controversial plays, for which they should be commended. Most questionable plays are now called correctly.

The Bullpen View

Peter Seitz's interpretation of the reserve clause in 1975 has to rank as one of the most influential events in baseball history. The arbitrator's ruling broke the power of the reserve clause, allowed players to become free agents, and enabled owners to purchase the missing pieces of their championship puzzles. Gary Gillette questioned whether George Steinbrenner could have brought a title to New York without the use of free agents. Bill McNeil cited two concerns with free agency: soaring salaries and the loss of the family atmosphere at ballparks. Thanks to free agency, fans were now looking at a whole new ballgame.

The AL's designated hitter rule created new jobs for aging veterans and the defensively challenged. What if the DH had existed even earlier in the 20th century? Gabriel Schechter suggested that Mickey Mantle, Ralph Kiner, Rogers Hornsby, and Hank Greenberg might have had extended careers; Mike Robbins predicted that unknowns like Buzz Arlett, Ike Boone, and Smead Jolley could have wound up as household names.

The crowning achievement in Hank Aaron's storied career came in 1974 when Hammerin' Hank superseded Babe Ruth as the all-time home run leader. The panelists mentioned several players who could have eclipsed

Ruth, given the right set of circumstances, including a few power hitters from the Negro Leagues. Jim Albright named Mule Suttles and Turkey Stearnes as two potential candidates, while Bill McNeil declared that Josh Gibson could have matched Aaron, if Gibson had received enough at bats in the majors. Meanwhile, Jim Vail studied several sluggers and concluded that only Willie Mays could have overtaken Ruth, if Mays had not missed two seasons to military service. Of course, Ruth himself toiled as a full-time pitcher early in his career. Had he served instead as an everyday player, Bill McNeil projected over 760 career homers for the Babe, perhaps forcing Aaron to play one more season to lay claim to the record.

One could argue that Cincinnati's Big Red Machine, one of the most potent dynasties of all time, might have fallen short of greatness had the Reds not acquired Joe Morgan from Houston. Reds broadcaster Marty Brennaman and Bruce Markusen insisted that Cincinnati would not have captured consecutive championships in 1975–76 without Morgan. Even with Morgan, Cincinnati barely squeezed by Boston in the 1975 World Series. If the Red Sox had enjoyed the services of Jim Rice in that series, Bill Lee predicted that Boston might have found the extra bit of offense needed to beat the Reds.

7

Strikes and Errors: 1980–2003

Historical Highlights

Over the past few decades, we have seen two damaging strikes and some glaring post-season errors committed by players, managers and umpires. 1981's work stoppage lasted approximately seven weeks, with the Dodgers emerging as world champions after an awkward and confusing playoff format. The strike of 1994 was an even greater nightmare, with the season cancelled in August, and the post-season noticeably absent.

When playoff games did occur, fans were treated to some unforgettable moments, such as Kansas City's hard-fought victory over St. Louis in the 1985 World Series and the Mets' amazing comeback against the Red Sox in 1986. The action was often controversial, as we saw in 1985 when an umpire's call may have cost St. Louis a World Series title.

Managers are also under the microscope as never before, with decisions heavily scrutinized by fans and the media. Take, for example, Jim Frey's pitching rotation for the Cubs in the 1984 NLCS and John McNamara's choices in Game Six of the 1986 World Series, as his Red Sox frittered away a lead against the Mets. More criticism was also heaped on Red Sox manager Grady Little in the 2003 ALCS for his failure to replace Pedro Martinez sooner in Boston's excruciating loss to the Yankees.

The Split Season

The 1981 season came to an abrupt halt June 12 when players opted to strike to protest a plan from owners, who insisted on compensation either in cash or comparable players for those players lost to free agency.[1] Over 700 games were canceled; by the time the schedule resumed August 10, owners had decided to use a split-season format for the playoffs. First place teams from each half of the season would meet in a best-of-five divisional series, guaranteeing playoff spots to the first-half winners, the Yankees, Athletics, Phillies and Dodgers. Kansas City, Milwaukee, Montreal and Houston then qualified for the post-season by winning their divisions in the second half of the season. Thanks to the flawed format, the team with the best overall record from both halves, the Cincinnati Reds, missed the playoffs.

The post-season belonged to Los Angeles. The Dodgers rallied to beat Houston in the NL West divisional series and then nipped Montreal 3–2 in the NLCS. With the score tied in the ninth inning of the critical fifth game, Montreal manager Jim Fanning dipped into his bullpen and brought forth a starter, Steve Rogers, in just the third relief appearance of his career.[2] Pinch hitter Rick Monday greeted Rogers with a two-out solo homer, sending the Dodgers onto a World Series date with the Yankees. Behind the hitting of Steve Garvey, Ron Cey and Pedro Guerrero, Los Angeles launched one more comeback, rallying from a 2–0 deficit to win four in a row, for the Dodgers' first World Series crown in 16 seasons.

What if the 1981 strike had not occurred?

BRUCE MARKUSEN: The split-season format was controversial in 1981 and remains controversial to this day. The team that really lost out was the Cincinnati Reds. The Reds fell short in the NL West in the first and second halves but had the best overall record in baseball at 66–42. There were a lot of games lost to the strike so we don't know how the Reds would have performed in those games.

Los Angeles won the 1981 World Series, but you can argue that if there was no strike, the Dodgers might not have made the playoffs that season. There were many factors in the second half of the 1981 season. Players had to get back in the swing of things after time off due to the strike, and teams that had won the first half of the season were already guaranteed playoff spots. Teams also had only so many games to work with in the second half of the season and there was an extra round in the playoffs as well.

REDS BROADCASTER MARTY BRENNAMAN: The Reds had the best overall record in baseball, and Cincinnati was on the outside looking in when the playoffs started due to the new and unique rules that were implemented for the post-season. I would say the Reds would have had a very good chance of going deep into the post-season. You can't ever predict that a team would have won a World Series title. There are simply too many factors that enter into it. The best club doesn't necessarily win the World Series. I think the 1981 Reds would have had a very good shot at winning the championship, had the strike not taken place, and the season not been split into two halves.

A World Series title in 1981 might have helped Cincinnati in 1982, when it comes to keeping some of the team's better players. Reds general manager Dick Wagner was still concerned that free agency was going to hurt Cincinnati. Had the Reds won it all in 1981, you have to feel that your perspective would be different, as to who stays in Cincinnati and who goes. When the Reds failed to make the playoffs in 1981, it changed the picture completely.

FORMER LOS ANGELES THIRD BASEMAN RON CEY: We had no idea how they were going to align the playoff system after the strike was over. We didn't know if they were going to resume the season where it had been before the strike. Then we got word that we're going to split the season in half and have the winner of the first half play the winner of the second half. We had no say about the way the playoff format was set up and we wound up playing Houston to decide who would win the NL West. The rules were established so it does a team no good to put up your team picture stating that you have the best record in baseball while you weren't in the playoffs. While I feel bad for a team like the Reds, the rules were the rules. The format gave everyone a chance to make the playoffs in the second half of the season.

What if Expos manager Jim Fanning had not used starter Steve Rogers in relief in the ninth inning of Game Five of the NLCS?

FORMER MONTREAL PITCHER BILL LEE: What hurt us was that our manager, Jim Fanning, didn't use me to face the Dodgers' left-handed hitters, including Rick Monday, in the ninth inning of the fifth game. We should have saved Steve Rogers for extra innings and pitched me against Rick Monday. The Dodgers hadn't hit me very well. Rogers tried his best but he always took time to get loose and it's difficult for starters to relieve. Rogers should have thrown longer in the bullpen and they should have allowed me to pitch to Monday.

We would have done very well against the Yankees in the World Series. I could have won a couple of games as a starter and the rest is history. That 1981 Expos team was a good club. We came close in 1979 but lost to the Pirates, and lost to the Phillies in 1980. Both those teams went on to be World Champions.

FORMER LOS ANGELES THIRD BASEMAN RON CEY: It's hard for me to speculate on decisions made by the opposition when you're in that kind of important playoff game. Steve Rogers was arguably Montreal's best pitcher in 1981. You don't want to use your best pitcher for just two hitters, so I'm not sure it would have been wise to replace Rogers with a left-hander to face Rick Monday. Rogers possibly could have gone three to four innings, and if you replace him with a lefty, then Rogers would have been wasted facing just two hitters. It's hard for me to sit back and manage Montreal's pitching staff. You don't know all of the factors. Steve Rogers may have been available for just one inning. If it's one inning, then maybe switching from Rogers to a lefty might have made sense. It's just hard for me to support using your best pitcher in the last game of the LCS for just two batters.

BRUCE MARKUSEN: You could argue a World Series appearance would have been a big shot in the arm for the Expos franchise. The Expos manager early in 1981, Dick Williams, was not a big supporter of Steve Rogers. Williams was let go before the end of the season and replaced by Jim Fanning. When Dick Williams came out with his book several years later, he really ripped Rogers, saying Rogers wasn't a clutch pitcher and wasn't a winner.

The big problem with Montreal in the late '70s and early '80s was that the team lacked a true closer, a dominant bullpen ace. Woody Fryman led the Expos in saves in 1981 with seven. The Expos had a bullpen by committee and lacked hard throwers coming out of the bullpen. Consequently, in the playoff with the Dodgers, the Expos were forced to use starting pitcher Steve Rogers in relief. Had Montreal had a big time fireman in 1981, perhaps the Expos get to the World Series that year and perhaps they make it to the post-season in a few other seasons as well.

Frey's Decision

Cubs fans thought 1984 was going to be the year that Chicago finally made it back to the World Series. With an offense spearheaded by second baseman Ryne Sandberg, and a pitching staff led by Rick Sutcliffe, the NL East champions jumped out to a 2–0 lead against San Diego in the best-of-five NLCS. When San Diego took the third game, Cubs manager Jim Frey faced a dilemma. Would he go with his top two starters, Rick Sutcliffe and Steve Trout, in the fourth and potential fifth game, or use another starter in Game Four and save Sutcliffe and Trout for Game Five? Frey elected to start Scott Sanderson in Game Four and the Padres rallied for a 7–5 victory.

Chicago's hopes now rested on the right arm of Rick Sutcliffe. The Cubs carried a 3–0 lead into the sixth inning, but Chicago miscues, including the mishandling of a routine ground ball by first baseman Leon Durham in the seventh inning, allowed San Diego to rally for a 6–3 win.[3] Although the Padres fell meekly to Detroit in the World Series, San Diego had deprived Cubs fans of a much anticipated world championship.

What if Cubs manager Jim Frey had gone with a different pitching rotation in the 1984 NLCS?

JOHN KUENSTER: I had quite a long talk with Steve Trout, the winner of Game Two. He felt Frey made a mistake by starting Scott Sanderson rather than Rick Sutcliffe in Game Four. Saturday's game, Game Four, was a night game. Sutcliffe started Game Five the following day, a Sunday. It was quite hot that day and Sutcliffe started tiring in the sixth or seventh inning. Steve Trout felt bad that he got only one start in the series. Trout wound up pitching one inning in relief in the fifth game and retired the side without any problem. In fact, Trout's ERA for the series was 2.00 and he pitched nine innings against the Padres. Trout told me later that Steve Garvey had said that the Padres were glad they didn't have to face Trout a second time as a starting pitcher.

I always felt the Cubs made a mistake and they should have used their top three starters, Sutcliffe, Trout and Eckersley in that order. I think the Cubs might have won the series, although you can never say for sure. Had the Cubs made it to the World Series, I think Chicago would have given Detroit more of a battle than the Padres did. The Cubs had an excellent team that year and might have provided the Tigers with more of a challenge.

FORMER CHICAGO THIRD BASEMAN RON CEY: We had the knockout punch available for Game Four with Rick Sutcliffe. He was ready to pitch that game and San Diego would have had to face a pitcher who had only lost one game all season. San Diego would have realized that not only would they have to beat Sutcliffe in Game Four, but they would also need to beat us in Game Five. When you change that situation over to a situation where San Diego is facing Sanderson in Game Four, and then Sutcliffe in Game Five, the outlook is completely different. I would have had no problem pitching Scotty Sanderson in Game 4 if he was healthy, but not under the circumstances that it happened in 1984.

I would have preferred us to go after the title in Game Four with Sutcliffe, because once you get to the deciding game of a series, anything can happen. Sutcliffe was pitching a great game in Game Five, but a few things happened that resulted in a tough loss for us. By saving Sutcliffe for Game Five, we gave San Diego hope and confidence.

I'm not sure our bullpen was used properly in that fifth game. When a guy like Sutcliffe is out there, you give him the ball and take your chances. If our team had not made a couple of mistakes, Sutcliffe probably would have finished the game against San Diego. He got a little tired in that game, but I think he would have been able to finish the game if we could have just caught the ball.

I also think we would have matched up a lot better with Detroit in the World Series than the Padres did. We would have had a lot of momentum going into the World Series. With the speed, the power and the good pitching we had, we would have provided Detroit with a much better match-up than San Diego did.

Bruce Markusen: Frey has been criticized for not using Sutcliffe in Game Four and then using Trout in Game Five. Another problem was that the Cubs' most dominant reliever, Lee Smith, did not pitch at all in the fifth and deciding game. Steve Trout was used in relief in Game Five in the seventh inning, and Warren Brusstar, a relatively mediocre pitcher, was used in the eighth inning. The Cubs' best pitcher was left in the bullpen in Chicago's biggest game of the year.

So rather than using the Cubs' most dominant starters, Sutcliffe and Trout in the fourth and fifth games, we saw instead Sanderson and Sutcliffe and it didn't work out for Frey, who always seemed to be under the gun, whether as the Cubs manager or the Royals manager. If Sutcliffe had pitched in Game Four, he would have been throwing on nearly four days 'rest. Even in 1984, the five man starting rotation was pretty well established. I honestly don't blame Frey for his pitching rotation for the series. Game Four was not an elimination game for the Cubs; if you don't have to win a game, why use a pitcher like Sutcliffe on short rest? I would blame the pitchers more than I would blame Jim Frey.

The Blown Call

Rarely do umpires decide the fate of World Series titles. However, in 1985, with St. Louis leading Kansas City 1–0 in the bottom of the ninth inning of Game Six, and the Cardinals just three outs away from the championship, an umpire's gaffe breathed new life into the Royals. Don Denkinger ruled that Kansas City pinch hitter Jorge Orta was safe at first base on an infield grounder, although replays clearly revealed that Orta was out. When St. Louis first baseman Jack Clark failed to grab a foul pop off the bat of Steve Balboni, the Cardinals disintegrated. A single by Balboni, a passed ball, and an intentional walk to Hal McRae loaded the bases for pinch hitter Dane Iorg, who capped Kansas City's comeback with a two-run single.[4]

Game Seven was simply no contest, as the Royals pounded St. Louis 11–0 for Kansas City's first World Series crown. It's said that great teams overcome adversity. In 1985, St. Louis proved to be incapable of shaking off an umpire's blown call.

What if Don Denkinger makes the correct call at first base in Game Six of the 1985 World Series?

JOHN KUENSTER: Sometimes one out can make a big difference in a game. St. Louis led 1–0 in the bottom of the ninth inning, and the Cards were just three outs away from the title with Todd Worrell on the mound. The films revealed that the first Kansas City hitter in the inning, Jorge Orta, was really out at first base, but Denkinger called him safe. The next hitter hit a pop up in foul territory that St. Louis first baseman Jack Clark failed to catch. Instead of two outs, there was a single and a passed ball and suddenly men were on second and third. A walk filled the bases and a single drove in the tying and winning runs. Getting the first out might have changed the complexion of the game. Whitey Herzog always felt the Cardinals would have won the series in the sixth game if they had recorded that first out in the ninth inning. Umpires have a tough job and most of the time they're pretty good.

ROB RAINS: If Don Denkinger makes the correct call, the Cardinals win Game Six and win the 1985 Series. I think a St. Louis victory in the Series changes a lot of things. Some people at the time said that the call did not cost St. Louis the World Series. It didn't allow the runs to score, but it did change the complexion of the inning. Even if St. Louis had lost Game Six, after Denkinger made the correct call, it changes the tone for the seventh game. As things turned out, Denkinger was behind the plate in Game Seven, Joaquin Andujar was pitching and he had a bad temper. Andujar and Herzog eventually got kicked out of the game and it was a very bad scene. Nothing against the Royals. They were a good club and I was glad Dick Howser got to win a World Series title before he passed away.

Following Game Seven, the brewery basically ordered the Cardinals to trade Andujar. St. Louis traded him to Oakland for Mike Heath. If Andujar didn't have that Game Seven blowup, I doubt the Cardinals trade him. Andujar was a fan favorite in St. Louis. St. Louis would have been a better team in 1986. I don't know that they would have beaten the Mets, but it would have been a good race. The carryover effect from a World Series title in 1985 would have been felt in 1986 and 1987. I think Whitey Herzog would be in the Hall of Fame. A title in '85 would have given Herzog two world championships and I think the Cardinals would have been a better ballclub in 1986 and may have beaten the Twins in the 1987 Series. If Denkinger had made the right call, fans wouldn't automatically say a blown call by an umpire today wasn't as bad as Denkinger's call in the '85 Series. Denkinger would be leading a calmer retirement in Iowa today.

BRUCE MARKUSEN: Don Denkinger's blown call at first base occurred with the leadoff batter for Kansas City. That was huge. There's no question that Denkinger made the wrong call. Had he made the right call, the inning and the game might have turned out completely different for the Cardinals. The call may have set the tone for the entire inning. I think a championship quality team has to find a way to recover. The Royals were able to come back and win Game Six and then won Game Seven when the Cardinals essentially never showed up. The Cards got their heads handed to them by Kansas City 11–0. The umpire's blown call was a factor and certainly had a direct impact on Game 6. I think a world championship caliber team has to find a way to put a call like that behind them for Game Seven and the Cardinals didn't do that.

Buckner's Miscue

While the Boston Red Sox have certainly experienced their full share of October frustration, the 1986 World Series has to rank as perhaps the team's most disappointing setback. Within a single strike of a magnificent World Series triumph, the Red Sox handed the title to the New York Mets, thanks to shoddy defense and a volatile bullpen.

Leading 3–2 in the series, and ahead 5–3 in the bottom of the tenth inning of Game Six, the Red Sox were ready to celebrate, especially after reliever Calvin Schiraldi retired the first two hitters. The next three Mets singled to slice Boston's lead to one. Long-time Red Sox reliever Bob Stanley replaced Schiraldi, and with two strikes on Mookie Wilson, Stanley uncorked an untimely wild pitch, allowing the tying run to score. Boston's nightmare was complete when Wilson rolled a grounder through the legs of first baseman Bill Buckner, capping New York's 6–5 come-from-behind victory. Forty-eight hours later, the Mets picked up the second World Series trophy in club history when the Red Sox blew a 3–0 lead in Game Seven and lost 8–5.

Despondent Red Sox fans searched for answers and for scapegoats. In his long major league career, Bill Buckner banged out more than 2,700 hits; unfortunately, many would choose to remember Buckner for his fateful error in Game 6.[5]

Could one more pitcher have made a difference for the Red Sox? Boston had acquired 41-year-old right-hander Tom Seaver from the White Sox in

June; Seaver responded by going 5–7 with an ERA of 3.80. Unable to play in the post-season due to an injury, Seaver watched from the dugout as the Mets, Seaver's first team, beat the Red Sox, Seaver's last team.[6]

What if Bill Buckner had come up with Mookie Wilson's ground ball in Game Six of the 1986 World Series?

BILL DEANE: A lot of things went wrong for the Red Sox in the last inning of Game Six against the Mets, but everyone remembers just Buckner's error and criticizes the Boston manager, John McNamara, for not replacing Buckner at first base. There were two outs and no one on for the Mets, so Boston was just one out from the championship. Calvin Schiraldi allowed singles by Gary Carter, Kevin Mitchell and Ray Knight before he was replaced by Bob Stanley, who threw a wild pitch that allowed the tying run to score. Stanley's wild pitch hurt the Red Sox more than Buckner's miscue because it turned a lead into a tie. Even if Buckner had fielded the ball cleanly, Stanley failed to cover first and I don't think Buckner would have beaten Mookie Wilson to the bag. Had Stapleton been playing first instead of Buckner, it might have been a different story.

BRUCE MARKUSEN: Dave Stapleton had been used as a late inning defensive replacement throughout the season for Boston. If Stapleton is at first base rather than Buckner in Game Six, Stapleton would have gotten to the ball and he would have had enough time to get Mookie Wilson at first. Wilson was a fast runner, but the ball wasn't that far behind first base and Stapleton could have made the play himself. The game was already tied up at that point. I think sometimes there's a misconception that Buckner's miscue cost the Red Sox the game. Even if Buckner or Stapleton makes the play at first, the game is still tied. In that kind of game, an extra inning affair, the home team always has the advantage. Even if the Red Sox are able to force another inning, there's no guarantee that Boston eventually wins the game.

ROB NEYER: I do believe McNamara screwed up big time by letting Buckner play first base. Wilson's grounder was a routine grounder. That kind of play should always be an out if the pitcher remembers to cover first. There's little question that Dave Stapleton makes that play if he's in the game, and Stapleton had replaced Buckner in games before Game Six of the World Series. McNamara should have played it the same way he had played it before. I also believe Buckner should have been lifted for a pinch hitter an inning or two before. There was a left-hander on the mound for the Mets, and the Red Sox were in a position to score some more runs. Don Baylor

Was Bill Buckner to blame for Boston's World Series loss in 1986? (Courtesy Boston Red Sox.)

was on the bench and his job was to face lefties in that kind of situation. However, McNamara let Buckner hit. Granted, Buckner had over 100 RBI in 1986, but he was gimpy and didn't do well at all against lefties that season (.218 batting average, .257 on-base percentage). Letting a gimpy Buckner face a left-handed pitcher in a key situation was like letting a pitcher bat when you're behind by three runs in the eighth inning. Just flat-out stupid. To me, it was an obvious move, and Baylor was apoplectic about not being used. Had McNamara used Baylor as a pinch hitter, even if the Red

Sox hadn't scored any more runs, then Stapleton goes to first base defensively for Boston and things almost surely turn out differently. We do have to remember, though, that the game was already tied when Buckner made his error. The Mets had the superior bullpen so chances are New York still wins the game. But then you go to Game Seven and who knows how things work out? The bullpen situations are different because Game Six goes extra innings. In my mind though, even if that play had been made at first base, the Mets still would have won the Series.

BILL McNEIL: Bill Buckner has been labeled as the goat of the 1986 World Series for 20 years, but I think he got a bum deal. Bill Buckner was a hard-nosed ballplayer who gave 110% at all times. He made a mechanical error in the Series that allowed the New York Mets to win Game Six and tie the Series. However, other members of the Red Sox were just as culpable, like Calvin Schiraldi who was 0–2 with a 13.50 ERA, and Bob Stanley who let in the tying run in the sixth game with a wild pitch.

But the failings of Buckner, Schiraldi, and Stanley were all physical errors. In my opinion, errors of character are more blameworthy, and the player who failed in the clutch was Red Sox pitcher Roger Clemens. The 24-year-old right-hander was coming off a Cy Young Award season in which he went 24–4 and led the American League in victories, winning percentage (.857), and ERA (2.48) Even though he was unable to complete five innings in his first Series start, the Boston Red Sox held a three games to two lead in the Series going into Game 6 and manager John McNamara selected Clemens to bring the World Championship back to Boston. For seven innings, Clemens made the decision look good as he protected a 3–2 lead. All he needed to do was throw two more shutout innings, and the Red Sox would have won their first World Championship in 68 years and would have buried the "Curse of the Bambino" forever. However, Clemens was not up to the task. He inexplicably asked McNamara to take him out of the game after the seventh inning because he had a blister on his middle finger. And that, in the final analysis, decided the Series.

Roger Clemens is one of the great pitchers in baseball history, but he lacks the magic ingredient that separates the men from the boys in the big games, as is evidenced by his record of completing only one game in 30 post-season starts through 2004. Compare that with the record of Bob Gibson who completed seven of nine World Series starts while compiling a Seven and two record slate. And with Sandy Koufax, who threw a 3–0 shutout at the Minnesota Twins in Game Seven of the 1965 World Series on two days' rest after telling his manager, "If you want to win the game, you'll pitch me."

What if the Red Sox could have pitched Tom Seaver in the 1986 World Series?

JEFF KATZ: When the Boston Red Sox acquired 41-year-old Tom Seaver from the White Sox for Steve Lyons on June 29, 1986, they felt that a veteran arm could only help their march to the playoffs. Seaver had come off a stellar 1985 campaign where he won 16 games with a 3.17 ERA. While he had only two wins in the first three months of the 1986 season, it would turn out that the Red Sox needed Seaver in the rotation, as Oil Can Boyd was suspended for his outburst after being snubbed from the AL All-Star squad. Also, Bruce Hurst was recovering from a groin injury.

However, after a September 13 start against the Yankees, Seaver's aging right knee stiffened and in the fourth inning of a September 19 start against Toronto, he felt something snap. He had torn the cartilage in his right knee. It was hoped that Seaver would be ready for the playoffs against the Angels or for the World Series, should the Red Sox make it that far. As it turned out, the Red Sox did make it to the 1986 World Series to face the New York Mets but sadly, Seaver would not be ready to pitch.

Perhaps he would have started Game Four rather than Al Nipper, a game that the Mets won 6–2. Had Seaver pitched and pitched well, the Red Sox could very well have won and gone up 3–1 after four games. It is also nice to speculate that Seaver could have been used in relief, perhaps closing the door on the Mets in either Game Six or Seven at Shea Stadium, the site of so many of his greatest moments. One can see Seaver slowly trudging in from the Red Sox bullpen for the bottom of the seventh inning of Game Six, pitching two scoreless innings before Calvin Schiraldi pitched a scoreless ninth inning for Boston's first championship since 1918. Or maybe coming into Game Seven in the sixth inning and pitching well enough to hold the Mets to a run or two in the sixth and seventh innings, instead of allowing the six runs the Mets scored as New York rallied for a Game Seven World Series—clinching victory. It never happened, and the Mets beat the Red Sox.

The Lost Season

With a new three-division format in place for each league, and with the introduction of wild card playoff berths, 1994 was shaping up to be one of the more entertaining seasons in recent memory. The season would be historic, but for all the wrong reasons. The 1994 schedule officially expired September 14, a little over a month after players decided to go on strike, rather than support a plan from owners to link revenue sharing with a salary cap. For the first time since 1904, there would be no World Series.[7]

Although MLB refused to name official division winners, the Expos and Yankees owned the best records in the NL and AL respectively at the time of the strike on August 12:

National League				American League			
East	W	L	GB	*East*	W	L	GB
Montreal	74	40	—	New York	70	43	—
Atlanta	68	46	6	Baltimore	63	49	6.5
New York	55	58	18.5	Toronto	55	60	16
Philadelphia	54	61	20.5	Boston	54	61	17
Florida	51	64	23.5	Detroit	53	62	18
Central				*Central*			
Cincinnati	66	48	—	Chicago	67	46	—
Houston	66	49	0.5	Cleveland	66	47	1
St. Louis	53	61	13	Kansas City	64	51	4
Pittsburgh	53	61	13	Minnesota	53	60	14
Chicago	49	64	16.5	Milwaukee	53	62	15
West				*West*			
Los Angeles	58	56	—	Texas	52	62	—
San Francisco	55	60	3.5	Oakland	51	63	1
Colorado	53	61	6.5	Seattle	49	63	2
San Diego	47	70	12.5	California	47	68	5.5

The strike also curtailed several outstanding individual performances. San Diego's Tony Gwynn was hitting .394, while San Francisco's Matt Williams had homered 43 times in 112 games, putting the Giants third baseman in position to challenge Roger Maris' single-season home run record. Lurking right behind Williams was teammate Barry Bonds with 37 home runs; in the American League, Seattle's Ken Griffey, Jr. had blasted 40 homers, followed by Chicago's Frank Thomas with 38 and Cleveland's Albert Belle with 36. Would Maris' record have fallen in 1994, rather than in 1998? Baseball returned in 1995, but 1994 would remain a bad memory for owners, players and fans.[8]

What if the 1994 strike had not occurred? What if a settlement had allowed the post-season to take place?

JOHN KUENSTER: I thought 1994 was going to be the White Sox' year. Frank Thomas was having a super season. Chicago also had a very strong pitching staff with Jason Bere, Wilson Alvarez, Jack McDowell and Alex Fernandez in the starting rotation and Roberto Hernandez as their closer. When the season ended due to the strike, Chicago was a game ahead of Cleveland. The Yankees had an excellent team, but I think the White Sox would have won the AL. In the NL, Montreal had pitchers like Pedro Martinez and John Wetteland, and hitters like Moises Alou, Marquis Grissom and Larry Walker. I could certainly see a World Series match-up of the White Sox and the Expos.

An Expos victory in 1994 might have had a favorable long-term impact on the Montreal franchise. It was just like the Cubs in 1969. Billy Williams told me that had Chicago won the NL East in 1969, the Cubs could have used the momentum to succeed for a few more years.

ROB RAINS: Montreal had such a good club in 1994 and it was a shame baseball had the strike. Montreal fans were excited, and I think the Expos would have won the NLCS and made it to the World Series. I also think a league pennant would have had a positive long-term impact on the Montreal franchise. A World Series appearance would have converted a number of casual fans, and we might have also seen a successful drive to build a new ballpark in Montreal. The Expos might also have had the money to sign some of their stars like Larry Walker, Pedro Martinez and John Wetteland.

A title in 1994 would have saved the Montreal franchise, perhaps not forever, but it would have saved it for the current generation. Montreal had several good young players. You can't count out the Braves but they would have had to come through as a wild card. Montreal had a better club than Atlanta and I really liked the Expos to win the National League. The strike and financial loss hurt the Expos, forcing Montreal to get rid of star players and ending the fan base. I think you can trace the death of the Montreal franchise to the strike of 1994.

ROB NEYER: It's pretty clear, when looking at the numbers, that the Expos probably had the best club. The Reds and Braves were both very good in 1994, and I think any one of those three teams could have emerged as National League champs. If you look at what happened in 1993 and 1995, perhaps you assume that the Expos were a bit of a fluke in 1994, and the Braves would have been the stronger team in the 1994 post-season. I think either the Braves or Expos would have gone to the 1994 World Series.

The Yankees were the best team in the American League. It's interesting to speculate how baseball history might have been changed if the Yanks had won the 1994 World Series under Buck Showalter. Showalter might still be the Yankees manager today. That means that Joe Torre's career would have had a significantly different shape. Showalter might not have been dumped, as he was after losing in the 1995 playoffs. I think Showalter is one of the great managers of our era. He doesn't get that much credit, one reason being that Showalter wasn't able to finish off the 1994 season.

Several players also lost out on potentially incredible seasons in 1994. Greg Maddux was on his way to another great season. Matt Williams was on pace to challenge Roger Maris' record. My guess is that Williams would not have set the single-season home run record. It's hard to maintain that kind of home run pace. A lot of players have been able to carry that kind of pace into early August and weren't able to maintain it. Tony Gwynn also had a chance in 1994 to hit over .400, but that probably wouldn't have happened either. Basically, the strike just might have cost the Expos an incredible season, but it might also have put Joe Torre in the Hall of Fame (in a back-handed sort of way).

SEAN FORMAN: I tried to project which teams would have made it into the playoffs, had they been able to play out the entire season. In the NL East, Montreal was well ahead of Atlanta, and I think the Expos would have won the division, although the Braves probably would have been the wild card. In the NL Central, Jeff Bagwell broke his wrist just before the strike occurred, so I think Cincinnati would have probably gone on to win that division. The Reds and Astros were neck and neck, but Bagwell was carrying the Astros, and I suspect the Reds would have pulled ahead of Houston down the stretch. In the NL West, the Dodgers would have beaten the Giants to win that division.

In the AL, the Yankees were the best in the East, and I think both the Indians and White Sox would have made the playoffs from the AL Central. In the West, we would have probably seen the commissioner's worst nightmare, a team with a record under .500 winning the division. 1994 was the year that every team in the West was at least ten games under .500 at the time of the strike.

In the playoffs, I could see Montreal beating Cincinnati for the NL pennant, and Cleveland beating the Yankees and White Sox in the AL playoffs. In the World Series, I would say Montreal would have won it all. A World Series title could have really boosted the Expos franchise. Montreal has been characterized as a poor baseball town, but there were seasons when Montreal was among the league leaders in attendance, such as in the early 1980s.

Matt Williams might have hit 62 homers in 1994. Williams had a chance to pass Maris since Barry Bonds was on that Giants team. If the Giants had fallen out of contention, every effort would have been made to get Williams to surpass 61 home runs. I don't think people remember just how fearsome a power hitter Matt Williams really was.

GARY GILLETTE: The 1994–1995 years were essentially a war. People say baseball has come all the way back, but it really hasn't. In terms of the number of people that count baseball as their favorite sport, or the number of people that follow baseball, the game has never recovered from the horrible strike years of 1981 and 1994. The trend usually is that the game takes a big dip in popularity due to a strike, and then you see a recovery after the strike is over, although it never recovers to the pre-strike level.

The Expos had the best record in the NL at the time of the strike and were headed for the post-season. Montreal would have broken the Braves' streak of consecutive divisional titles. Even if Montreal had lost the World Series in 1994, such a Series appearance might have been enough to save the franchise.

The 2003 Postseason

For one brief moment, the 2003 post-season looked to be magical for two of baseball's most beloved underdogs, the Red Sox and the Cubs. The two teams appeared to be virtual locks for the World Series, until fate stepped in to deal each team a cruel blow.

In Game Six of the NLCS, Chicago's Mark Prior took a 3–0 advantage against Florida into the eighth inning, and with the Cubs just five outs away from the Fall Classic, a fan by the name of Steve Bartman intervened. Bartman interfered with Chicago left fielder Moises Alou's effort to grab a foul ball in the stands. The umpires decided not to call fan interference and Chicago promptly imploded: the Marlins scored eight times thanks to an error by shortstop Alex Gonzalez and a Cubs bullpen that poured fuel on the fire. Florida also rallied to win the seventh game 9–6, forcing Cubs fans to put their World Series plans on hold one more time.[9]

As heartbroken as Cubs fans were, New York's victory over Boston in the 2003 ALCS could easily be viewed as an even bigger disappointment for Red Sox supporters. In Game Seven, with Boston ahead 5–2 in the bottom of the eighth inning, and with ace Pedro Martinez on the hill, you couldn't blame Red Sox fans for ordering their World Series tickets. New York had other ideas, putting two men on base, and with two lefties due up, Red Sox manager Grady Little visited the mound to talk to his tiring superstar. Southpaw reliever Alan Embree seemed to be the logical choice. However, Little stuck with Martinez, and Hideki Matsui and Jorge Posada promptly smacked back-to-back doubles to tie the game.[10] Aaron Boone's 11th inning homer then concluded New York's stirring comeback and sent the Yankees on to the World Series. The Red Sox would avenge the loss with an amazing rally of their own the following season, but many would continue to blame Grady Little for Boston's failure in 2003.

What if Steve Bartman had not reached for a foul ball in Game Six of the NLCS?

JOHN KUENSTER: I don't blame the Cubs fan at all for trying to catch the ball. We would probably do the same thing he did, if we were in that situation. The left field umpire was Mike Everett and he has been around for a few years. He was coming toward the play at an angle to see if there would be interference, if a fan reached over the railing to try to catch the ball. In my opinion, the fan did reach over the wall just briefly. He deflected the ball and then pulled his hands back, so a lot of the photos show his hands inside the fan seating area. The umpire saw the catch from an angle that might have hampered his judgement. Had he been right in line with the wall, he would have seen that the fan did reach over briefly to deflect the ball, and that it was fan interference. That's why Moises Alou got so upset and threw down his glove in frustration, from being denied making the catch. That would have been the second out and would have changed the complexion of the game. At that point, the Cubs were just five outs away from the World Series. Instead of there being two outs, Luis Castillo drew a walk and the Cubs shortstop made an error on a potential double play ball. The gates then swung open for Florida. I think Prior could have finished off the inning, had the Cubs gotten the second out when Castillo hit the foul fly to left.

Had the Cubs won and played in the World Series, it's hard to say how Chicago would have done against New York, or even Boston, had the Red Sox beaten the Yankees. You have to remember that both Kerry Wood and Mark Prior were used pretty strongly in the NLCS, and they might not have been able to carry the Cubs to a World Series victory. It would have been great to have a Cubs-Red Sox match-up in the 2003 World Series but it just wasn't to be.

ROB NEYER: The fan interference was a problem but I think Cubs manager Dusty Baker left his starting pitcher in too long as well. I think managers err on the side of machismo in the playoffs, trying to let their big horse get the job done. That kind of philosophy cost the Cubs and Red Sox in 2003. I think managers also tend to get more conservative in the postseason. I think the spotlight, from the media and the fans, make managers much less likely to do something that later might be criticized.

What if Red Sox manager Grady Little had replaced Pedro Martinez earlier in Game Seven of the ALCS?

BILL DEANE: Everyone was saying, after the fact, that the Boston manager should have replaced Martinez with Al Embree, the lefty reliever. That's the way it's always done. You let Pedro go into the seventh inning, put in Embree to face the Yankees' lefties and then you use your closer. Remember though that Embree's ERA was 4.25 and Pedro's ERA was 2.22, so I don't see how that strategy makes the Red Sox a better team. Pedro was still throwing in the mid–90s and told the Red Sox manager Grady Little that he was ready to go. The catcher and other teammates said nothing to contradict Pedro. I supported the decision to leave Martinez in, and I thought Little was unfairly criticized, especially by Tim McCarver, whom I admire as a broadcaster. Of all people, McCarver should have remembered the final game of the 1964 series when McCarver was catching and Bob Gibson was pitching against the Yankees. Gibson was running out of gas, but the Cardinals manager allowed Gibson to complete the game, and the Cards hung on for a 7–5 win. I thought it was a similar situation for the Red Sox. You have your best pitcher on the mound, and like Gibson, Pedro has a lot of heart. You live or die with your best.

DAVID SHINER: In the seventh game of the 1964 World Series, St. Louis manager Johnny Keane let his ace, Bob Gibson, stay in the game as the Yankees pulled from a 7–2 deficit to within 7–5 before losing. Keane let Gibson successfully finish the game and the Cards won the series. Afterwards, Keane said he had a commitment to Gibson's heart. That's noble, but in some ways it has cursed managers for the last 40 years. Grady Little had a commitment to Pedro's heart and it didn't work out for Boston. Rationally, if Little had pulled Pedro out of the game and gone to his bullpen, the Red Sox probably would have won. The Red Sox pen was doing a great job in the series. Timlin and Wakefield were doing an especially good job. Still, who knows? As the Red Sox proved in 2004, sometimes you can throw the history lessons out the window.

ALAN SCHWARZ: When I was watching the game, I admired Grady Little's decision to stick with Pedro, his ace. Then again, I wasn't aware of the fact that the numbers showed that Pedro basically imploded after 105 pitches in a game. Grady was aware of that trend. However, despite all this, you have to remember that other pitchers give up hits, too! We'll never really know how the other Red Sox pitchers might have done, had they been brought in to replace Martinez. It wasn't like the Red Sox were up by eight runs and Martinez was left in for an unbelievable amount of time. If the Red Sox had made a change, there's no guarantee that Boston's bullpen would have saved the lead.

Managers do tend to get more conservative in the playoffs due to media scrutiny. It's difficult to be as daring as you might want to be with today's amount of media attention. Consequently, managers tend to go with the option that causes the least amount of trouble. Obviously, in this case that backfired horribly.

ROB NEYER: I think Boston manager Grady Little completely blew Game Seven by leaving Pedro Martinez in to pitch. It was obvious to me that Martinez didn't have anything left. He escaped the seventh inning and should have been removed. He shouldn't have been allowed to pitch in the eighth. The seventh inning had been a very tough and stressful inning for Martinez. The Red Sox should have pulled Pedro after that inning, and the failure to do so cost Boston the game and the series.

The Bullpen View

It's only natural for fans to fantasize about what might have happened, if the strikes of 1981 and 1994 had never arisen. Despite owning the best overall record in 1981, Cincinnati failed to qualify for the post-season, and Reds broadcaster Marty Brennaman indicated that Cincy could have made it to the World Series, rather than Los Angeles, the eventual champion. At least there was a champion in 1981. In 1994, the season ended in mid-stream, forcing fans to use computers and tabletop games to play out the post-season. Who had the best team in 1994? John Kuenster named the White Sox and the Expos as his top two clubs. Sean Forman, Gary Gillette and Rob Rains also voiced their opinion that a World Series appearance by Montreal might have expanded the club's fan base and extended the life of the franchise.

Dubious decisions by managers often decided post-season match-ups in the '80s. Chicago lost three in a row to San Diego in the 1984 NLCS, leaving some to criticize Cubs manager Jim Frey's pitching rotation for his road games in San Diego. John Kuenster and long-time third baseman Ron Cey stated that Rick Sutcliffe and Steve Trout should have started Games Four and Five, and both Cey and Bruce Markusen questioned Frey's use of the Cubs bullpen. Bill Buckner's failure to field Mookie Wilson's grounder in Game Six of the 1986 World Series is often pinpointed as the play that killed Boston's title hopes. Bill Deane argued that Bob Stanley's wild pitch hurt the Red Sox more than Buckner's error, although both Rob Neyer and Bruce Markusen agreed that Dave Stapleton should have replaced Buckner at first base earlier in the game.

Red Sox and Cubs fans may never stop castigating Grady Little and Steve Bartman respectively for crushing their World Series aspirations in 2003. John Kuenster didn't fault Steve Bartman for attempting to grab a foul ball in Game Six of the NLCS, and he suggested that the umps might have ruled fan interference if they had enjoyed a better view of the play.

The experts also locked horns over Grady Little's decision to stick with a fatigued Pedro Martinez in Game Seven of the ALCS. Bill Deane supported Little's judgement; Rob Neyer and David Shiner claimed that Boston might have won the series if Little had turned the game over to his bullpen. The Red Sox would have to wait a year to avenge the loss, but vengeance would be sweet in 2004.

Appendix:
Surveying the Experts

Many of the experts who provided commentary on the counter-factual issues also agreed to extend the fantasy a bit further by taking part in the following short survey. Whether dealing with Hall of Fame might-have-beens, time travel or seventh game preferences, these are issues guaranteed to spark debate.

The Hall of Fame

Getting to the Hall of Fame is no easy matter. You need talent, consistency, and good health. At times, good fortune also comes into play. For example, hitters would prefer to stroke the ball in a bandbox like Philadelphia's Baker Bowl than in a cavernous stadium like the Houston Astrodome.

The top vote getters in this survey question were Pete Reiser and Tony Oliva. Both appeared headed for Cooperstown, but outfield walls stopped Reiser, and bad knees diverted Oliva.

Who might have made the Hall of Fame, if they had not experienced injuries, or other roadblocks, during their career?

Bill James: A lot of things have to go right for a ballplayer to make it into the Hall of Fame. Not too many things have to go wrong to keep you out of the Hall of Fame. For every player in the Hall of Fame, there are probably 20 players who might have been in the Hall, if not for an injury. Hal McRae was a young player in the Reds organization, when the Big Red Machine was being put together. McRae was very fast, and was an outstanding baserunner. He had an accident in a minor league game. He broke his ankle, which cost him his speed. It cost him his chance to play center field for the Big Red Machine. It delayed the start of his career by several years. That's three big hits to his career, all stemming from one injury.[1] Even with those factors working against him, McRae still got over 2,000 hits and hit over .300 several times. I have no doubt he would have been a Hall of Famer, if not for his injury. There are more players like that than there are actual Hall of Famers.

Ballparks also come into play. Some hitters spend a majority of their career in a park made for hitters. Others aren't so fortunate. Chuck Klein played his best years in the Baker Bowl. He was a good player whose home park made him look better than he was. Then you have guys like Jose Cruz, who had to play most of his career in the AstroDome; it made him look less impressive than he really was.[2] So that has a lot to do with who gets into the Hall of Fame.

Thom Henninger: The successful Minnesota Twins teams of the late 1960s featured two Hall of Famers— Harmon Killebrew and Rod Carew — yet arguably the most gifted all-around player for those clubs was Tony Oliva.

Showing surprising power with a quick, fluid swing, Oliva exploded onto the American League scene as a rookie in 1964. Three years after leaving the family farm near the western tip of Cuba, the little-known prospect won the AL batting crown with a .323 average and stroked 32 home runs. In his debut season, he led the league in runs, hits, doubles and total bases.

In 1965, when the Twins put an end to the New York Yankees' dynasty with their first-ever trip to the World Series, Oliva became the only player in major league history to win batting titles in his first two seasons. He was a key to the Twins' pennant drive. After a slow start, he hit .374 from July 1 through the end of the season. He was batting .275 on July 9, and he trailed the American League's leading hitter, Boston's Carl Yastrzemski, by 65 points. Oliva went on a 50-for-130 tear (.385) to overtake the Red Sox' star in September.

Once again Oliva led the league in hits in 1965, and he did so in five of eight seasons through 1971. Only four players generated more hits over those eight years: Pete Rose recorded the most, followed by three Hall of Famers, Lou Brock, Billy Williams and Roberto Clemente.

No major leaguer collected more doubles during those eight summers, a tribute to Oliva's speed as well as his bat. While Tony-O was a threat to drive almost any pitch deep for extra bases, he was just as likely to beat out an infield hit, steal a bag or take an extra base on an unsuspecting outfielder. Only his defensive game was lacking when he arrived in the majors, but with a remarkably strong arm and some extra work, he quickly developed into a complete player who seemed well on his way to Cooperstown after claiming his third batting title in 1971.

Oliva wasn't the same ballplayer after tearing cartilage in his right knee, diving for a Joe Rudi fly ball at Oakland Coliseum on June 29, 1971. Oliva was in the midst of his best big league season when he was hurt. He was leading the American League batting race by a wide margin at .375 and looked like the league's MVP. After missing a few weeks, he returned but struggled through the season's final two months. A career-best .337 mark secured his final AL batting title, and Oliva led the circuit in slugging for the only time in his career.

From 1964 through 1971, he averaged 22 homers and 90 RBI a season — impressive numbers in an era that was extremely pitcher-friendly. Over those eight years, Hank Aaron led the National League, averaging 37 dingers and 105 RBI a year. Killebrew paced the AL at 37 and 103. Oliva also mixed in a major league best 35 doubles a season and batted .313 through those eight summers.

Injured a month shy of his 31st birthday, Oliva would endure seven knee operations to keep himself in the game. There would be endless hours of rehab and even more knee pain, but there wouldn't be any more seasons like 1964 or 1971.

The Hall of Fame has honored excellence generated over an injury-shortened career. Sandy Koufax was elected based on six years of Hall of Fame credentials. Pitcher Bob Lemon was a Veterans Committee selection in 1976, admitted based on nine solid seasons before a leg injury forced him to retire in 1958. Don Drysdale, who was felled by a torn rotator cuff at age 33, was elected largely based on six successful seasons with the Dodgers.

After consistently ranking among the American League's best hitters for each of his eight healthy seasons — a complete player who could excel at all facets of the game — Oliva should be in the Hall of Fame. Yes, he lacked the milestone numbers, the big totals accumulated over a long career, but his brilliance over an eight-year period deserves recognition.

Bill McNeil: Pete Reiser was, according to no less an expert than Leo Durocher, who managed Willie Mays, the greatest natural talent that ever played the game. He could hit with either hand and throw with either hand. He was as fast as greased lightning and as smooth as silk. When he arrived in Brooklyn in 1940 he was a shortstop, but the Dodgers already had Pee Wee Reese at that position, so Reiser was asked to play center field. He just smiled and said, "You mean all I have to do is chase the ball and catch it. That's easy." And it was easy. Everything was easy for the kid known as "Pistol Pete."

The 22-year-old Reiser became the youngest National League batting champion in 1941 when he hit a torrid .343. He also led the league with 39 doubles, 17 triples, 117 runs scored, and a slugging average of .558. The next year he was hitting .356 on July 19 when his world came tumbling down. That day in St. Louis he collided with the center field wall while running down a fly ball, and had to be carried from the field on a stretcher, suffering from a fractured skull. He was never the same player after that accident. According to sportswriter Red Smith, the aggressive Dodger outfielder had to be carried off the field 11 times during his career. In 1946, he set a major league record by stealing home seven times while leading the league with 34 stolen bases. The following year, after another collision with an outfield wall, he was given the last rites of the Catholic Church.

Pete Reiser's career was snuffed out brutally before he could realize his full potential, but for 727 days, from his major league debut on July 23, 1940, until his tragic collision with the outfield wall in St. Louis, Pistol Pete Reiser was the greatest baseball player who ever lived.

Jim Vail: Joe Jackson is the most obvious answer, as his stupid involvement in the 1919 Black Sox fix was perhaps the ultimate "career setback." Injury-wise, Herb Score and Tony Conigliaro are probably the poster boys among young guys of obvious greatness whose careers were diminished or cut short early on. Carl Mays and Dick Allen may qualify as the two most deserving players whose Hall of Fame chances were torpedoed by the "setback" of having a nasty, hyper-sensitive and/or selfish personality. Among 19th century players, Harry Stovey comes to mind, as spending most of a career in the old American Association has proved to be an insurmountable Hall of Fame disadvantage to everyone except Bid McPhee, and it took McPhee a century to get elected through the Cooperstown back door.

Would Pete Reiser be in the Hall of Fame if he could have avoided run-ins with outfild walls? (Courtesy Los Angeles Dodgers, Inc.)

Beyond them, Johnny Pesky's Cooperstown chances probably suffered the most as result of World War II military service, given that it took away youthful seasons sandwiched between two years when he led his league in hits. But in my view, although the injury that slowly ended his career isn't much of an issue with regard to his Hall of Fame credentials, Vern Stephens suffered from the most whammies in this category. Some but not all of them include: (1) he played for the hapless, and generally HOF-voteless Browns; (2) voters apparently discounted his stats during that period due to the wartime talent shortage; (3) when he later played for the Red Sox it seems that everyone ignored his run production as the mere windfall of batting cleanup in a lineup that featured Dom DiMaggio, Pesky, Ted Williams and Bobby Doerr, without ever considering that his presence inevitably enhanced their stats as well; (4) he had the misfortune to play at the same time as a half-dozen other HOF-credible shortstops, including Luke Appling, Lou Boudreau, Pee Wee Reese and Phil Rizzuto (who are in Cooperstown), plus Pesky and Marty Marion (who are not), three of whom (Reese, Rizzuto and Appling) played in much bigger cities where they got more press; and (5) he also suffered from blatant voter stupidity, as those other six men, none of whom was head-and-shoulders better, received a combined total of 5,640 votes from Hall of Fame electors, while Stephens never got one, despite retiring with the (then) all-time record for most home runs at a position where home run hitters were (and remain) historically rare. In my view, he certainly qualifies as the most overlooked player in the history of Cooperstown voting.

Dream Player

Time travel is the ultimate fantasy. When it comes to remembering baseball stars of yesteryear, quite often all we have is faulty memories and grainy photographs. What if we had the ability to travel back in time, to watch Christy Mathewson pitching in a pinch or Ty Cobb sliding into third base spikes high? In fact, the spirited Cobb was the top choice of eight of the respondents, while six expressed a desire to see Babe Ruth up close and personal.

If you could go back in time to watch just one player, who would it be?

David Shiner: Ty Cobb. It's almost forgotten now, but at the time they said Cobb's baserunning skills might have been his greatest ability. I'd like to see that.

Gene Carney: It would be Joe Jackson during the 1919 World Series. I would watch him very carefully!

David W. Anderson: It would be easy to say Babe Ruth or Ty Cobb but for my money, I would pay to see Honus Wagner. He was a great teammate and a valuable player for most of his career. I could watch him from 1900 to 1909, when he had an average of .944 in OPS, and was among the leaders each year in just about every offensive category.

Jim Vail: My parents were both from Missouri, so I was inevitably raised as a Cardinals fan. In turn, Stan Musial was my boyhood hero, but I was born the same year as his best season (1948) and never got a chance to see him play when he was under the age of 37. So, selfishly, I'd like to see his entire season of the year I was born.

In terms of historical significance, and despite the fact that Babe Ruth is a more obvious choice in that regard, career-wise I would pick Josh Gibson simply because Ruth's achievements are demonstrable through his numbers, but Gibson's have no meaningful statistical support, thereby stranding him as an unverifiable giant in the mythology of baseball. Like Gilgamesh or Hercules, everyone has heard of him, but compared to white major leaguers it's hard to prove he really existed beyond legend.

Dean Sullivan: Since my memory of watching baseball extends back to only 1972, I could include such modern players as Sandy Koufax, Ted Williams and Roberto Clemente. However, I have seen all of these players, and many other great players, on film. I have had the opportunity to study their statistics and read many accounts of their games.

I cannot say this about Negro League stars. Almost no footage of Negro League contests exists, and despite the effort of many dedicated researchers, meaningful statistics for these players will never be recreated. Of all the great Negro League stars, the most intriguing for me is Josh Gibson. I know his stance is roughly reminiscent of Albert Belle, but I know nothing of his swing, or his stride. How did he handle pitchers? How well did he run or field? I really don't know, and that's a shame.

Bill McNeil: I would love to have seen 'Pistol Pete' Reiser as a 20-year-old superstar in 1941. The 5'11, 185-pound outfielder had blinding speed and possessed the five prerequisites for greatness. He could hit, hit with power, run, field and throw. Even in 1946, when he was just a shadow of his former self, he excited fans with seven steals of home, setting a major league record.

Fall Classics

Wouldn't it be fascinating to travel back in time to watch a legendary World Series? There are so many choices. How about experiencing a stunning upset, like when the 1914 Miracle Braves knocked off Connie Mack's Athletics? Would you rather attend a series that featured a fabled defensive play, such as Willie Mays' over the shoulder catch against Vic Wertz and the Cleveland Indians in 1954?

While the panelists listed several World Series classics, the number one choice, listed by five of the respondents, was the scandalous 1919 World Series.

If you could go back in time to watch just one World Series, which would it be?

Gary Gillette: The 1919 World Series, to see for myself how much the press and the public were talking about the fix at the time it was happening.

Bill McNeil: I would love to revisit the 1955 World Series. As a Dodger fan since 1946, I suffered through several tragedies, including the 1946 playoff loss to St. Louis, the 1950 defeat at the hands of the Philadelphia "Whiz Kids," and the worst day of my life, when Bobby Thomson hit a 315-foot chip shot into the left field stands at the Polo Grounds to snatch the 1951 pennant away from us. Game Seven of the 1955 Series was the crowning achievement for Brooklyn baseball fans, with 23-year-old Johnny Podres handcuffing the New York Yankees for nine innings, and little Sandy Amoros saving the day with his great catch against Yogi Berra.

Dean Sullivan: Since I would be happy watching any of dozens of possibilities, I'll have to almost pick one at random, and I select 1912. I'd love to have seen one-year wonder Smokey Joe Wood (another Hall possibility if not for injury) face off against Christy Mathewson, nearing the end of his dominance. Just how good was the legendary Boston outfield of Harry Hooper, Duffy Lewis and Tris Speaker? Just how bad was the so-called Snodgrass muff, and how great was the catch Snodgrass made immediately afterwards? What was it like to see Boston fans celebrating a World Series win? It would be nice to know.

Thom Henninger: I think I'll go with the 1923 Giants-Yankees World Series. The Yankees claimed the first championship in franchise history in a six-game series with five close affairs. Casey Stengel hit a ninth inning inside-the-park home run to give the Giants Game One, and Stengel homered for the game's only run in Game Three. In Game Two, Ruth hit a moon shot over the right field roof at the Polo Grounds. The Yankees claimed the final three contests in a Series with plenty of Hall of Famers on both sides (Babe Ruth, Frankie Frisch, Herb Pennock, Stengel and others).

Honorable mention: 1951 Giants-Yanks with Mays and Mantle as rookies. Great Yanks-Dodgers Series in 1952, '55, '56.

Jim Vail: At other times in my life I would have answered this differently (e.g.: 1926 Yanks against the Cardinals, just to see Grover Alexander come out of the bullpen to get those three strikeouts with a hangover, and to watch Babe Ruth cut down stealing to end the series; or 1944 Cardinals versus Browns, so I could see my hero Stan Musial play in a World Series in which the Cardinals won and he batted over .300). But the 1905 all-shutout Series appeals to me most right now, because it would present the absolute antithesis of Bud Selig/steroid ball, and it might be the quintessential example of how great baseball was played for the ultimate prize before Babe Ruth, outlawing the spitball and really good fielding gloves changed the game.

Changing the Rules

Baseball is constantly evolving. We have seen some big changes in the way the game operates over the years, including the designated hitter rule, wild card spots, and even inter-league play. What was the worst modification? Twelve of the respondents placed the DH at the top of their list.

What was the worst change in baseball history?

Jerry Eskenazi: The DH is the most perfidious rule ever invented in the history of baseball. Baseball should be nine guys who hit, run and field. To change one-ninth of the equation changes about 20 percent of the game. I always thought it was fabulous to have the pitcher due up, and have the manager decide whether he should get a pinch hitter. It's more of a challenge if you have a one or two run lead, or if the game is tied, to have to make the decision to pull your pitcher for a pinch hitter. The DH removes a lot of strategy from the game. I miss having pitchers deliver surprising hits in crucial situations. Some pitchers, guys like Warren Spahn and Don Newcombe, were pretty good hitters. Newcombe was actually used as a pinch hitter at times.

David Shiner: The advent of the DH was really bad, particularly because it was adopted by only one league. Now that we really don't have leagues anymore, except as a convenience, it's even worse.

Gil Bogen: All of the rules making it a hitter's game, starting with the lowering of the mound from 15 to ten inches, to the DH, followed by a smaller strike zone, expansion, smaller ballparks and exhaustive weight training by batters.

Steve Steinberg: Banning the spitball. The spitter added color to the game and gave pitchers a much-needed weapon against hitters.

Bill McNeil: The worst rule change was probably shrinking the strike zone to the size of a postage stamp. The strike zone had been from the shoulders to the knees from 1887 to 1950. There were minor adjustments in 1950, 1963, and 1969 that identified the strike zone as the area between the batter's armpits and the top of his knees, but in 1988 the top limit of the strike zone was identified as "a horizontal line between the top of the shoulders and the top of the uniform pants." Today's pitchers, if they want to throw a strike, have to put the ball in the batter's wheelhouse and hope for the best.

Dean Sullivan: I vote for the institution of the save in 1969. It's not that relief pitchers don't deserve credit for their efforts, but that the rule is so liberal that the save signifies nothing. There are at least 50 pitchers capable under the right circumstances of achieving a 30-save season, still considered to be an impressive figure. Even the greatest relievers rarely enter the game with runners on base, or with the potential tying or winning run at the plate. If the definition of the save demanded candidates to face this situation upon entering the game, I would be satisfied.

The problem is that the existence of the save has radically changed the way relievers are utilized. Overprotective managers often shield their anointed closer from genuinely difficult situations by utilizing one-batter specialists to do the dirty work. Only after the lead is safe, and the drama is gone, is the closer allowed to take the stage. I have read that even the worst teams win over 90 percent of their games when they enter the ninth inning with a two or three run lead. If a reliever can't save a game in this situation, he doesn't belong in the majors.

Jim Vail: Among the relatively recent changes, I could go on for 20 pages or more with sound and statistically defensible arguments against the adoption of the wild-card playoff format. But it wouldn't achieve anything, because Bud Selig and the owners are not about to retreat from the lucrative benefits of the current, multi-tiered playoff status quo, and absent thoughtful and widespread coverage by the media of the salient arguments against the wild card, the majority of fans seem content to see relatively mediocre teams advance to the World Series on an annual basis, whether or not those clubs merited a post-season berth on the basis of comparative regular-season play.

Fantasy Hitting

With the game on the line, you need a hitter that can drive in the winning run. Do you prefer a slugger who can reach the upper deck, a contact specialist who can slap a ball past the infield, or a patient batsman who will work the pitcher for a walk? Although the panelists mentioned several different possibilities, two lefties drew the most attention, with Ted Williams and Barry Bonds deadlocked with four votes apiece.

It's the bottom of the ninth in the seventh game of the World Series. The game is tied and the bases are loaded with two outs. Name the hitter you would like to have at the plate.

David W. Anderson: Yogi Berra. He had 117 total bases and he could always deliver the base hit when needed. There are other players with higher batting averages but Yogi is the one.

Dean Sullivan: Anyone who watched the 2001 Series knows that it doesn't take much of a hit to deliver in that situation — just a flare over second, in that case. A similar hit won the 1997 Series for the Florida Marlins. The best batter in that situation is one who can put the ball in play, ideally "hitting the ball where they ain't." Who better to do that than Willie Keeler? Keeler had a lifetime .345 average and almost no strikeouts. Then there's Luke Appling, famed for his ability to foul off pitch after pitch. Of course, I'd take the Babe, too.

Jim Vail: This really depends on who's on the mound and how good he is: a righty or lefty; Mariano Rivera or Calvin Schiraldi? It also depends a little on who is the baserunner at third. If the runner is someone in the Jackie Robinson, Lou Brock or Rickey Henderson mold, then I might select Nellie Fox out of spite and call for a suicide squeeze! (After all, if it fails we go to extra innings, I've got the home-field advantage, and the added suspense maximizes my chances as manager for a myocardial infarction.) But assuming the guy on third possesses average speed and baserunning skills, implying that my batter has to earn the Series-winning run with his stick, then I'll take the matchup-appropriate hitter of the two I've chosen, Thurman Munson and Keith Hernandez, as they both seemed to get far more than their fair share of those (according to many in SABR) nonexistent clutch hits in their careers. Then again, if Mariano Rivera is pitching, I might have to opt for Luis Gonzalez and a seeing-eye baseball.

David Shiner: George Brett. He was the best post-season clutch hitter of the last 60 years, perhaps of all time.

Fantasy Pitching

We have seen whom the experts prefer at the plate. Which pitcher would you want to take the mound in a decisive seventh game of a World Series? Do you go with one of the early 20th century hurlers, like Walter Johnson or Christy Mathewson? How about fireballers like Lefty Grove and Bob Feller, or perhaps one of the aces from the '50s and '60s, like Whitey Ford, Bob Gibson or Sandy Koufax? Would you prefer a more recent pitcher like Nolan Ryan, Randy Johnson or Roger Clemens? The respondents settled on two proven World Series winners, Koufax and Gibson, each of whom received eight votes.

If you had to pick one pitcher to start the seventh game of a World Series, who would you select?

David Shiner: Bob Gibson. He was the best post-season clutch pitcher of the last 60 years, perhaps of all time.

Dean Sullivan: Christy Mathewson. Big, strong, hard thrower with a trick pitch (the fadeaway, or screwball) and could "pitch in the pinch." Look it up.

David Anderson: Whitey Ford. He had ten wins in the World Series. There is nothing more to say. He was a brilliant strategist and picked his situations to make the right pitch. My second choice would be Christy Mathewson, who won five World Series games, including three shutouts in 1905.

Gary Gillette: Pedro Martinez, who has the best Adjusted ERA of all time and who was an incredible pitcher in his prime.

Fantasy Managing

If you own a team heading into a decisive seventh game, whom would you employ as your manager to bring home the title? Long-time Giants manager John McGraw grabbed the top spot with eight votes, with Casey Stengel listed as the runner-up.

If you had to pick one manager to lead your team in the seventh game of the World Series, who would it be?

Bill McNeil: John McGraw was a hard-nosed player and manager, who asked no quarter and gave none. In addition, he used whatever means he had at his disposal to win games, including the stolen base, the hit-and-run, the sacrifice, and the squeeze play. Today's managers, especially the American League managers who have the designated hitter, use very little strategy. They all sit back and wait for the three-run homer. And the American League managers don't even have to struggle with the decision of whether or not to remove their pitcher for a pinch hitter at a critical moment in the game. The designated hitter has taken care of that.

David Anderson: There would be only one manager that I would select and it would be Casey Stengel. He won 37 games in the World Series and always seemed to have the right combination to win the key game.

Thom Henninger: Casey Stengel, who was an expert in using his pitching staff during the Yankees' dynasty of the '50s and early '60s. His pitching moves always seemed to pay off, whether conventional or not. He used platoons effectively, long before platoons became common in the modern era.

Jim Vail: I've long been convinced that managers have good and bad seasons, just like players. If so, the same is probably true regarding post-season performance, unless we're talking about Tony LaRussa, whose teams just never seem to play to their talent in October, and often seem psychologically vexed by his post-season moves. In almost 50 years of watching baseball, I think Dick Howser's 1985 performance was the best I've ever seen by a skipper in the post-season. During Kansas City's comeback from a three-games-to-one deficit against Toronto, he seemed to know the Blue Jays' roster (strengths, weaknesses and who was available for what) better than Bobby Cox did, and at times appeared to have totally manipulated Cox's lineup moves with his own maneuvers. He capped that by bringing his club back from another three-to-one disadvantage against St. Louis in the World Series (albeit with a little help from Don Denkinger), once again out-managing a skipper of far greater renown and reputed genius.

The Fantasy World Series

It would not have taken much for baseball's real-life World Series pairings to take on a completely different look. Quite often, the best teams never make it to the Fall Classic, so I decided to give some of the game's near misses a second chance at October glory. It is up to the panelists to decide which clubs were of championship caliber, and which ones should have stayed at home.

1908

While the Cubs easily handled Detroit in the 1908 World Series, the New York Giants could have represented the NL, if Fred Merkle had just bothered to touch second base. Either Cleveland or Detroit might have wound up as the AL's entry, if the Tigers had played a full schedule of games.

1908—NEW YORK GIANTS VS. DETROIT TIGERS OR CLEVELAND NAPS

Gabriel Schechter: I like this one! Two of my favorite pitchers, Mathewson and Joss, would have squared off if New York had faced Cleveland, and that matchup could have gone either way. Overall, however, the Indians (Naps) just didn't have much offense, and the Giants had enough good hitting to take the series.

Dan Holmes: Tigers win in six as Ty Cobb bangs out 13 hits, with six RBI and two stolen bases. A Game Two collision between Cobb and Giants pitcher Christy Mathewson renders Matty useless for much of the series.

Darryl Brock: The Giants would have beaten either the Tigers or Cleveland.

Dean Sullivan: The Tigers may have had the better offense, but New York's vast superiority in pitching would have given them the edge. Christy Mathewson was a proven World Series performer; Ty Cobb was not. Giants in six.

1920

Cleveland grabbed its first World Series title by winning five of seven from Brooklyn. Chicago might have repeated though as AL champions, if the Black Sox could have taken part in the final few games of the season, rather than sitting out those games due to suspensions stemming from the 1919 World Series scandal.

1920—CHICAGO WHITE SOX VS. BROOKLYN DODGERS

Rob Neyer: The White Sox win the series. The Dodgers had to rank as one of the weaker World Series teams of all time.

Gabriel Schechter: The White Sox had a much better offense than the Dodgers in 1920, plus four 20-game winners, so they would have to have been the betting favorite, as they were a week before the 1919 Series. If they were still the betting favorite when Game One began in 1920, I'd say they'd win.

Marshall Wright: The Dodgers beat Chicago. The White Sox would have been too distracted by their legal problems.

Dean Sullivan: Let's see: did Chicago win the pennant because the Black Sox Eight were not thrown out of baseball by new commissioner Kenesaw Mountain Landis at all (or were expelled after the season), or because the remaining Sox were inspired to victory by the loss of their comrades (or to prove they were a good team in spite of the corruption of the Eight)?

Because it's more fun, I'll say that Shoeless Joe and gang were at least temporarily spared the axe and participated in the Series. They would be extraordinarily motivated to prove that they should have beaten the Cincinnati Reds the previous year, and will easily dispose of the Dodgers, even if they don't hit into a triple play. Sox in six.

David Shiner: I'm reasonably certain that the full-strength White Sox, if playing on the level, would have beaten Uncle Robbie's Dodgers. The American League was the stronger circuit at the time, and the Dodgers were the weakest pennant-winner in years. A nine-game Series only makes it more likely that the better team would have won.

1922

In reality, the Giants rolled over the Yankees without suffering a loss. Would the Giants have had the same kind of success against the St. Louis Browns?

1922—NEW YORK GIANTS VS. ST. LOUIS BROWNS

Gabriel Schechter: A good battle and fun to think about. The Browns had a *much* better offense than the Yankees in 1922 and never should have lost the pennant to them in the first place. Their two big guns, Sisler and Williams, batted lefty, and except for Nehf the whole Giants staff was righties. Still, the Giants had .300 hitters up and down their lineup, and McGraw directing traffic. This is a tough call, but I think the Giants would have won in seven exciting games.

Dan Holmes: In one of the most controversial series in World Series history, the Browns took out the Giants in six games. New York manager John McGraw retired in the middle of the series amidst rumors of a gambling scandal and fixed games, and later was banned from baseball along with several Giants, including Heinie Groh and Phil Douglas.

Marshall Wright: McGraw's Giants win it. Never vote for the newcomer.

1946

The Cardinals barely survived the Red Sox in a seven game World Series thriller in 1946. Then again, St. Louis had to win a best-of-three playoff against Brooklyn to wrap up the NL crown. What if the Dodgers had won that playoff instead?

1946—BROOKLYN DODGERS VS. BOSTON RED SOX

Dean Sullivan: The Dodgers lost the first-ever playoff series to the St. Louis Cardinals after they tied for the NL pennant, but if Brooklyn had reversed that outcome and beaten St. Louis in the Series, it might have permanently impacted baseball history.

Think about it: if Dem Bums had managed to win the World Series, would Branch Rickey have been as motivated to take the risk of immediately promoting and starting the first African American player, Jackie Robinson, the following season? The victory might have allowed Rickey to postpone Robinson's debut in the name of preserving the chemistry of a championship team. That, in turn, might have forced Bill Veeck to wait before bringing Larry Doby to the majors. On the other hand, if Doby had been the first player to integrate the majors, it might have forced the American League to take the lead in signing Negro League players, which could have changed the balance of power between the leagues for decades.

Back to the subject at hand. In addition to possibly slowing or altering the pace of integration in major league history, the insertion of the Dodgers in the 1946 Series would have ended The Curse before that term ever was coined. The Red Sox would have won in five games, with Ted Williams playing a starring role.

1948–1949

The 1948 and 1949 seasons had to be the most disappointing back-to-back years for Red Sox fans. In 1948, Cleveland won the AL title by knocking off Boston in a playoff game, and then beat the Braves in the World Series. In 1949, on the final weekend of the regular season, the Red Sox lost the AL pennant to the Yankees, who then defeated the Dodgers to win the world championship. The Red Sox could have easily represented the AL in both Fall Classics.

1948—BOSTON RED SOX VS. BOSTON BRAVES
1949—BOSTON RED SOX VS. BROOKLYN DODGERS

Gabriel Schechter: The 1948 Red Sox didn't have the pitching the Indians did, but they had a very potent offense, and I don't think it would have rained enough to save the Braves. Ted Williams would have atoned for his weak showing in the 1946 Series, leading the Red Sox to the title.

The 1949 Red Sox were better overall than they were in 1948. The Dodgers, despite a lineup full of HOFers, just didn't get it done, and I think the Red Sox would have won.

Jeff Katz: Red Sox bats come alive in 1948 as Boston wins in six. Dodgers win their first series in 1949 as Jackie Robinson leads Brooklyn to victory in five games over Boston.

Dean Sullivan: Riding on their triumph in the 1946 Series, the Red Sox would have crushed the Braves in four straight games. Even Sox fans would have been bored with this one.

In spite of their tremendous offense in 1949, which could overwhelm any pitching staff, I don't think the Red Sox had the pitching to win three Series in four years. Although I think that Boston had the better team, I counterfactually predict that the Dodgers would have won in five games. Yankees fans had better hope so; if the Sox had indeed won three World Series championships in four years, they might have become a dynasty for the next several decades. On the other hand, if the last team in major league history to integrate was also the dominant team, it might have discouraged other clubs from integrating.

Marshall Wright: I'll take the Red Sox in '48. The Braves overachieved to win the National League that year. The Red Sox win again in 1949 as Ted Williams dominates the series.

1950–1951

The Brooklyn Dodgers could easily relate to Boston's agony in 1948–49. In 1950, the Phillies outlasted the Dodgers for the NL title; in 1951, Bobby Thomson's homer gave the New York Giants the pennant. Both the Phillies and the Giants wound up losing to the Yankees in the World Series. How would Brooklyn have fared?

1950—BROOKLYN DODGERS VS. NEW YORK YANKEES
1951—BROOKLYN DODGERS VS. NEW YORK YANKEES

Gabriel Schechter: An interesting proposition. The Yankees weren't as strong as they were later in the decade, and in both of these years they benefited from playing teams that were emotionally spent by the time they won the NL pennant. If the Dodgers had played the Yankees both of these years, that would mean the two teams played five years in a row, and I have to think the Dodgers would have won one or two of those. I don't think Stengel could have pulled a title out of nowhere every year. Or could he? The Dodgers were hot at the end of 1950, so I think that, of these two years, that's the year they would have beaten the Yankees.

Dean Sullivan: If my previous counter-prognostications had come true, then the Dodgers would have been a more experienced, more successful Series team than the Yankees in recent years. Since the teams were closely matched in talent, I think this would give the edge to Brooklyn, which would have won both Series in six games, and might have convinced Robert Moses to allow Walter O'Malley to build a new stadium in Brooklyn. In turn, it might have caused the Yankees to consider moving West in order to recapture their dominant market share they lost to the ascendant Dodgers.

Marshall Wright: The Yankees would have beaten Brooklyn in 1950. New York was statistically a better team than Brooklyn in 1950. The Dodgers would have won in 1951 because they were the superior team that season.

1965–1966

Los Angeles, with its dominating pitching staff, rallied to defeat Minnesota in the 1965 World Series. The following year was a different story however, as the Dodgers scored just two runs in four games while being swept by Baltimore. In both seasons, Los Angeles barely nipped San Francisco for the NL pennant. What if the Giants, rather than the Dodgers, had faced the Twins and the Orioles?

1965—SAN FRANCISCO GIANTS VS. MINNESOTA TWINS

1966—SAN FRANCISCO GIANTS VS. BALTIMORE ORIOLES

Gabriel Schechter: I think the Giants would have lost to both of those teams. In 1965, the Twins were the better team, and it took a superhuman effort by Koufax to beat them. The Giants had a three-man offense (Mays, McCovey, Hart) and were weak otherwise. They were about the same in 1966, and the Orioles were better than the 1965 Twins. I don't think much would have changed here.

Jeff Katz: Giants beat Twins in six and the Orioles in five thanks to the hitting of Mays, McCovey and Cepeda.

Marshall Wright: San Francisco wins in 1965 and 1966. The Giants get the edge in '65, thanks to Willie Mays and Juan Marichal. San Francisco had more pop than Baltimore did in '66.

Thom Henninger: I believe Minnesota would have beaten San Francisco. The explosive Twins were shut out just three times all season, but the Dodgers turned the trick three times in the World Series. The difference was Sandy Koufax, who blanked the Twins on four hits in Game Five. Then on two days' rest, he threw a three-hit shutout in Game Seven. I don't see the Giants' starters shutting down the Twins like that.

The Dodgers were shut out in the final three games of the 1966 World Series. Baltimore's Jim Palmer, Wally Bunker and Dave McNally did the honors. The Dodgers ranked eighth in the ten-team National League in runs scored that summer, and placed ninth in team slugging. On the other hand, Willie Mays, Willie McCovey and Jim Ray Hart all surpassed 30 homers and 90 RBI for the 1966 Giants. Perhaps the Orioles' pitching still would have prevailed, but a Giants-O's match-up should have been good for at least six games.

1969

The Amazing Mets' victory over the seemingly invincible Baltimore Orioles has to rank as one of the greatest upsets in World Series history, if not the greatest. Don't forget that the Cubs owned a sizeable lead over the Mets in August. What if Chicago had held on, won the NL East, and defeated Atlanta in the NLCS?

1969—CHICAGO CUBS VS. BALTIMORE ORIOLES

Dean Sullivan: I think this would be a more competitive series than others might think. The Cubs were a very talented team, and Ferguson Jenkins was good enough to beat even the awe-inspiring Orioles once or twice. However, the Cubs would have to play perfectly (one might say miraculously) to prevent Baltimore from winning in less than six games.

Gabriel Schechter: The Orioles all the way in this one. The Cubs had a lot of talent, but the Orioles had more. If they hadn't run into a miracle, they would have won easily. The Orioles and their fans still haven't figured out how it happened.

Jeff Katz: Orioles crush the Cub's pitching staff in a four game Series sweep.

Marshall Wright: Baltimore beats the Cubs. Without the Mets' momentum, there would be no National League victory.

1972

Oakland edged Cincinnati in the 1972 World Series, the first of three straight world championships for the Athletics. For a brief moment, it looked like Pittsburgh would get the NL's World Series ticket. The Pirates led 3–2 in the ninth inning of Game Five of the NLCS, but Cincinnati's Johnny Bench tied the game with a homer off reliever Dave Giusti, and the Reds won the pennant on Bob Moose's wild pitch. Roberto Clemente, who would die in a tragic New Year's Eve plane crash while helping earthquake victims in Nicaragua, had narrowly missed one final World Series appearance.

1972—PITTSBURGH PIRATES VS. OAKLAND ATHLETICS

Dean Sullivan: How I wish this series had happened. Roberto Clemente would have had another showcase in his final games, taking advantage of Oakland's vast outfield to demonstrate his defensive prowess, and Willie Stargell could hit the ball out of any stadium. The A's were not yet a juggernaut, and the Pirates, the defending Series champions, would have continued their success by winning in six games. Perhaps, on the heels of a second consecutive Series title, Clemente could have gotten more attention and more help for his fund-raising efforts following the Nicaraguan earthquake, and might have been able to rent a better plane.

1978

While the Yankees were beating the Dodgers for their second straight World Series crown, the team with the second-best record during the regular season was wondering how they had blown a double-digit lead to New York. The Boston Red Sox won 99 games in 1978, but fell victim to Bucky Dent's unlikely three-run homer in a one-game playoff for the AL East crown, as the Yankees rallied from a 2–0 deficit to beat Boston 5–4.

1978—BOSTON RED SOX VS. LOS ANGELES DODGERS

Jeff Katz: The Red Sox are too powerful for Los Angeles as Jim Rice's six homers lead Boston.

Marshall Wright: Los Angeles is the winner. The Red Sox would have been bruised by the close race for the American League East pennant.

Dean Sullivan: In his first World Series (after missing the 1975 Series with an injury), Boston's Jim Rice would have single-handedly bludgeoned the Dodgers, with help from Fred Lynn and a pair of victories by the entertaining Bill Lee. Sox in six.

1980

Led by pitchers Steve Carlton and Tug McGraw, Philadelphia captured its first World Series title ever, with a six-game triumph over Kansas City. Houston nearly made it to the Fall Classic instead. The Astros blew eighth inning leads in Game Four and Game Five of the NLCS, as Philadelphia rebounded to win one of the wildest post-season series ever.

1980—HOUSTON ASTROS VS. KANSAS CITY ROYALS

Gabriel Schechter: This would have been a great series. The 1980 NL playoffs remain arguably the most exciting ever, and the fact that the Phillies were able to survive that series and still have enough left to defeat the Royals tells me that the Astros probably would have done the same thing. They had more pitching depth than the Phillies, and an offense that wouldn't quit. The Astros in Seven.

Marshall Wright: Kansas City is the winner. Houston would have been spent after beating the Phillies in the NLCS.

Jeff Katz: Nolan Ryan wins three games in a seven-game Series win for Houston.

1986

In reality, Boston came within a strike of winning the World Series, before the Mets claimed the championship in the seventh game. In another reality, the World Series pairings might have had a different flavor.

Leading 3–1 in the ALCS, California took a 5–2 advantage into the ninth inning of Game Five, but Boston rallied behind Dave Henderson's two-run homer off reliever Donnie Moore. The Red Sox wound up winning the game and the series.

The NLCS nearly had an alternate ending as well. Houston pitcher Mike Scott, who had overwhelmed the Mets in Games One and Four, was set to pitch Game Seven in Houston, if the Astros could find a way to win Game Six. With a 3–0 lead in the ninth inning, Astros fans had every reason to be confident, but a frenzied Mets' comeback gave New York the NLCS crown.

1986—CALIFORNIA ANGELS VS. NEW YORK METS OR HOUSTON ASTROS

Gabriel Schechter: Nobody could touch Mike Scott, and if the Astros had beaten the Mets in Game Six of the NLCS, Scott would have gotten them into the World Series. I do think the Mets were the best team in '86 (they did win a dozen more games than everyone else, after all), yet they clearly got lucky to go all the way. I think either NL team should have defeated either AL team.

Dean Sullivan: Both the Angels and the Astros lost in the playoffs in the most agonizing fashion. If they had faced each other in the Series, it would have meant that Nolan Ryan would be pitching against one of his former teams. As unpredictable as Ryan could be in clutch situations, I think he would have pitched well enough to split his starts. The invincible Mike Scott, who in this scenario won the seventh game of the NLCS, could only have pitched in games three and seven. This would give Houston the edge to beat California in seven tight games.

If the Angels had instead faced the Mets, then they would have had the upper hand. Their star power would have overcome the scrappiness of the Mets, and Gene Autry would have taken home the trophy after six games.

Jeff Katz: Angels win behind solid pitching and great relief work from Donnie Moore.

Marshall Wright: California beats New York as Reggie Jackson relishes a return to the World Series.

1997

A late rally in the decisive seventh game boosted Florida past Cleveland, as the Marlins became the first wild card team to win the World Series. The Marlins almost didn't make it past Atlanta in the NLCS. With the series tied at two, Florida starter Livan Hernandez went the distance to stifle Atlanta 2–1. While the Braves would later complain about umpire Eric Gregg's liberal strike zone in Game Five, the Marlins closed out Atlanta in Game Six, beating the Braves 7–4.

1997—ATLANTA BRAVES VS. CLEVELAND INDIANS

Gabriel Schechter: The Braves got robbed in their playoff series against Florida. Eric Gregg's umpiring behind the plate in Game Five was the worst travesty I have ever seen. If Atlanta had won that game, the Braves would have won the series and gone on to beat the Indians in the World Series.

Dean Sullivan: Everyone knows that in 1997 the Braves were robbed by the atrocious umpiring of Eric Gregg in the NLCS against the Florida Marlins, the rented team of destiny. As good as the Indians were, I think for the second time in three years the Braves' vaunted pitching would have shut them down and Atlanta would have won the Series in six games.

Jeff Katz: Indians avenge 1995 loss by beating Atlanta in six and have, for the first time, three hitters (Belle, Thome and Ramirez) with four homers in a Series.

Marshall Wright: Cleveland wins its first World Series since 1948.

2003

Florida knocked off the Yankees in six games to win the 2003 World Series. As detailed earlier, however, the 2003 World Series could have easily featured the Cubs and Red Sox, had Chicago and Boston found a way to maintain leads in their respective League Championship Series.

2003 — CHICAGO CUBS VS. BOSTON RED SOX

Gabriel Schechter: A joke I heard was that these teams were going to meet in the Series, and in the ninth inning of the seventh game, an asteroid was going to strike Earth, destroying everything and leaving these two teams unfulfilled after all. But seriously, I think the Red Sox had the best team and would have won.

Marshall Wright: Boston's curse disappears in 2003, as the extra base prowess of the Red Sox sparks Boston past the Cubs.

Darryl Brock: The Cubs win, thanks to better pitching.

Dan Holmes: In a thrilling seven game Series, Boston edges by Chicago. The Red Sox hang on to win the seventh and deciding game 2–1, as Boston manager Grady Little removes Pedro Martinez in the eighth inning with runners on the corners and two out. Reliever Alan Embree works out of the jam and knuckleballer Tim Wakefield is called upon in the ninth inning to preserve the victory. With two out and pinch runner Tom Goodwin on third, Wakefield's pitch gets by catcher Jason Varitek. Varitek quickly recovers the ball and flips it to Wakefield, who lays the tag on Goodwin, who had chosen not to slide. Boston shortstop Nomar Garciaparra is named the MVP of the series after hitting .425 with two home runs.

Chapter Notes

1. Beginnings

1. Thorn, Palmer, Gershman and Pietrusza, *Total Baseball*, p.6.
2. Ibid., p.3.
3. Burns and Ward, *Baseball: An Illustrated History*, p. 20; Rhodes and Snyder, *Redleg Journal*, p. 14–15.
4. Gershman, Pietrusza, and Silverman, *Baseball: The Biographical Encyclopedia*, p. 1257; Rhodes and Snyder, *Redleg Journal*, p. 16.
5. Rhodes and Snyder, *Redleg Journal*, p. 29.
6. Thorn, Palmer, Gershman and Pietrusza, *Total Baseball*, p. 212; Rhodes and Snyder, *Redleg Journal*, p. 25.
7. Gillette and Palmer, *The Baseball Encyclopedia*, p. 1363.
8. Gillette and Palmer, *The Baseball Encyclopedia*, p. 1367; Gershman, Pietrusza and Silverman, *Baseball: The Biographical Encyclopedia*, p. 535.
9. Gershman, Pietrusza and Silverman, *Baseball: The Biographical Encyclopedia*, p. 1200.
10. Gillette and Palmer, *The Baseball Encyclopedia*, p. 1388; Gershman, Pietrusza and Silverman, *Baseball: The Biographical Encyclopedia*, p. 1200.
11. Gillette and Palmer, *The Baseball Encyclopedia*, p. 1370; Burns and Ward, *Baseball: An Illustrated History*, p. 26.
12. Gillette and Palmer, *The Baseball Encyclopedia*, p. 1372,1387.
13. Ibid., pp. 1389–1390
14. Burns and Ward, *Baseball: An Illustrated History*, p. 4; Gershman, Pietrusza and Silverman, *Baseball: The Biographical Encyclopedia*, p. 178.
15. Burns and Ward, *Baseball: An Illustrated History*, p. 6.
16. Gershman, Pietrusza and Silverman, *Baseball: The Biographical Encyclopedia*, p. 189.
17. Gillette and Palmer, *The Baseball Encyclopedia*, p. 1369, 1376.
18. Ibid., p. 1373, 1392.
19. Ibid., p. 1394, 1399

2. Deadball Days

1. Thorn, Palmer, Gershman and Pietrusza, *Total Baseball*, p. 6.
2. Gillette and Palmer, *The Baseball Encyclopedia*, p. 1406.
3. Thorn, Palmer, Gershman and Pietrusza, *Total Baseball*, p. 148.
4. James, *The New Bill James Historical Baseball Abstract*, p. 105.
5. James, *The New Bill James Historical*

Baseball Abstract, p. 71; Dewey and Acocella, *Total Ballclubs*, p. 71, 478.

6. Burns and Ward, *Baseball: An Illustrated History*, p. 65.

7. Thorn, Palmer, Gershman and Pietrusza, *Total Baseball*, p. 52.

8. Snyder, *The World Series' Most Wanted*, p. 45.

9. Gershman, Pietrusza and Silverman, *Baseball: The Biographical Encyclopedia*, p. 363.

10. Ibid., p. 363.

11. Ibid., p. 363.

12. Anderson, *More than Merkle*, pp. 159–160; Dewey and Acocella, *Total Ballclubs*, p. 375.

13. Anderson, *More than Merkle*, pp. 172–173.

14. Gillette and Palmer, *The Baseball Encyclopedia*, p. 1415.

15. Anderson, *More than Merkle*, p. 179; James, *The New Bill James Historical Baseball Abstract*, p. 84.

16. New York outfielder Fred Snodgrass muffed a routine fly in the bottom of the tenth inning, a defensive lapse that helped the Red Sox rally from a 2–1 deficit to beat the Giants 3–2 and win the 1912 World Series. Thorn, Palmer, Gershman and Pietrusza, *Total Baseball*, p. 329.

17. Gillette and Palmer, *The Baseball Encyclopedia*, pp. 1428–1429.

18. James, *The New Bill James Historical Baseball Abstract*, p. 105.

19. Lewine and Okrent, *The Ultimate Baseball Book*, p. 98.

20. Lieb, *Connie Mack*, p. 181.

21. Ibid., pp. 182–183.

22. Ibid., p. 184.

3. Between the Wars

1. James, *The New Bill James Historical Baseball Abstract*, p. 122.

2. Thorn, Palmer, Gershman and Pietrusza, *Total Baseball*, p. 141.

3. Asinof, *Eight Men Out*, p. 118.

4. Gershman, Pietrusza and Silverman, *Baseball: The Biographical Encyclopedia*, p. 341.

5. Gillette and Palmer, *The Baseball Encyclopedia*, p. 1441.

6. Gershman, Pietrusza and Silverman, *Baseball: The Biographical Encyclopedia*, p. 381.

7. Sowell, *The Pitch That Killed*, p. 174; Gershman, Pietrusza and Silverman, *Baseball: The Biographical Encyclopedia*, p. 195.

8. James, *The New Bill James Historical Baseball Abstract*, pp. 121–122.

9. Huhn, *The Sizzler*, p. 97.

10. Ibid., p. 140.

11. Lieb, *Connie Mack*, pp. 249–251.

12. Ibid., pp. 252–254.

13. Gershman, Pietrusza and Silverman, *Baseball: The Biographical Encyclopedia*, p. 275.

4. Careers Lost, Teams Lost

1. Burns and Ward, *Baseball: An Illustrated History*, p. 278.

2. Gershman, Pietrusza and Silverman, *Baseball: The Biographical Encyclopedia*, p. 347.

3. Ibid., p. 1237.

4. Robbins, *Ninety Feet from Fame*, p. 183.

5. Gershman, Pietrusza and Silverman, *Baseball: The Biographical Encyclopedia*, p. 1141.

6. James, *The New Bill James Historical Baseball Abstract*, p. 210.

7. Snyder, *The World Series' Most Wanted*, p. 25.

8. Lewine and Okrent, *The Ultimate Baseball Book*, p. 236.

9. Burns and Ward, *Baseball: An Illustrated History*, p. 288.

10. Gillette and Palmer, *The Baseball Encyclopedia*, p. 1374.

11. Thorn, Palmer, Gershman and Pietrusza, *Total Baseball*, p. 495.

12. Ibid., pp. 497–498.

13. Gillette and Palmer, *The Baseball Encyclopedia*, pp. 1492–1494.

14. Robbins, *Ninety Feet from Fame*, pp. 72–75.

15. Gillette and Palmer, *The Baseball Encyclopedia*, p. 1497.

16. Gershman, Pietrusza and Silverman, *Baseball: The Biographical Encyclopedia*, p. 391.

17. Dewey and Acocella, *Total Ballclubs*, p. 235.

18. Gershman, Pietrusza and Silverman, *Baseball: The Biographical Encyclopedia*, p. 37.

19. Ibid., p. 950.

20. Miksis scored the winning run in the

ninth inning of Game 4 of the 1947 World Series. Yankees pitcher Bill Bevens lost the game, and a no-hitter, when Cookie Lavagetto lined a two-run pinch double off the right field wall. Gershman, Pietrusza and Silverman, *Baseball: The Biographical Encyclopedia*, p. 649.

21. Robinson, *The Home Run Heard 'Round the World*, p. 151.

22. Ibid., p. 205.

23. Erskine, *Carl Erskine's Tales from the Dodgers Dugout*, p. 63; Robinson, *The Home Run Heard 'Round the World*, p. 225.

24. Burns and Ward, *Baseball: An Illustrated History*, p. 343.

25. Gershman, Pietrusza and Silverman, *Baseball: The Biographical Encyclopedia*, p. 26.

26. Snyder, *The World Series' Most Wanted*, p. 33.

27. James, *The New Bill James Historical Baseball Abstract*, p. 240.

28. Ibid., p. 241.

29. Gershman, Pietrusza and Silverman, *Baseball: The Biographical Encyclopedia*, p. 1011.

30. Ibid., p. 1012.

5. Decade of Growth

1. Gershman, Pietrusza and Silverman, *Baseball: The Biographical Encyclopedia*, p. 705.

2. Dewey and Acocella, *Total Ballclubs*, pp. 297–298.

3. Snyder, *The World Series' Most Wanted*, p. 27.

4. Gershman, Pietrusza and Silverman, *Baseball: The Biographical Encyclopedia*, p. 726.

5. Kashatus, *September Swoon*, p. 138.

6. Gershman, Pietrusza and Silverman, *Baseball: The Biographical Encyclopedia*, p. 726.

7. Ibid., p. 129.

8. Ibid., p. 710.

9. Gillette and Palmer, *The Baseball Encyclopedia*, p. 1530.

10. Gershman, Pietrusza and Silverman, *Baseball: The Biographical Encyclopedia*, p. 955.

11. Ibid., p. 620.

12. Leavy, *Sandy Koufax*, p. 155.

13. James, *The New Bill James Historical Baseball Abstract*, p. 840.

14. Robbins, *Ninety Feet from Fame*, p. 148.

15. Ibid., p. 148.

16. Gershman, Pietrusza and Silverman, *Baseball: The Biographical Encyclopedia*, p. 230.

17. Snyder, *The World Series' Most Wanted*, p. 239.

18. Gillette and Palmer, *The Baseball Encyclopedia*, p. 1537.

19. Dewey and Acocella, *Total Ballclubs*, p. 427.

20. Ibid., p. 150.

6. A Whole New Ballgame

1. Gillette and Palmer, *The Baseball Encyclopedia*, p, 1550.

2. Dewey and Acocella, *Total Ballclubs*, p. 206.

3. Gillette and Palmer, *The Baseball Encyclopedia*, p. 1547.

4. Gershman, Pietrusza and Silverman, *Baseball: The Biographical Encyclopedia*, p. 410.

5. Ibid., p. 844.

6. James, *The New Bill James Historical Baseball Abstract*, p. 284.

7. Burns and Ward, *Baseball: An Illustrated History*, p. 443.

8. Commissioner Bowie Kuhn canceled both sales, stating that they were not in the best interests of baseball. Dewey and Acocella, *Total Ballclubs*, p. 444.

9. Ibid., p. 85.

10. Rhodes and Snyder, *Redleg Journal*, p. 519.

11. Robbins, *Ninety Feet from Fame*, p. 12.

12. Dewey and Acocella, *Total Ballclubs*, p. 411.

7. Strikes and Errors

1. Burns and Ward, *Baseball: An Illustrated History*, p. 447.

2. Gershman, Pietrusza and Silverman, *Baseball: The Biographical Encyclopedia*, p. 964.

3. Ibid., p. 316.

4. Snyder, *The World Series' Most Wanted*, p. 14.

5. Gershman, Pietrusza and Silverman,

Baseball: The Biographical Encyclopedia, p. 140.

    6. Ibid., p. 1016.

    7. Gillette and Palmer, *The Baseball Encyclopedia*, p. 1589.

    8. Ibid., pp. 1588–1589.

    9. Dewey and Acocella, *Total Ballclubs*, p. 156.

    10. Ibid., pp. 93–94.

Appendix

    1. After a brief stint with Cincinnati in 1968, McRae suffered an injury in the off season while playing in the Puerto Rican Winter League. Sliding into home, McRae broke his leg in four places, wiping out his 1969 season and hampering his running ability. Reduced to a part-time role with the Reds, McRae was traded to Kansas City in November of 1972, and went on to hit .280 or better in nine of his first 12 seasons with the Royals. McRae finished his career with a .290 average. Gershman, Pietrusza and Silverman, *Baseball: The Biographical Encyclopedia*, p. 767.

    2. Cruz spent 13 seasons playing his home games in the Astrodome. He hit .300 or higher in six of those seasons and turned in a lifetime batting average of .284, finishing his career with more than 2,200 hits. Gershman, Pietrusza and Silverman, *Baseball: The Biographical Encyclopedia*, p. 253.

Bibliography

Anderson, David. *More Than Merkle*. Lincoln: University of Nebraska Press, 2000.

Asinof, Eliot. *Eight Men Out*. New York: Rinehart and Winston, 1963.

Burns, Ken, and Geoffrey C. Ward. *Baseball: An Illustrated History*. New York: Alfred A. Knopf, 1994.

Dewey, Donald, and Nicholas Acocella. *Total Ballclubs*. Toronto: Sports Media Publishing, 2005.

Erskine, Carl. *Carl Erskine's Tales from the Dodgers Dugout: Extra Innings*. Champaign, Illionois: Sports Publishing L.L.C., 2004.

Gershman, Michael, David Pietrusza, and Matthew Silverman, eds. *Baseball: The Biographical Encyclopedia*. Kingston, New York: Total Sports/*Sports Illustrated*, 2000.

Gillette, Gary, and Pete Palmer, eds. *The Baseball Encyclopedia*. New York: Barnes & Noble Books, 2004.

Huhn, Rick. *The Sizzler: George Sisler, Baseball's Forgotten Great*. Columbia: University of Missouri Press, 2004.

James, Bill. *The New Bill James Historical Baseball Abstract*. New York: The Free Press, 2001.

Kashatus, William C. *September Swoon*. University Park: The Pennsylvania State University Press, 2004.

Leavy, Jane. *Sandy Koufax: A Lefty's Legacy*. New York: HarperCollins, 2002.

Lewine, Harris, and Daniel Okrent, eds. *The Ultimate Baseball Book*. Boston: Houghton Mifflin, 1981.

Lieb, Frederick G. *Connie Mack: Grand Old Man of Baseball*. New York: G. P. Putnam's Sons, 1945.

Markusen, Bruce. *Roberto Clemente: The Great One*. Champaign, Illinois: Sports Publishing L.L.C., 2001.

Rhodes, Greg, and John Snyder. *Redleg Journal*. Cincinnati: Road West Publishing, 2000.

Robbins, Mike. *Ninety Feet from Fame*. New York: Carroll & Graf, 2004.

Robinson, Ray. *The Home Run Heard 'Round the World*. New York: HarperCollins, 1991.

Snyder, John. *The World Series' Most Wanted*. Washington, D.C.: Brassey's, 2004.

Sowell, Mike. *The Pitch That Killed*. New York: Collier Books, 1989.

Thorn, John, Pete Palmer, Michael Gershman, and David Pietrusza, eds. *Total Baseball*. New York: Total Sports, 1999.

Index

Numbers in **_bold italics_** indicate photographs